Why Politics Matters

Term-time openi

Why Politics Matters

Making Democracy Work

Gerry Stoker

First published 2006 by
PALGRAVE MACMILLAN
Houndmills, Basingstoke, Hampshire RG21 6XS and
175 Fifth Avenue, New York, N.Y. 10010
Companies and representatives throughout the world

PALGRAVE MACMILLAN is the global academic imprint of the Palgrave
Macmillan division of St. Martin's Press, LLC and of Palgrave Macmillan Ltd.
Macmillan® is a registered trademark in the United States, United Kingdom
and other countries. Palgrave is a registered trademark in the European
Union and other countries.

ISBN-13: 978-1-4039-9739-5   hardback
ISBN-10: 1-4039-9739-X   hardback
ISBN-13: 978-1-4039-9740-1   paperback
ISBN-10: 1-4039-9740-3   paperback

This book is printed on paper suitable for recycling and made from fully
managed and sustained forest sources.

A catalogue record for this book is available from the British Library.

A catalog record for this book is available from the Library of Congress.

10   9   8   7   6   5   4   3   2   1
15   14   13   12   11   10   09   08   07   06

Printed and bound in Great Britain by
Creative Print & Design (Wales), Ebbw Vale

To **Deborah**, **Bethany**, **Robert** and **Ben**
with all my love

Contents

List of Tables and Figures

Tables

Figures

Preface

This book owes its life to a sense that too many people I meet seem to loathe politics. When they then find that I am a professor of politics they either look at me as if I am mad for spending my time having anything to do with politics, or proceed to tell me all the things that annoy them about politics. This book is essentially my answer: it tries to explain why people find politics such a pain in the neck and hopefully to persuade them that politics is not that bad and actually crucially important to our freedom and wellbeing. Making the democratic form of governance that now dominates the world work better is the only way we can avoid something worse taking its place and I try, especially in the last part of the book, to set out what sort of changes are necessary, and why.

The initial inspiration for writing the book came when Katy Donnelly and John Williams – two fairly politically engaged people – brandished a copy of Bernard Crick's book *In Defence of Politics* – an earlier attempt to achieve a similar purpose – and indicated that as a guide to understanding politics in the modern era it was somewhat lacking. Now I had always rather liked Bernard's book, but when I started to read it again, I saw what they meant. It is dated, written in the Cold War era when fewer than a third of all countries were democratic and when the main opposition to democracy was Soviet and Chinese authoritarianism and a range of dictatorships (military or otherwise). In today's world, in contrast, democracy has achieved a dominant position in political thinking and is practised in about two-thirds of all countries. But the difficulty is that, while democracy has triumphed, respect for and willingness to engage in politics has declined. This book explores why that has happened and what we should do about it.

Because it ranges widely over countries and research topics that I have not previously addressed, this book inevitably relies enormously on the scholarship of others. I apologize now for the simplifications and maybe even distortions that may have been inflicted by my attempts to synthesize a complex literature into a coherent narrative of politics in our times. However, I do think that there is great value in being able to stray way beyond one's normal comfort zone as an academic. I enjoyed the journey, and I hope you enjoy the product. That journey would not have been possible without the financial support of the Economic and Social Research Council (ESRC) that provided me with a four-year professorial fellowship from January 2004 (ref no: RES-051-27-0067). I thank the ESRC for their support, and the time and opportunity it has provided.

Many academic colleagues have helped me refine and develop my arguments. I particularly benefited from an early presentation of some of the ideas in the book at the Australian National University, Canberra, in June 2005. Several colleagues read all or part of the book. They include Vasudha Chhotray, David Farrell, Francesca Gains, Vivien Lowndes, Peter John, Mick Moran, Tony Payne, Graham Smith and David Wilson. I also received very helpful comments from David Goodhart, Emily Robinson and Miranda Lewis. Three anonymous publisher's reviewers of the book also made many very helpful suggestions. I also inflicted the book on several of my neighbours who had better remain nameless but who generally said nice things like 'yes, it's readable' although it was never entirely clear how much of it they had read. But that's not the kind of thing you push with neighbours, is it?

I had great support from within the Institute of Political and Economic Governance at the University of Manchester. Two PhD students – Tessa Brannan and Catherine Durose – helped to get the typescript into shape. Two administrators – Deborah Woodman and Angie Lewis – also helped improve the text and provided supportive and encouraging comments. Angie in particular deserves praise for restoring the formatting to the text each time I managed to mess it up!

My publisher, Steven Kennedy, was just fantastic, always offering the right mix of challenge and support and buying me at least two good dinners along the way. He is rightly regarded as a giant in political science publishing. Thanks are also due to Keith Povey and his excellent copy-editing team.

Finally, of course, there is my family. Now normally what I do at this stage is thank them for putting up with me while I was writing. But actually I was a rather happy fellow while writing this book as I was enjoying my new learning and understanding. So I don't think they had to put up with much, although they might disagree. But what they did this time is enter more into the production of the book. Robert, my eldest son, is just completing his politics degree, so he was never short of an opinion about the book. Bethany is a scientist but took pity on her Dad and not only did a lot of the initial research behind the book but also undertook the survey analysis reported in Part I. Ben and Deborah listened to many versions of arguments in the book as they were at home and could not escape. Deborah is still holding out the prospect that this is a book of mine that she might finally read beyond the Preface. Anyway, I dedicate the book to them with my love.

GERRY STOKER

Acknowledgements

The author and publishers acknowledge with thanks permission to reproduce Table 3.2, slightly adapted from Yaojun Li *et al.*, 'Dynamics of social capital: trends and turnover in associational membership in England and Wales, 1972–1999', *Sociological Research Online*, 7(3), 2002. Every effort has been made to contact all the copyright-holders, but if any have been inadvertently omitted the publishers will be pleased to make the necessary arrangement at the earliest opportunity.

List of Abbreviations

BPR	Business process re-engineering
CEE	Central and eastern Europe
CEO	Chief executive officer
COP	Budget council (Porto Alegre, Brazil)
CPI	Corruption perception index
EU	European Union
FSU	Former Soviet Union
FTA	Free-trade agreement
FYR	Former Republic of Yugoslavia
GDP	Gross domestic product
GM	Genetically modified
ICT	Information and communications technology
ILO	International Labour Organization
IMF	International Monetary Fund
IT	Information technology
MNC	Multinational corporation
MP	Member of Parliament (UK)
NGO	Non-governmental organization
PB	Participatory Budgeting (Porto Alegre, Brazil)
SES	Social and economic status
SME	Small and medium-sized enterprise
TI	Transparency International
TNC	Transnational corporation
UAE	United Arab Emirates
UK	United Kingdom
UKIP	UK Independence Party
UN	United Nations
UNDP	UN Development Programme
USA	United States of America
WHO	World Health Organization
WTO	World Trade Organization

Introduction

The Dynamics of Politics

Democracy as an idea is more popular than ever, but citizens in democracies appear disenchanted with the political process. A worldwide opinion survey, covering more than 50,000 people in sixty-eight countries published in 2005, reveals that most people believe that their government does not act according to their wishes.[1] Lack of confidence in governments is highest in the former Soviet bloc, where 75 per cent say that their country is not governed by the will of the people, but similar views are held by most Europeans (64 per cent) and North Americans (60 per cent). Worldwide, politicians represent the least-trusted occupation in the survey, scoring only 13 per cent. Religious leaders are the most trusted, at 33 per cent. People like the idea of democratic governance in the abstract, but do not generally find the practice a positive experience.

While many in countries under dictatorial rule struggle bravely to achieve democracy, many people living in democracies are alienated from politics and feel that it does not work properly. The central argument of this book is that politics matters, and getting it right matters. The book takes a broad view of the main issues confronting all democracies in the twenty-first century world, but given the limitations of space and the experiences and capacities of the author it gives more attention to the politics of longer-established industrial democracies. While the problems and solutions to the current malaise of democratic politics will vary from country to country, I believe that my focus on common features and key comparisons provides a good starting point for discussion of where we are, and what needs to be done.

When asked which types of people they would like to see have more power, the survey put 'intellectuals' (writers and academics) in first place at 35 per cent, followed by religious leaders at 25 per cent. As an academic, it is good to see this vote of confidence from world public opinion, but I fear that it may be based on rather defective reasoning. Politics is not a difficult process simply because of the flawed characters of politicians, and I am not convinced that there would be any fewer problems if I and my academic colleagues took over! The real problem with politics, even in democracies, is that it is inevitably destined to disappoint because it is about the tough process of squeezing collective decisions out of multiple and competing interests and opinions.

1

The negative response to politics that many of us share is, I think, a very human reaction to the way politics works. As an intricate mechanism in our multifaceted and complex societies, politics exists because we do not agree with one another. Politics is about choosing between competing interests and views often demanding incompatible allocations of limited resources. Crucially, because it is a collective form of decision making, once a choice has been made then that choice has to be imposed on us all. There is no point having a rule that vehicles on a road must stop when a traffic light turns red unless it is generally observed and enforced. Politics at the level of today's large-scale, inter-connected and diverse societies is on a tough beat. Our collective will – which is what politics is supposed to express – is not easy to fathom, or always comfortable to accept once it is decided upon.

The central focus of this book is on these challenges that are internal to the political processes of democracies, but the external environment for politics has also got harder. Globalization appears to be taking decisions out of the hands of politicians and citizens rooted in nation states. The rapid scale of our technological development and issues such as the global warming of our planet create challenges that some fear may be beyond the capacity of our science and politics to tackle effectively. Finally, a wide range of social and cultural changes seem to be making many of our societies more individualistic and less cohesive. Added together, these factors may well have made politics harder, and may explain in part our sense of disenchantment with it. But politics is failing not just because the challenges are tougher.

There are a number of internal pathologies to the dynamics of politics that need to be examined. People have, according to what psychologists tell us, a number of common fears or preconceptions when it comes to living in human societies and politics by its nature tends to bring those fears and preconceptions to the fore.[2] People don't like to be taken for a sucker or treated as an idiot. Politics as experienced on a daily basis often seems calculated to feed that fear. When politicians debate issues in simplistic terms, when they imply that we can have it all at no cost and when politicians appear at times to manufacture a range of arguments that they think will play well to different groups, it is hardly surprising that we think that they are taking us for a ride. Nor is it odd that cynicism becomes a common coping response. People often find it difficult to think beyond their own experiences and therefore tend to judge political decisions according to their own interests and circumstances. Naïve aspirations and assumptions about politics often flow from these preconceptions. People tend to assume that most other people agree with them (or would do if only the issue was explained to them properly) and that the ideal outcome is one that suits them in every detail. People generally do not like making a lot of effort for little reward.

Accordingly, offloading responsibility on to others is a very common coping mechanism in political exchanges.

I argue in this book that politics matters more than most people in democracies give it credit for, and it is more demanding of them than they fully realize. You can have politics without democracy – that is, you can have authoritarian government with people making collective decisions on your behalf without accountability to you – but you *can't have democracy without politics*. There is no form of collective decision making that can be described as 'democratic' that does not rest on a process of engaging those affected by a decision in the making of that decision. Yet thinking about politics for many citizens of democracies goes along the following lines:

> Politics is not intrinsically interesting. Ideally, what I would want are politicians who know instinctively what I want. I do not really care much about most issues and indeed I am happy to see someone else with more interest make the effort of sorting things out. What I do want should I deign to participate, because something grabs my attention or affects me in some way, is that the political system then responds to my demands with courtesy and attentiveness.[3]

Now I hope that you are laughing at this point, because you recognize that this kind of reasoning about politics contains aspirations about the way democracy should work that are hopelessly and spectacularly unrealistic. If you are laughing, then I hope you will enjoy reading this book as it explores how we can construct a realistic understanding of how democracy works and how it could be improved and made sustainable in the twenty-first century. If you are not laughing and read the passage wishing that politics was done in this way, I hope that you will read this book and become convinced that you should have been laughing at this point.

Why Politics?

This book is premised on a belief that politics matters, and that it matters so much we can't afford to be stupid, naïve or cynical about it, and moreover we cannot afford to entirely offload our responsibilities to engage in it. To explore this statement a little further it is first worth dwelling on the issues of what politics is, and whether it has to exist. There have been many disputes over these two questions stretching over centuries.[4] I have already suggested that politics reflects the existence of conflicts of interests and opinions. But is it inevitable that politics must exist? You might argue that politics persists only because humans make the wrong choices: if they followed the right path, set down by religion or some other moral guide, they would all choose the same thing and as a result politics would not be necessary. You might alternatively argue that politics operates only in societies that are structured so that people's interests are fundamentally opposed, but that it might be possible to structure a society where people's interests were always aligned and as a result politics would not be required. The former argument has at various times been made by some religious and other moralizing opinion leaders. The latter is one used by some radicals and utopians of various hues. Neither is particular convincing to me, and neither can take much succour from the historical record to date. There is little to suggest that human beings or human societies are perfectible, as implied by these contrasting under-standings.

It is difficult to be certain about human nature. But I think it is reasonable to take as a starting point the idea that people are capable of terrible deeds, but also capable of great acts. It is equally difficult always to be sure what is in someone's best interests, so it seems impossible to establish a society where some interests do not clash. Given human society as it has been, and as it might reasonably be expected to be in the future, people will make their own judgements about what is right for themselves and for others and there is no basis to assume that those judgements will be shared. Equally, it is clear that as humans we need to find ways to act together, to engage in collective action and to resolve the problems and challenges of living together. So poli-tics, as John Dunn, defines it, can be seen as:

> [T]he struggles which result from the collisions between human purposes: most clearly when these collisions involve large numbers of human beings . . . It takes in, too, the immense array of expedients and practices which human beings have invented to cooperate, as much as to compete, with one another.[5]

Politics is constructed in order to express conflicts and allow different inter-ests to shape our collective endeavours. So politics is about trying to get what you want for yourself, or alongside others, for a common cause. Politics is also ultimately something to do with rule, with the ordering of our societies. Politics is about reaching a compromise, and finding ways for those who disagree to rub along with one another.

Some people argue that there is a strong distinction between a 'big P' politics of government conducted at a national (or perhaps an international level) and a 'small p' politics of civil society that takes place in communities and associations of citizens.[6] There are, indeed, different sites or locations for politics, and part of a better approach to politics in democracies might be to extend the scope of a politics of civil society alongside allowing citizens greater access to the more mainstream 'big P' politics. We shall cover these issues in Part III of the book. For now, it is important to emphasize that there is no escape from politics. Whether at a 'big P' level or 'small p' level, politics involves expressing and resolving differences and findings ways of cooperating to achieve collective actions. In civil society differences exist as much as they do in the 'big politics' of nation states and international relations. Romantic thinking about community and civil society should not blind us to the reality that because we are human we disagree and seek different things and we need politics not only to express but also to manage those disagreements and if possible find ways to cooperate.

Why Politics Matters

Politics matters because collective decisions matter. Perhaps the very richest in society are in a position where they could opt out and live on a desert island free from the rest of us, but even there they can't today escape the impact of global warming and our collective effect on our environment as sea levels rise. For almost everyone else, what happens in the wider society makes a huge difference to their ability to get a job, access education or receive health care. What happens in the wider society matters to us all – and that means that politics matters too, because it is through politics that we can influence what happens in that wider world. And that does not only apply to politics on the grand stage of national and international politics, but also to the politics of civil society, the communities in which you live and the associations that structure your life.

Politics matters because there are conflicts and differences of perspective in society about what to do, what resources to collect for public use and how those resources should be spent. The idea that people disagree may seem at first take uncontroversial; but one constant suspicion that people have about politics is that a lot of disagreements are trumped up and that the great show of difference that politicians and the media sometimes try to emphasize is somehow false.[7] Sometimes it is true that disagreements are a result of misunderstanding and that discussion and debate can mitigate it, but on many occasions conflict has a very solid base. To understand politics, one must above all understand the inevitable *partiality* of judgement. Judgement is particular to an individual because it reflects their unique set of experiences. Throughout the ages, people have hoped that wise and incorruptible individuals could be found to make judgements on all our parts, avoiding the unpleasant necessity of politics by allowing others, more expert and gifted, to decide. Such hopes perhaps lie behind the opinion survey finding, quoted at the beginning of this chapter, which claims people think that intellectuals or religious leaders should be given a greater say in democratic and political decision making. But judgement is always partial because it comes from the whole breadth of human experience. As John Dunn puts it: 'what partiality rests on is the lives which each of us live'.[8] No one else can live our life and no else can therefore make all judgements for us.

People can value some things more than others. At the very grand level, a lot of politics is about different views of 'the good life'. A central divide for much of the last two centuries has been between those who prefer liberty over equality and those who privilege equality over liberty. At a more prosaic level, a lot of politics is about hanging on to what you have got, and politics often involves crude power struggles over who gets what. Politics does not always involve grand visions of right and wrong, but rather its focus is on fighting to get or keep a share of resources. More challenging still can be political arguments about identity and entitlements. Issues of ethnicity and the rights of different social groups can often lead to great problems in finding sustainable political solutions if those basic rights are disputed or challenged by another group. The concern to define who and what you are is a constant source of political conflict in our diverse societies, and it is a form of disagreement that is very hard to manage within democracies. Violent conflict, civil wars and even genocide can result from these types of conflict.

Some matters are just more important to some people than others. And at different stages of your life you may be concerned about different things from student loans to pensions. So a lot of politics involves the 'don't cares' on a particular issue versus the 'care-a-lots', because they are directly affected. Indeed, one of the main things that people disagree about is what should be on the political agenda of society and be something therefore that politics should do something about. A lot of politics is about getting something on the 'to-do-list' of governments at all levels.

If everyone agreed we should value the environment and the future of the earth (and it is difficult to argue we should not) there would be plenty of scope for disagreement about what to do, what course of action to take and at what level of urgency. So if people agree about the goal there remain a lot of arguments to be had about the means to achieve the goal. A lot of collective decision making involves *redistribution*, and so politics can involve intense arguments about who gets what. Politics often involves regulation or intervention that passes costs on to some rather than others. And in the details of implementation – the way that a policy is put into effect – there is plenty of scope for further differences of opinion and interest.

Politics matters because it reflects the tensions created when human beings rub up against each other and at times it does more than just express those conflicts, it finds a way of settling them. Politics is one of the ways we know of how to address and potentially patch up the disagreements that characterize our societies without recourse to illegitimate coercion or violence. Politics, especially in democratic societies, enables people to compromise and reach an agreement. It is a means to orderly and legitimate self-rule. As Bernard Crick puts it in his classic book, *In Defence of Politics*:

> Politics is simply the activity by which government is made possible when differing interests in an area to be governed grow powerful enough to need to be conciliated ... Other paths are always open. Politics is simply ... that solution to the problem of order which chooses conciliation rather than violence and coercion, and chooses it as an effective way by which varying interests can discover that level of compromise best suited to their common survival.[9]

In other words, politics can provide a means of getting on with your fellow human beings that aims to find a way forward through reconciliation and compromise without recourse to straightforward coercion or outright violence. It provides a way to live in an ordered manner with your neighbours, but one that unavoidably often calls on you to sign up to deals and compromises that might not be your first or even tenth choice, but which nevertheless have something in them that enables you to put up with them. It might not be very inspiring, but when it works politics delivers one great benefit: it enables you to choose, within constraints, the life you want without fear of physical coercion and violence being used against you. Politics creates space for human choices and diverse lifestyles. Politics, if done well, creates the positive context and stable environment for you to live your life. That's why politics matters.

Democratic Politics in Trouble: An Overview of the Argument

Democracy as a particular way of practising politics has gained considerable ground in the last few decades. Around two-thirds of all the countries in the world have a basic set of democratic institutions built around competitive elections that enable all adult citizens to choose and remove their government leaders. Yet paradoxically, at the moment of democracy's triumph, there appears to be a considerable amount of discontent and disenchantment about the operation of democracy both in those countries that have prac-tised democracy for decades and those who are more recent converts. Mass democracy, practised with a universal suffrage, has less than a century's worth of experience. Democracy is a demanding way of doing the politics of compromise and reconciliation because it rests on the fundamental idea that all adult citizens have a right to a say in matters that affect them. So perhaps we should not be surprised that democratic politics is proving to have difficulties in practice that we still need to learn to overcome. According to the social theorist Max Weber:

> Politics is a strong and slow boring of hard boards. It takes both passion and perspective . . . And even those who are neither leaders nor heroes must arm themselves with that steadfastness of heart which can brave even the crumbling of all hopes.[10]

Max Weber, writing at the beginning of the twentieth century, thought that modern democratic politics would be the preserve of professional politicians and activists for whom politics was a vocation. These activists and leaders would require imagination and commitment but also willingness to compro-mise and make hard choices. Yet even the mostly unengaged citizenry would require a certain steadfastness of heart to stay with the political process. But today many citizens appear to be alienated by the professional-ization of politics and dissatisfied with their allocated position as passive and patient observers of the decision making of others.

The book is not a dispassionate analysis, although it aims to offer clear analytical frameworks for thinking through the issues and provide an accu-rate account of some of the most important ways that we currently conduct politics in democracies. Alongside the analysis there is a concern with how things ought to be, as well as a focus on how they are. This book looks at the rights and wrongs of our current democratic politics and eventually, in Part III, how we might go about improving our practice of politics. Part I of the book provides an analytical and empirical account of our discontents with democracy and how they might be explained, alongside normative judge-ments about what democratic politics is about and by implication how it should be conducted. Part II of the book is the most heavily empirical. It analyses the ways that citizens are engaged, or not engaged, in politics in democracies, but it too does not shy away from normative judgements about whether certain types of engagement are good or bad for democracy. Part III of the book is the most straightforwardly normative, in that it turns its atten-tion to how politics in democracies might be made to work better. However there are strong analytical and empirical strands even in this section as the aim of the book is not to just explore ideas about what might be done, but also point towards new practices.

Mass Democracy: Triumph and Disappointment

Chapter 1 begins our exploration by arguing that getting politics in democracies to work is a worthwhile challenge. Democracy is rightly a celebrated guide to how we should take collective decisions in our societies. The starting idea of democracy is that all adult citizens should have a voice in respect of decisions made in the societies in which they live. The practice of democratic governance requires free and fair elections to choose government leaders and a range of other freedoms (such as freedom of speech and assembly) and basic respect for human rights. Beyond these basic starting points there are, of course, differences of view about how democracy can best be expressed and achieved. Above all, democracy needs to be seen as a universal value. It is not simply a western ideology. People everywhere have reason to see its basic premises as valuable. It is an integral part of human nature to value the opportunity to be involved in decisions about issues that affect you. Democracy, in turn, protects a wider commitment to freedom and respect for human rights. Your right to engage is only validated by the rights of others to engage also being respected. Democracy also delivers at a basic level. It cannot guarantee you a happy life, but it makes government and power-holders in society inclined to look after your basic necessities. Finally, democracy helps by using the knowledge embedded in different parts of society to find solutions to intractable problems. The ideas behind democratic governance appear to have wide support in many countries of the world, across a range of cultures and contexts. Most people think that democracy may have some problems, but they are clear that it is better than other forms of government. Yet establishing and maintaining effective democratic practices are no easy tasks, especially in divided societies.

As already noted, one of the paradoxes of our age is that democracy is more dominant as a form of governance than ever before, but within both established and newer democracies there appears to be a considerable disenchantment with politics. Detailed evidence from all regions of the globe is provided to illustrate this point in Chapter 2. What emerges is a complex picture of overall decline and a set of discontents that range from a lack of confidence in the way that politics works to extreme cynicism about the process. Some degree of scepticism about politics might well be considered healthy and there may be a cycle to public engagement in politics, depending on the nature of the issues at stake. But it is difficult to escape the idea that the scale and breadth of discontent about politics raises some questions about the long-term health of democracy. People perhaps naturally do not trust politicians but, more than that, many of the key institutions of democracies – parties, parliaments and polls – do not command sufficient respect and engagement. Democracy cannot survive if its lifeblood of politics is seen as a sort of necessary evil – or, worse still, a pointless waste of time.

Chapter 3 explores various explanations of why disenchantment might have grown. One idea is that maybe politics has come to be disparaged because the world has got so out of control that it is no longer possible to change the world through our collective will. Politics is about people deciding to take action, but what is the point if political forces cannot exercise influence over it. Some appear to think that globalization represents just such a force, and through its economic, social and technological demands takes choices away from human societies. But there is much counter-argument and evidence to suggest that government at local and national levels can influence global trends and that the growing capacity for global governance gives us an embryonic way of addressing issues in a new way. In short, globalization provides a new terrain for politics and not the case for its abolition. Some argue that technology rather than globalization provides the biggest threat to our capacity to control our societies and therefore the meaningfulness of politics. The rampant exploitation of the earth's resources and the prospect of new and untried genetic and other technologies mean that economic growth and the pressures of scientific development will create impacts that politics will not be able to contain. Again, Chapter 3 presents evidence to suggest that the doomsayers are presenting an over-exaggerated argument. What is clear is that politics is in challenging and hard times, and that observation is compounded by a realization that the societies in which politics operates are fragmented in complex ways.

Chapter 4 presents a general statement of the argument that lies at the heart of this book – namely, that the increased discontent with formal politics is best explained by a number of misunderstandings of the political process that have taken hold in the discourse of democracies. The pressure from the increased prominence given to market-based consumerism in the culture of many democracies has led key aspects of politics to be overlooked. As a result, many citizens fail to fully appreciate that politics in the end involves the collective imposition of decisions, demands a complex communication process and generally produces messy compromise. Politics is designed to disappoint – that is the way that the process of compromise and reconciliation works. Its outcomes are often messy, ambiguous and never final. Part of the trick is to recognize that it is possible to return to an issue later. Politics involves that hardest of human skills: listening carefully to the opinions of others and their expressions of their interests. Doing politics in a small group is hard enough and the greater prospects of misinformation, muddle and malaise in our large complex societies is bound to create some frustration. Democracy cannot wish away that reality.

The Pathologies of Political Practice

Part II of the book explores the argument that it is not just that we characterize and understand politics in a mistaken way, but that there are problems and difficulties with the way we practise it as well. Most citizens' engagement has a sporadic and mundane character and an uneven and very limited quality. As Chapter 5 shows, for all the opportunities that in theory might be afforded them most people engage very little beyond occasionally casting a vote; and as we know that declining numbers worldwide appear willing to do even that. Research indicates that when citizens do engage they tend to undertake relatively simple acts such as signing a petition or boycotting a product as a way of sending a political message. Even in terms of these types of political activity there are significant differences between the civic capacity of different countries and within countries between more and less educated people. In terms of the quality of the engagement there is a sense in which what counts as 'politics' for most people is not much more than an extension of their activities as consumers. There is nothing wrong with such expressions of citizenship; they are just rather limited. Much engagement is directed towards something that brings personal benefit or perhaps provides an expressive statement about a person's sense of themselves and their identity. These atomized forms of citizenship mean that people often have only a surface engagement with political issues and complexities. There is hope in the range and diversity of engagement in democracies, but there are also concerns because of its uneven spread and shallow quality.

Most of the real politics is done in a space where we are spectators. It is the sphere of professionals not amateurs. Chapter 6 examines the roles of high-intensity activists in party politics, citizen lobby groups and protest movements. The cohesion brought by parties, the advocacy of special interests by the lobby and the challenge and dissent offered through various forms of protest offer vital links in the democratic chain between governors and governed. But all are failing to engage citizens-at-large in politics. The committed activists for democracy constitute maybe fewer than 1 in 600 in any population. Activists are odd people, very much in a minority in our society. They do a lot of the work of politics for us, and we should be grateful to them; but the way their organizations work is in part responsible for people's sense of alienation from politics.

As parties have lost membership, they have become reliant on professional campaigners and organizers and operate in a way that treats citizens as passive political observers that just need to be mobilized at elections times to back the party. Citizen lobby organizations – such as Friends of the Earth – have large-scale memberships, but their involvement is generally restricted to providing the necessary funding. They, too, rely on professional organizers and experts. Members provide the cash but the professional politicos in the lobby organizations decide what to campaign on. Citizens are a passive audience to be exhorted about particular campaigns through the media and occasionally galvanized to send in letters or cards of support or join a public demonstration based on often rather simplistic messages. Citizens are offered little in terms of depth of analysis or understanding of the issues at stake by these organizations. Even more radical protest organizations tend to be professionalized in their style of behaviour and their use of the media. The occasional engagement by a wider group of citizens in a protest 'event' or rally is in danger of being more a lifestyle statement than a serious engagement with a political debate.

Chapter 7 argues against the corrosive influence of cynicism in the way that so many of us view politics and politicians. It challenges the academic literature that lends support to a very cynical take on politics. A central part of the chapter addresses the issue that might make the most direct case for cynicism – namely, that politicians lie all the time. There is no point in denying that politicians do lie some of the time, but the case for the defence rests on two main points. First, we all lie some of the time. Second, between lying at one end of the spectrum and the full, unvarnished truth at the other, there are many halfway houses that our expectations and the circumstances under which they may operate often force politicians uncomfortably to occupy.

The final section of Chapter 7 examines the role of the media in promoting a culture of cynicism. There are several aspects of this argument to consider. First, there has been a 'dumbing down' in news coverage, which means that people are less likely to understand underlying issues or complexities in respect of politics and politics can often be seen to fail when what it is delivering is judged in a simplistic framework. Second, the fusing of news reporting and comment, which is a characteristic of modern media coverage of politics, probably feeds a culture where fact, opinion and speculation merge into one another and which lends itself to a cynical take on political life. A third argument is that the media in some countries has actively spread a culture of contempt; a fourth argument is that we have seen the emergence of a style of journalism that presents itself as the champion of the people and takes a strongly adversarial position to politicians, asking all the time why is this politician lying to me and you, the viewers and listeners.

The first two arguments perhaps hold true across more countries than the last two. However, we should stop glorifying journalists and journalism that makes its reputation by being constantly cynical about politics and politicians. The problem with cynicism is that it is ultimately a fatalistic creed: it feeds disengagement, because it tells us that in the end selfishness and mendacity will triumph, so why bother?

I am not arguing that you should trust politicians without qualification. I am happy to agree that politicians sometimes make politics worse by their behaviour. Some politicians are dishonest, some are time-serving compromisers and some are dangerous ideologues. In some senses, in all of these ways they are representative of us, the citizens. But beyond that, many politicians are not as venial, incompetent or divisive as we sometimes think. Democracy needs us to strike a pose of healthy scepticism towards politicians, rather than corrosive cynicism.

Chapter 8 looks at another problematic approach to democratic politics that is commonly to be observed in today's world: *populism*. Populists see themselves as true democrats, defending the neglected interests of the people. Modern populism finds an accommodation with democratic practice and thought and is reflected in the rapid rise of 'anti-politicians' of various hues and persuasions: right-wing, left-wing and centrists. It is often reflected in the spectacular rejection of political elite-supported referendum propositions that are put to the people. Modern populism draws in people from all walks of life, not just the uneducated or the underclass. It feeds on the discontent with politics and produces short bursts of engagement, but offers little that could sustain a tolerant and viable approach to politics.

My main criticism of populism is that it fails to see the complexities of politics. Ironically for a creed that holds that the commonsense of the people should be lauded, populism tends towards a very high-octane faith in redemptive politics. Changing the world in the direction you want is a matter of capturing the will of the people. Democracy should deliver what the people want, and if it does not it's down to corrupt politicians or the malign influence of do-gooders, big business or some other unrepresentative lobby. It tends to a view that a powerful personality and strong leadership could overcome all the problems and institutional complexities that appear to bedevil the practices of democratic governments. The irony is that commonsense might tell you to be more pragmatic and view politics as the art of the possible, a matter of compromise, its tone as driven by respect for toleration and diversity, its rewards as stability and peace rather than any utopia. Populism should not be viewed as simply anti-democratic or as undesirable. Populism can express a belief central to democracy – that the people can change their world for the better. Where it falls down is when it collapses into aggressive intolerance of other people's legitimate viewpoints and generally the rather simplistic understanding of political processes and prospects that it conveys.

Searching for Solutions

The understanding of politics in democracies offered here provides a framework for interpreting the sense of disenchantment and divorce from politics that pervades those democracies and simultaneously points towards ways to improve the practice of politics in democracies. We now need to consider what changes are needed, and how positive change could be delivered. This book takes a long hard look at how people participate in politics. It finds that people are often cynical about politics, that many have naïve aspirations about what it can offer and achieve, that people tend to offload responsibilities for engagement and that most prefer to join in themselves only in a way that minimizes effort and maximizes potential gain.

The troubling issue is that these dominant forms of citizen engagement are not sustainable as a way of conducting democratic politics. They feed a cycle of disaffection that ultimately runs the risk of undermining public support for democracy. Rampant cynicism, populism and a stark gap between high-intensity activists and the political practice of the rest of us makes politics more difficult and less likely to succeed. We need to rethink the way that we do politics. It matters for the future of democracy that we do.

In Chapter 9 I argue, however, that we should start from where people are and then seek to mould political institutions and a wider civic infrastructure to enable people to engage in politics more effectively without transforming them into new model citizens. When it comes to politics, most people are amateurs: they have no intention of making it their vocation or career. There is nothing wrong with being an amateur, but there is a difference between a vaguely competent amateur and a completely inadequate layperson – as any golfer, sailor, or bird-watcher will tell you. Moreover, being an incompetent amateur when it comes to these leisure activities can be very irritating to others, and occasionally even dangerous. The same argument can be applied when considering democratic politics. So the first plea of this book is that people should be more self-critical and reflective about their approach to politics. They should seek to become more competent amateurs.

Politics is a place for amateurs, but we need to design institutions, structure processes and develop support systems to make it easier for people to engage. My solution to the problem of disenchantment with politics is thus deceptively simple. It is to expand the opportunities for citizens to have a say about the issues they care about. There are two insights hidden away in this formula that run as threads throughout this book. First, it is vital to recognize the *range of issues* that people think are important. One person's 'big issue' can mean nothing to another. This is so because politics rests on a fundamental truth about human beings: because we, and only we, can live our different lives, we all see the world through the lens of that experience. Most of us probably carry around in our heads a set of (usually unarticulated) understandings of what range and type of issues matter to us; they will be different to those held by others. We need a politics that allows citizens to have a say over what is important to them, not what professional politicians, lobbyists, journalists or scientists tell them is important. The second is that having a say does not mean, for most people, having a veto or being the final judge. As amateurs, citizens are cautious about claiming decision taking responsibility. Having a say means wanting to *influence*, but not having to *decide*.

The implications of these challenges are taken up in Chapters 10 and 11. Chapter 10 explores how to make representative politics more legitimate and open. Representative politics needs to be understood as a more active exchange between citizen and representative and restructured to give more scope for local and global decision making. Chapter 11 looks at the broader civic arena that surrounds politics and explores imaginative ways in which people can engage in the public realm by trying to influence public policy, and more generally by taking responsibility by taking action to meet collective difficulties together. It goes on to examine the roles of key civic institutions, and in particular the media, in creating a positive environment for democratic politics and engagement. The book concludes with a plea: politics is not an unpleasant sideshow that wastes the energies of freedom-loving individuals, but rather it is an arena in which the challenge of living together in a shared world can be met. In short, it matters.

Part I

Mass Democracy: Triumph and Disappointment

1

The Triumph of Democracy?

> In the summer of 1997, I was asked by a leading Japanese news-
> paper what I thought was the most important thing that had
> happened in the twentieth century. I found this to be an unusu-
> ally thought-provoking question, since so many things of grav-
> ity have happened over the last hundred years ... I did not,
> ultimately, have any difficulty in choosing one as the pre-
> eminent development of the period: the rise of democracy. This
> is not to deny that other occurrences have been important, but I
> would argue that in the distant future, when people look back at
> what happened in this century, they will find it difficult not to
> accord primacy to the emergence of democracy as the preemi-
> nently acceptable form of governance.[1]

Amartya Sen, 1998 Nobel Laureate in Economics

Amartya Sen picks out democracy as the crowning achievement of the
twentieth century. It has to be admitted that it is possible to think of many
other developments in the century worthy of praise, from widespread
advances in economic welfare to space travel. But I think the establishment
of democracy deserves to be placed at the top of that century's achieve-
ments. A powerful wave of democratization closed the twentieth century,
and as a result most politics now takes place in mass democracies whose
citizens have been given a voice in the processes and institutions that determine how power is exercised and how decisions are made. This chapter
shows how democratic governance has become a widely accepted and celebrated guide to how we should make decisions on a collective basis in our
societies. It explores the nature of this democratic governance, arguing that
democracy is a system worth defending and showing that it is not just a
'western' idea but also a universal value. The chapter continues by examining the spread of democratic practice. It concludes by looking at the 'dark
side' of democracy in multiethnic nation states where the arguments of
democracy have been distorted to justify the 'cleansing' of one ethnic

group by another. Nevertheless the overall message of this chapter is: hooray for democracy.

The Nature of Democratic Governance

Large-scale democracy, based on voting rights for all adults, is a very new form of governance that got underway in the early decades of the twentieth century, although the concept of democracy has a longer history stretching back at least to the Greek states more than 2,000 years ago. In recent decades, it has become the world's preferred form of governance.

Let us define democratic governance as a political system that meets the following three criteria:

• Universal suffrage – that is, the right to vote in elections for all adults
• Governments chosen by regular, free and competitive election
• The presence of a set of political rights to free speech and freedom to organize in groups.

By these far-from-tough criteria, no nation state in 1900 could be called 'democratic' because none had universal suffrage. By 1950, about a third of all nations could meet all three criteria to a reasonable extent; and in the last quarter of the century, a great wave of change saw democratic governance extended to about two-thirds of all countries.[2] Democracy now has pole position as the world's preferred form of governance.

The struggle to achieve democracy has often involved inspirational acts both by leaders and by populations at large. The experience of Nelson Mandela and South Africa in the 1990s stands out in our memories, but there have been countless other steps towards democracy taken in difficult and trying circumstances. In the 1980s, there were the long struggles of peoples in Poland and other eastern European countries to establish democracy. Further back, the early years of the twentieth century saw the continuation of a campaign to win votes for women, with the honour of first granting universal women's suffrage going to Finland in 1906.[3]

There have been a number of key influencing factors behind the spread of democracy in the last quarter of the twentieth century.[4] The most obvious is the break-up of the earlier colonial arrangements of western powers such as the UK, France and others. A second has been the fall of authoritarian regimes in some parts of western Europe including Spain, Portugal and Greece. A third is the collapse of the former Soviet Union (FSU) and the liberation of an associated group of satellite central and eastern European

(CEE) states held under its influence. Fourth, there has been a resurgence of democracy in Latin America and Asia.

Economic development that in turn supports changes in the social structure – shifting the position of classes, ethnic groups and women – has been a key driver for democratization, as exemplified by the experience of South Korea, Taiwan, Brazil and Mexico. In some cases, the failure of authoritarian regimes to deliver economic performance has opened them to the challenge that democratic forces might do better. Crucially, in order for such a transition to occur a form of compromise between established elites and new political forces has had to emerge. The experience of some parts of Europe, Latin America and Africa can be seen as following this path.

But to an extent, the debate about democratization has changed. Traditional explanations focused on national structures or players to see if they were ready to provide the conditions and context for democracy, with the in-built assumption that democracy was an unusual form of governance and needed the right conditions to become established. More recently, the emphasis has been on global and international factors. Since the end of the Cold War more international pressures have been brought to bear advocating the cause of democracy. Both the USA and the European Union (EU), although not always consistently, have promoted democratization as the right path to follow for other countries. Finally there has been more international pressure to support human rights and democracy as a basic right. Extending democracy is now the stated project of important and powerful global actors.[5]

Democracy as a Universal Value

What exactly is 'democracy'? Our starting point should be a straightforward definition of democratic governance, identified above as a set of procedures and institutions through which decisions by societies are filtered. As a governance system – that is, as a way of making collective decisions in society – democracy requires free, fair and competitive elections, underwritten by universal suffrage in order to choose government leaders; it is also necessary that the results of those elections be respected. Democracy also entails respect for the freedoms and the basic rights of citizens, a capacity to deliver justice and respect for the rule of law. It also demands a capacity for free exchange of views among citizens and an uncensored distribution of news and opinion. Democracy, even to achieve what might be regarded by many as these minimum conditions, asks a lot of a society.

Some argue that democracy is about much more than a set of arrangements for making decisions in society, as set out above. The starting concept of democracy that is used in this book rests firmly in what can be described as the 'realist camp', in that its focus is on an *operating system of decision making* rather than some far-off goal. The model is egalitarian, in its emphasis on equal rights to participation and protection, but it does not insist on a wider economic or social equality as a precursor to democracy. What I would say is that, ultimately, democracy must involve citizens in more than simply selecting leaders to govern them. It must be about the capacity of citizens to engage in and influence policy debates and outcomes. Democracy, rather than democratic governance, rests on the idea of those being affected by a decision having a right to a say in that decision. Exactly how much of a say, and what citizens should expect from a system of democratic governance, are matters that are returned to again and again in this book, and most explicitly in Chapter 9.

For the present, it can simply be noted that there are other narratives of democracy, many of them emphasizing to a much greater degree than I do the need for direct participation and the need for egalitarian conditions to be established before democracy can flourish.[6] Indeed, in the processes that contribute to democratization in different countries there are likely to be different views about what democracy will bring and what it means, and these are in turn a source of inspiration, dispute – and, if undelivered, disappointment.[7] In some of the newer democracies, for example, the processes of democratization ran alongside other developments such as a shift to a market economy or (in the case of South Africa) the attempt to create a post-apartheid society. If democracy fails to support economic development or a more equal society, it may lose legitimacy and public support. Such matters will be considered later in the book, as will the possibility that more participation might help to revitalize politics in mass democracies.

Democracy, it is sometimes argued, is an exclusively western concept. While it is true that some politicians in the West tend to claim democracy as their own, such claims should be disputed. Some institutions dominated by powerful western countries – such as the World Bank – have pushed western-style democracy as part of a package of good governance from the 1980s onwards, but it would be a mistake to assume that democracy is just another export of the West.

Democracy is better understood as a universal value. As Nobel Prize winning academic Amartya Sen points out:

> In any age and social climate, there are some sweeping beliefs that seem to command respect as a kind of general rule – like a 'default' setting in a computer program; they are considered right unless their claim is somehow negated. While democracy is not yet universally practiced, nor

indeed uniformly accepted, in the general climate of world opinion, democratic governance has now achieved the status of being taken as generally right.[8]

Democracy is not a universal value because everyone agrees with it. Indeed, any value that achieved such general acclaim would be likely to fall into the 'motherhood and apple pie' category of empty ideas that no one could object to. Democracy is a tougher concept than that. It has been hard fought over, and won respect. What makes it universal is that 'people anywhere may have reason to see it as valuable'.[9]

But, there are still commentators who claim that particular sections of the world's population are culturally or practically incapable of democracy. Samuel Huntington[10] argues that the world has reached a historical period in which it is faced by a fundamental clash of civilizations, with the West versus the rest. The West's power and dominance is a source of antagonism, but fundamentally there is also a clash of *values*. Liberalism, democracy, the rule of law and a range of other 'western' values have little resonance in Islamic, Confucian and other non-western cultures. According to this Harvard professor, the reality is that: 'modern democratic government originated in the West. When it has developed in non-western societies it has usually been the product of western colonialism or imposition'.[11] A less academic way of putting it would be to say that 'Arabs or Africans just can't handle democracy'.

Samuel Huntington may well be right to suggest that the West's use of its power to get its own way causes resentment elsewhere in the world, and a brash western commercial and political imperialism of ideas and products are sources of antagonism. Where he is mistaken is in suggesting that democracy is a western preserve. It is, to say the least, wide of the mark historically to suggest that, outside western democracies, democracy exists because of western colonialism or intervention. The people of India or South Africa could explain to him that democracy exists in their countries despite, not because of western input. Since his article about the clash of civilizations was published in 1993, democracy as a form of governance, as noted earlier, has become ever more widely established and present in Islamic, Confucian, African and Latin American regions, and by no means confined largely to the West.

There is a more fundamental reason for objecting to the 'clash of civilizations' thesis: it places a false emphasis on a homogeneity of thought and practice in broad cultures or civilizations. As Amartya Sen points out, 'diversity is a feature of most cultures in the world', so to suggest that western thought has shown 'a historical commitment of the West – over the millennia – to democracy, and then to contrast it with non-Western traditions (treating each as monolithic) would be a great mistake'.[12] Islamic and other traditions allow scope for democratic practice; western thought is not exclusively democratic. Authoritarianism – the major alternative to democracy – has been a core part of western thought and historical practice.

Democracy is attractive to a great many people for three fundamental reasons. Again following Amartya Sen, we can view democracy as having *intrinsic*, *instrumental* and *constructive* features that make it desirable. The intrinsic value of democracy is something much celebrated by political philosophers and rests on the idea that it is an integral part of being human to share decisions and choices with other humans. Participation in the political life of a community makes us more whole as people and gives us a chance to express ourselves as human beings.

Some may find the intrinsic value argument convincing, and others may not. It seems to rest on a rather romantic or even woolly view of politics, and I for one need some more practical arguments to support the case for democracy. How sustainable is the love of a procedure such as democracy unless it helps you achieve something? It is a better sell for democracy to claim that it will 'help you achieve the outcomes which are the things closest to your heart'.[13] This is the point where the *instrumental* argument for democracy kicks in. But in this case the marketing of what politics can do needs to be cautious. Democracy cannot guarantee you a happy life, but it can make some disasters of human life less likely to be imposed on you. One study suggests tentatively 'there is a robust correlation between democratic institutions and health, resulting in greater life expectancy in democracies'.[14] Amartya Sen, in part, won his Nobel Prize for showing that major famines generally do not occur in democracies; recent famines in Ethiopia and Somalia occurred under dictatorships, and great historical famines such as those in the Soviet Union in the 1930s or China in 1958–61 took place in authoritarian regimes. The evidence is clear and so, too, is the explanation:

> Famines are easy to prevent if there is a serious effort to do so, and a democratic government facing elections and criticisms from opposition parties and independent newspapers, cannot help but make such an effort.[15]

When things are going fine, then the instrumental value of democracy may not be missed. It is when things go wrong, as they always will, that democracy is needed, because of the particular incentives it gives governments to behave in way that takes the welfare of citizens into account. Democracy provides the mechanism to ensure that governments are only able to get away with so much.

Finally, democracy does positively help in the search for solutions to intractable problems and challenges. This is the *constructive* value of democracy. Open dialogue can be the key to resolving many of the most challenging issues we confront; it enables the sharing of ideas, learning and the thinking through of problems. It is that public airing of issues that can make all the difference. Sometimes, however, contrary to the view of some theorists of deliberative democracy, politics does its work through smoke and mirrors. By enabling people who fundamentally disagree to find a way forward by sometimes giving different meanings to the same words, politics does much valuable work. Democracy – more often than we often care to admit – relies on 'weasel phrases', hidden compromises or delayed gratification and various other forms of ambiguous construction that enable all sides to claim victory, or at least emerge defeated but with their honour intact.

So democracy deserves its status as a universal value. It is not an exclusive western form of governance, but rather the preferred system of making decisions for people throughout the globe. It does its work in a variety of ways and with a considerable degree of messiness and compromise. It is constrained and limited. But in the last few decades it has become a living practice for the majority of countries on the planet, as the next section will show.

The Triumph of Democracy

Here are five important facts about democracy:

- The most powerful nation in the world, by far, at the beginning of the twenty-first century – the USA – has a system of democratic governance
- India – one of the world's most populated countries – has had a system of democratic governance for over fifty years and, despite enormous religious, social and ethnic divides, it has survived
- The EU consists of a group of twenty-five countries, each operating a system of democratic governance, and constitutes a powerful bloc in economic, trading and foreign affairs
- Most of the Latin American and Caribbean countries have some form of democratic governance, as do many African and Asian nations
- Democratic governance and human rights are the largely unquestioned international standard for countries.

These facts do not command universal rejoicing. Some people think that the USA is powerful, but also an aggressive and dangerous actor on the global stage. Some citizens of Europe do not like the EU. The strength of the internal democracies of all nations – but particularly those in Africa, Asia and Latin America – are often questioned. Some fear that double standards and national self-interest cloud the rhetoric about international commitment to human rights and democracy: the West favours democracy when it suits its interests and opposes, or at least fails to support, it when it does not; western countries stick up for human rights when trying to put other countries in the dock, but are willing to ignore human rights issues themselves. Democratic governance may be an international standard, but many express doubts about whether democracy can be imposed from the outside. Yet for the first time in human history it is possible to imagine a future in which authoritarian rule might be eliminated within two or three decades.[16] That should be a matter for universal rejoicing.

The rise of democracy is a story that stretches beyond the boundaries of this book. At the beginning of the 1970s – when I first studied politics – writers about the constitutional arrangements of different nation states classified regimes under three headings. First, there was relatively small group of democracies concentrated mostly in advanced industrial nations. Second, there was a larger group of communist states, and finally there were the developing countries, a few of which operated democratic forms of governance but most of which were prone to military or one-party dictatorships, or at least authoritarian rule. At the beginning of the 1970s, there had been no great surge in the growth of democratic governance and as a result the position was similar to that already noted in 1950. In total, around a third of the countries in the world could be classified as meeting the criteria of democratic governance of universal suffrage, regular elections to choose government leaders and basic political rights, in that period.

The great drive to democracy that dominated the last quarter of the twentieth century started with the collapse of the European dictatorships in Portugal, Spain and Greece in the 1970s.[17] Between 1979 and 1985 the military withdrew in favour of civilian governments in nine Latin American countries. In the 1980s and 1990s democratization began to spread to previously untouched parts of Asia. The Philippines saw the end of the Marcos dictatorship in 1986 and Taiwan, South Korea, Bangladesh, Nepal and Pakistan all strengthened their democracies or became democracies in this period, although in the last case, democracy did not survive. The fall of the Berlin Wall in 1989 and the collapse of the Soviet Union saw the start of a process that spread democracy throughout central and eastern Europe. In Africa, Benin led a move to democracy in 1990, followed by a process that

Table 1.1   Democracies, by region, 2002

Region	Number of countries	Number of democracies (per cent)
Western Europe and Anglophone states	28	28 (100)
Latin American and Caribbean	33	30 (91)
Eastern Europe and the FSU	27	18 (67)
East, South, South East Asia	25	12 (48)
Pacific Islands	12	11 (91)
Africa (sub-Sahara)	48	19 (40)
Middle East and North Africa	19	2 (11)
Total	192	120 (63)

Source: Data extracted from Table 5 in Larry Diamond, 'Can the whole world become democratic? Democracy, development and international politics', Center for the Study of Democracy, paper 03.05, University of California, Irvine, 2003.

led to democracy being established in South Africa in 1994. Other African states also established democratic rule during this period. As a result nearly three in five states had achieved some strong aspects of democratic governance by 1994, and the process has become firmly established, so that by the start of the twenty-first century nearly two-thirds of all countries met the basic criteria. Table 1.1 gives a breakdown by regions of the world.

Of course, the quality of democracy in all countries can be questioned. After all, it was in the 'model' democracy of the USA that the presidential election of 2000 collapsed into an acrimonious dispute over whether George Bush or Al Gore had actually won because of irregularities or uncertainties in vote-counting. A detailed democratic audit of any country is unlikely to produce a clean bill of health.[18] All of the countries included in Table 1.1 meet the minimum requirement that they hold regular, free, fair and competitive elections to fill the positions in their governments. Citizens in these countries all have a secret ballot, fair access to a range of media and basic rights to organize, campaign and solicit votes. But many still suffer from significant human rights abuse, corruption and a weak rule of law.

As Table 1.1 shows, the democratic form of governance has a major foothold, if not a dominant position, in most regions of the world. Democratic governance exists in rich and poor countries and in countries with a range of cultures and traditions. It has been established in small and large countries, although more so in the former than the latter. Yet eight out of eleven countries with populations greater than 100 million have a form of democratic governance. Democratic governance is practised in countries with every major philosophical and religious tradition: Christian, Jewish, Buddhist, Confucian, Hindu and Muslim. All this suggests that comments about certain cultures not being suited to democracy are difficult to sustain. The region that is the missing link in the spread of democracy is the Middle East and North Africa, where in 2002 only two countries meeting the criteria of democratic governance could be found. But I think that this reflects the politics of the region and the negative impact of past western influences and interventions, rather than a cultural issue for the population.

Public opinion survey evidence backs up this judgement that the idea of democratic governance is popular in all parts of the globe. In particular, the survey research indicates that many Muslims prefer the idea of democracy to authoritarian rule, as do clear majorities of the population in all other parts of the world. The *World Values Survey*, a spectacular public opinion research effort covering over eighty nations, reveals the scale of the support for democratic governance. Table 1.2 provides detailed results: members of the public in many countries appear to agree with the direction of thought offered by Winston Churchill, that democracy may not be a perfect or all-wise form of government, but it is less bad than all the alternatives.[19] Specifically in relation to the issue of Islamic-populated states and democracy, Ronald Inglehart, a key mover behind the *World Values Survey*,

Table 1.2   Support for democracy

Per cent agreeing that 'Democracy may have problems but it's better than any other form of government'

Region	Highest (per cent agreeing)	Lowest (per cent agreeing)
Western Europe and Anglophone states	Denmark (99)	Britain (78)
Latin America	Uruguay (96)	Mexico (79)
Eastern Europe and FSU	Croatia (96)	Russia (62)
East, South, South East Asia	Japan/India (92)	Indonesia (71)
Africa (sub-Sahara)	Uganda (93)	Nigeria (45)
Middle East and North Africa	Algeria (88)	Iran (69)

Note: No figures are available for Caribbean states and Pacific islands.
Source: Data from the *World Values Survey* (1999–2002) wave for most countries (drawn from a fuller analysis by Ronald Inglehart, 'The worldviews of Islamic publics in global perspective', 2005, available at www.worldvaluessurvey.org).

concludes: 'Islamic publics, including the Arab publics, overwhelmingly view democracy as the best form of government'.[20]

Although a response to one survey question – the evidence provided in Table 1.2 – is hardly likely to be the last word on the issue of world public opinion and democracy, it does provide support for the view that support is widespread and fairly strongly held in most countries. If you are British – as this author is – it is not too comforting to see the self-proclaimed 'mother of democracy' as the lowest ranked of the 'western' democracies when it comes to support for democracy. The response of citizens in many countries also suggests that they are able to distinguish between the *idea* of democratic governance and its, often less than perfect, *practice*. In short, people may well see failings in their own system of governance, but recognize that democracy is an ideal worth striving towards.

Conclusions: A 'Dark Side' to Democracy?

Broadly, we can be positive at this point. Democratic governance is widely supported in the public opinion expressed by the peoples of the world, regardless of culture, religion or other factors. If we had more time, we could probably identify some significant differences between the perceptions and value placed on democracy in different countries. People in many countries are not so sure that democracy is working for them, and there are substantial portions of many populations who it appears would not take much persuasion to consider a more authoritarian form of rule. In Latin America, East Asia and the post-communist countries of Eastern Europe and the Soviet Union there is much evidence of people being less than convinced by the development of democracy, as Table 1.2 makes clear. But it would be churlish not to recognize the degree to which the idea of democracy has become a dominant force in world public opinion. Moreover, two-thirds of the countries of the world are attempting to put democracy into practice in some form.

We know that if democracy is to work, it needs more than the establishment of a particular set of institutions. It has to be a lived practice, with at least two key elements.[21] The maintenance of democracy requires an effective state to regulate society, agree compromises and organize the distribution of public goods. It also requires a civil society of non-state actors that is organized, active and engaged and capable at a minimum of holding the state to account and at a broader level offers the seed bed for the development of democratic ideas and practice.

It is because of these realities that even if the global order now in a formal sense favours democracy, the arrival of democratic practice in former authoritarian countries cannot be guaranteed. Certainly it is difficult to see how democracy can be imposed from the outside: the active engagement and commitment of key players within a nation state is an essential basis for the reform of the state and the strength of civil society, as exemplified by the struggles in Iraq following the US-led invasion that brought down Saddam Hussein. Establishing democracy in areas that have seen deep internal division is not an impossible task, as shown by the example of South Africa. But democracy is not easy to establish, and even in mature democracies it may not be easy to sustain commitment to it as a form of governance.

The assumption made in the discussion so far is that democracy is something that develops in nation states. We operate with a territorially bound idea of what a political community is, and the community of citizens granted universal suffrage and political rights are seen as delimited by the boundaries of different countries: democracy exists in India or Portugal; the right to have a say means the right to have a say in your own country. One challenge that can be raised to this assumption is the growing impact of global decision making and forces that are taking issues beyond the boundaries of our national political communities. The implications of these developments are explored in Chapter 3. For now, I want to note how democracy can be in trouble when the definition and status of the political community is based on the promotion of one group at the expense of another. Northern Ireland, Kosovo, Sri Lanka, Fiji and Rwanda – to pick a range of cases from around the world – exemplify 'a dark side' to democracy,[22] in the form of ethnic divisions and, most tragically, ethnic cleansing.

The trouble comes when, in ethically mixed nation states, the demos (the people) becomes defined as one ethnic group (the ethnos). Michael Mann explains:

> But if the people is to rule in its own nation-state, and if the people is defined in ethnic terms, then its ethnic unity may outweigh the kind of citizen diversity that is central to democracy. If such a people is to rule, what is to happen to those of different ethnicity? Answers have often been unpleasant . . . Murderous ethnic cleansing is a hazard of the age of democracy since amid multiethnicity the ideal of rule by the people began to entwine the demos with the dominant ethnos, generating organic conceptions of the nation and the state that encouraged the cleansing of minorities.[23]

When rule by the people comes to mean rule by a particular ethnic group, then democracy can be a harbinger of brutal attacks on the minorities that fall foul of the majority. This is not to suggest that ethnic cleansing is justified by democratic ideals, but rather to recognize that the rhetoric of democracy can and has been used to justify barbaric acts. In modern colonies, settler democratic communities have in certain circumstances proved truly murderous. Mann describes in detail some of the activities of settlers in the USA and Australia. The break-up of former authoritarian regimes in Europe has created the conditions for ethnic conflict to flourish under democratic regimes: Mann examines the case of the former Yugoslavia (FYR). In democracy's defence, it can be said that by no means is ethnic cleansing a strategy that emerges from democratic states alone; authoritarian regimes are capable of such atrocities – think of Nazi Germany or Stalin's Soviet Union (both cases documented by Mann). Moreover, at the heart of the main practices of democratic governance is a commitment to formal political rights for all citizens and groups that make the case for the inclusion of all groups in decision making rather than the exclusion of some ethnic groups. Indeed, many democracies have developed quite elaborate mechanisms to enable different ethnic groups to share in decision making, as the cases of South Africa or Canada, in different ways, show.

Democratic governance as discussed in this chapter is about the protection of the rights of the minority, rather than the simple imposition of rule by the majority. So the 'dark side' of democracy, that lends itself in some cases to ethnic cleansing, is a distortion of the democratic ideal, but it reflects a tension in democratic thought that cannot be wished away. Democratic governance, as advocated here, is committed to enshrining freedoms and constitutional protections into a system of collective decision making that opens access to decision making to include all social groups. That is the model of democratic governance that has gained a dominant grip on politics throughout the world, and is the model of democracy that we should be celebrating. Yet as Chapter 2 shows, many citizens in democracies struggle to find much to celebrate about the practice of democratic politics in their countries.

2

Global Dissatisfaction with Politics

> The general temper of the world is one of profound disillusion-
> ment and despair. Our generation seems to have lost its scheme
> of values. Certainty has been replaced by cynicism; hope has
> given room to despair.[1]

> Harold Laski, 1931

The opening quotation from Harold Laski was written to describe the western democracies in the middle of the Great Depression in the late 1920s and
early 1930s. It reminds us that cynicism and disillusionment with politics
and the democratic system were quite widespread in earlier periods of
history.[2] Unemployment, large-scale poverty and the seeming incapacity of
the system to respond gave a distinctive flavour to the disillusionment of the
1930s. There were fears – some of then realized – that because of political
failures people would give up on democracy.[3] In the 1970s there was a wave
of concern about the 'ungovernability' of democracies,[4] and a concern that
people would give up on democracy because there were too many demands
from citizens and not enough capacity on the part of governments to
respond. These fears proved largely unfounded as a generation of politicians
responded with programmes to limit government. The challenge for the
purpose of this book is to understand the particular nature of the crisis in
politics at the beginning of the twenty-first century. The striking paradox
that provides its leitmotif is that popular confidence in political process
appears to be very low in many countries, while support for the idea of a
system of democratic governance is globally high. People appear to like the
idea of democracy, but not like the politics that goes along with it.

Dissatisfaction finds a reflection in a falling turnout in elections, especially among the young. In competitive elections across the globe, turnout
rose steadily between 1945 and 1990 to reach 68 per cent; but in the 1990s it
started to dip and is now heading back towards 60 per cent,[5] Throughout the

world, disgruntlement is expressed with governmental processes, parties and the whole political system. Government processes are regularly portrayed in the media and in everyday conversations as wasteful and inefficient. Political parties struggle to attract membership and the long-term commitment of voters.

This chapter provides evidence to support the proposition that people are distrustful of politicians and disillusioned with how democracy works in democracies. It concentrates its initial analysis on the advanced industrial democracies, but goes further and suggests that in some of the developing world and post-communist world – the new adopters of democratic governance – it is also possible to see a considerable frustration with political processes in democracies. The heart of this chapter, then, is a global tour of the politics of dissatisfaction in democracies.

In the concluding section of the chapter I ask: 'does it matter that citizens are disenchanted with the political process?' There is nothing wrong with citizens being sceptical about politicians and cautious about the dynamics of politics. Indeed, some suggest that what has happened at the beginning of the twenty-first century is a reflection of rising citizen expectations and their willingness to be critical: citizens, they argue, are simply more willing to complain about more things. But I argue that the scale of disengagement and disenchantment from politics is such that the goals of democratic politics may be undermined by people's lack of faith in the system. Without some faith, some system loyalty, politics cannot function.

The Changing Pattern of Politics in the UK

Let us start our tour in the country with which I am most familiar, namely the one in which I live, the United Kingdom of Great Britain and Northern Ireland. There is little doubt that many people think there is something wrong with politics here and the UK case is, I think, illustrative of the issues that are being confronted in many advanced industrial democracies.

Turnout in general elections from a high of 83.9 per cent in 1950 reached a low of 59.4 per cent in 2001, although as recently as 1992 a turnout of 77.7 per cent was achieved. The 2005 general election saw no substantial 'bounce back' in turnout, with 4 of every 10 eligible voters staying at home – a figure rising to 6 of every 10 among 18–25-year-olds.[6] Turnout in local elections is at around 30–40 per cent and has been low for some time; and in recent years turnout by young people in local elections has been estimated to be as low as 1 in 10.

Trusting politicians to tell the truth has been, at best, the preserve of only

1 in 5 of British citizens in various surveys between 1983 and 2004. The British seem to have found their politicians untrustworthy for at least two decades[7]. It does appear that there was greater trust in government in earlier periods such as the 1950s and 1960s.[8] One could argue that an increased amount of distrust of politicians is a healthy thing, since otherwise why would accountability through elections be seen as important? But it is perhaps more worrying when a lack of trust in politicians spills over into a lack of trust in information provided by government bodies. According to a MORI survey in 2005, 68 per cent think that official figures are changed to support politicians' arguments; 59 per cent think that the government uses such figures dishonestly; 58 per cent think that official figures are politically manipulated.[9]

Interest in politics seems to have maintained a roughly 60:40 or 50:50 split between those engaged by politics and those uninterested in it, in various polls between 1973 and 2003.[10] But there has been a substantial decline in the membership of political parties in the UK from over 3 million in the 1960s to around 800,000 in 1990s.[11] Many of today's members are 'paper members' who hand over their fees but are not engaged. In practice, most parties have 'severely depleted memberships' and an 'increasing dependence on limited numbers of activists'.[12] In the UK's mature democracy, not only has membership in parties plummeted, but so has party loyalty. In 1964, nearly half of Labour and Conservative voters were very strong identifiers with their chosen party, but by 2001 only, respectively, 14 per cent and 16 per cent could be so described: a three-fold drop. Strong Liberal identifiers in the same period fell from 32 per cent to 7 per cent.[13] Parties struggle to get any sort of commitment from voters who appear unattached and free-floating from the formal institutions of politics.

Alongside the trend to disengagement from formal politics, we have seen a rise of activism around particular issues and campaigns. Large numbers of people can be mobilized and engaged, but not through established parties and for only limited periods of time: for example, there were large-scale protests against the Iraq War in 2003. When asked in 2004 if they got involved, would they be able to change things, 4 in 10 thought not; 2 in 10 were not sure; but close to 4 in 10 did believe that if they engaged they would influence the outcome.[14] A sense of collective political efficacy remains for some, but close to two-thirds are not convinced that if they did engage, anything much would change.

It would be a mistake to suppose that British people are regularly or frequently taking to the streets or forging a new form of mass collective politics. Political practice is much more humdrum and based around a series of low key individual actions. Doing politics for most British citizens is more likely to involve signing a petition rather than taking to the streets. According to a survey conducted at the beginning of the twenty-first century by Charles Pattie and colleagues[15] the most common political action beyond voting is donating money to some organization, this has been done in the previous twelve months by nearly two-thirds of citizens. After that the next most popular form of engagement is signing a petition (undertaken by 4 in 10 in the past year). The next most likely political action involves taking up a grievance through some sort of formal or informal channel by contacting an organization or individual that could be involved in the decision making process (up to 25 per cent had engaged in that type of activity). Finally, and by far the least likely, political action involves engagement in collective action through forming a group or joining in a protest (only 5 per cent claim to have engaged in these types of activity in the last twelve months). The average person in Britain undertakes between three and four of these political interventions each year.

Politics is an *ad hoc* activity from which people tune in or tune out according to the circumstances that are confronting them. What they lack is any sense of sustained engagement with political institutions and the political system. It is, I think, difficult to see here great evidence of a wider surge of more critical citizenship. Rather, the picture is one of many citizens alienated from formal politics and trying as best they can to cope with the world of politics and government, but only when they have to because of some pressing need.

Disenchantment in Other Advanced Industrial Democracies

The position in most other advanced industrial democracies is similar in most important respects to that outlined for the UK. The most comprehensive and intensive survey of the position of those democracies by Russell Dalton concludes:

> Contemporary democracies are facing a challenge today. This challenge does not come from enemies within or outside the nation. Instead the challenge comes from democracy's own citizens, who have grown distrustful of politicians, sceptical about democratic institutions, and disillusioned about how the democratic process functions.[16]

Another review of politics in the same range of countries from North America, western Europe and Japan – referred to as the 'trilateral democracies' – takes a similar line:

Whatever the 'normal', background level of public cynicism and censure of politics, citizens in most the trilateral democracies are less satisfied – often much less satisfied – with the performance of their representative political institutions than a quarter of a century ago.[17]

Without going into the same depth as the UK, supporting evidence for the general thrust of the arguments presented above is provided by the experiences of North America, western Europe, Australia, New Zealand and Japan.

The USA

The case of the USA is well documented. Joseph Nye and his colleagues, in a book whose title tells the main story – *Why People Don't Trust Government* – review the US evidence and show quite a sharp decline in confidence in government there, too. In 1964, three-quarters expressed confidence in the federal government, but by the late 1990s that level had reduced to a quarter, with a similar pattern of decline being replicated at state levels of government.[18] What comes across in the sifting of evidence is a big shift in opinion. The mid-1960s appears to be the high point in confidence in government and politics. One US political scientist, writing in 1965, reported an increase in trust in government since the 1930s. Robert Lane argued that years of affluence had brought contentment, and that as a result there had been 'a rapprochement between men and their government and a decline in political alienation'.[19] The author even found that in 1945 a quarter of parents would be happy for their son to go into politics and that that proportion had gone up to a third by 1965; he concludes that this positive attitude on the part of a substantial proportion of Americans reflected 'a growing attitude that political life is both rewarding and honourable'.[20] So confident was the author that he went on to predict a 'growing state of confidence between men and government, perhaps especially between men and politics, during the Age of Affluence'.[21] This has not proved one of the better predictions made in twentieth-century political science.

If we add the extensive evidence of declining voter turnout, social disengagement and a weakening of civic institutions, assembled by Robert Putnam in his thesis of declining social capital in the United States (see pp. 55–8), then it is clear that confidence in the American political system has ebbed away.[22] Putnam records a drop of about 20 per cent in the public's following of current affairs in the last quarter of the twentieth century and a similar level of decline in interest in politics.[23] Against a range of measures of political participation, Putnam finds a 25 per cent drop in activity between the mid-1970s and the mid-1990s.[24] Some remain citizens, some remain civic activists, and others civic slugs, as Putnam puts it, but there has been a steep decline in the former and a substantial rise in the latter.[25] As Putnam notes, in the 1960s Americans felt that they were politically effective and even in times of crisis were prepared to give their government the benefit of the doubt, at least in respect of its good intentions. But by the 1990s, all that had changed, with cynicism becoming a more dominant theme. Putnam concludes:

> Today's cynical views may or may not be more accurate than the Pollyannaish views of the early sixties, but they undermine the political confidence necessary to motivate and sustain political involvement.[26]

In comparative terms, America remains a country of active citizens, but the evidence suggests strongly that it is much less engaged than it was.

The controversial Michael Moore would have had no market in the 1960s for his scathing books about politics that have been bestsellers over the last decade.[27] The USA is at the very least a country not at ease with itself over its politics. A team of authors writing under the auspices of the American Political Science Association in 2005, go further:

> American Democracy is at risk. The risk comes not from some external threat but from disturbing trends: an erosion of the activities and capacities of citizenship. Americans have turned away from politics and the public sphere in large numbers, leaving our civic life impoverished. Citizens participate in public affairs less frequently, with less knowledge and enthusiasm, in fewer venues, and less equally than is healthy for a vibrant democracy.[28]

This stark judgement suggests that people are indeed disengaging from formal politics in the USA, and provides little to support the view that a new spread of critical citizen politics has stepped into the vacuum.

Canada

The picture from Canada provides similar evidence of withdrawal from formal politics.[29] Turnout in federal elections has fallen for three straight elections, from 75 per cent in 1988 to 61 per cent in 2000, although in provincial elections the picture is more mixed. Turnout in the 1980s and 1990s fell in five provinces, but went up by a small amount in three, and has remained roughly at the same level in two. Young Canadians are considerably less interested in current affairs and formal politics, and for those that are engaged and active the focus is rather different. Young Canadians are not necessarily more cynical than their elders, but they have become more disengaged from traditional political institutions. What appears to be a factor is that when young people do engage it is over international issues, rather than domestic ones. There may be some evidence here of critical citizens, but it is far from clear to what extent such activity spreads beyond a small social group.

Western Europe

The evidence suggests that Europeans – with the possible exception of the Nordics – display most of the same symptoms of political disenchantment and unease with formal politics. Admittedly starting from a higher base that that generally achieved in Anglophone countries, 'European' voter turnout – that is, votes in European nations in national elections – has decreased from 88 per cent in 1980 to 74 per cent in 2002. After years of relative stability, the downturn in recent years is noteworthy. Party membership also displays a marked downward drift, especially in the long-established democracies of western Europe. Party membership had fallen to closer to 5 per cent of the population in 2000 compared to a figure of nearly 9 per cent a decade or so earlier. This phenomenon builds on a more long-term trend of decline.[30]

Figures from the *European Social Survey* – undertaken at the beginning of the twenty-first century – tells us clearly that all is not well with the state of European politics.[31] The survey covered most of the established democracies of Europe, together with a few of the newer democracies such as Poland, Hungary, the Czech Republic and Slovenia, and because of the limits and variable coverage of the survey it is important to be cautious about the degree of validity around some of the figures and percentages produced below. It is nonetheless clear that the survey shows a pattern of some considerable alienation. Asked if politicians cared what people like them think, over half the Europeans surveyed said they thought that hardly any or very few politicians did care. Less than 4 per cent were prepared to sign up to the proposition the most politicians do care what people think. The Nordics generally felt that their politicians were more responsive, and Portugal took top prize for having politicians that do not listen. The survey also shows that 10 per cent of people have no trust in politicians; and a further 30 per cent have what could be defined as 'low trust'. Against the 40 per cent with no or low trust, only 10 per cent have what might be described as 'high trust'. Trust of politicians is generally at its highest in the Nordic countries, but in

Greece, for example, nearly 1 in 5 has no trust at all in politicians. Interest in politics is pretty modest, with half of those surveyed saying that they were hardly, or not at all, interested. The Spanish take the prize for the least interested in politics and the Dutch appear to be the most – nearly 80 per cent of Spaniards claim not to be interested in politics much or at all; that figure drops to 34 per cent for the citizens of the Netherlands.

Notwithstanding these figures, some see talk of a crisis in representative democracy in Europe as being wide of the mark. Klingemann and Fuchs, two German-based scholars,[32] point to people being more prepared to consider a wider repertoire of ways of engaging politically. Representative democracy, at least in the established democracies of western Europe, is not on its last legs, but people are focusing their judgements on the ability of democratic politicians, not so much to engage them but to *deliver better performance*. The difficulty of achieving such effective performance may undermine the political system still further.

The authors of a report on democracy in Europe published in 2004 by the Council of Europe[33] are much clearer that there is a major problem in the ways that politics is working. They define two broad types of discontent that can be observed among citizens. One form of alienation, which is familiar and long-standing, stems from people who fear that they lack the skills to intervene effectively in politics. Such people tend to have a rather low level of education, social status, political information and sophistication. They may feel a personal political incompetence and lack marked political preferences, but fear being 'had' by politicians. They lack an interest in politics: it is something done to them and what they observe is bickering point-scoring among politicians that in the end makes no difference to the often difficult life circumstances they find themselves in.

A second type of alienated citizen has 'more sophisticated feelings of discontent'. This group tends to have a higher (but not necessarily a very high) level of education. They are confident in their ability to cope with politics, but alienated from its current practice. They pay enough attention to politics to be able to criticize political actors with informed arguments, but they are far from convinced that there is any longer any point to mainstream politics. They tend to think that politics no longer offers real choices to them, or that governments simply lack the capacity to intervene effectively because of the power of 'big business' and the impact of globalization.

Japan

What about the position of the advanced industrial democracies on the other side of the globe from Europe? In Japan, disaffection with politics has a number of distinctive features,[34] but is nevertheless high. First, trust in politicians has for a long time been low; almost from its launch on the democratic path in the late 1940s Japan appears to have had a low opinion of politics. Dissatisfaction with politics stayed at 50–70 per cent between 1978 and 1995. In 1992, 74 per cent of Japanese endorsed the view that many dishonest people were running the country, and that the key issue was the connection between candidates, 'big business' and money. A series of reforms pushed through in the 1990s appeared to make little immediate difference. A second distinctive feature of Japanese disenchantment was that it was focused on politicians and politics, rather than bureaucrats and bureaucracy. But scandals during the 1990s dramatically reduced the levels of trust in the elite group of central bureaucrats, so that two-thirds in one poll said that they had no confidence in them. A third feature of Japanese politics is the way that distrust has been directed at national, much more than local, politicians.

Australia and New Zealand

Australian politics is, for many of its citizens, characterized by a sense of cynicism and frustration. As one commentator puts it:

> Popular forms of political discourse are peppered with anti-politician and anti-government rhetoric. The persuasiveness of political slogans, such as 'Vote No to the Politicians' Republic' during the 1999 referendum campaign, and the Australian Democrats' once famous 'Keeping the Bastards Honest', exemplify the resonance of anti-politician sentiment in the Australian electorate.[35]

Survey material from 2003 confirms that:

> Respondents were satisfied and proud of a general conception of Australian democracy but were mistrustful of politicians, the federal parliament, the legal system and the public service. Thus . . . citizens support democratic ideals whilst being critical of the practical workings of democracy.[36]

The picture in New Zealand is similar. Recent reforms, and in particular the establishment of proportional representation in elections, appear to have done little to shift attitudes towards politics in a positive direction.[37]

Political Disenchantment beyond the Industrial Democracies

Central and eastern Europe

There seems to be clear evidence of disenchantment when it comes to the advanced industrial democracies. But can the same be said of the newer democracies? It would appear so. The alienation from politics and governance systems is striking in the newest democracies of central and eastern Europe. There has been a marked decline in electoral participation with a fall in average in voter turnout from around 70 per cent at the beginning of the 1990s to 60 per cent just ten years later. Global Barometer surveys[38] (covering Belarus, Bulgaria, Croatia, the Czech Republic, Estonia, Hungary, Latvia, Lithuania, Moldova, Poland, Romania, Russia, Serbia, Slovakia, Slovenia and Ukraine) conducted in the late 1990s and early 2000s reveal that among the citizens of these countries nearly a third are of the view that almost all public officials in their country are corrupt, and a further 40 per cent think that most are. Only 1 per cent of citizens think that almost no officials are corrupt. Nearly two-thirds distrust their political institutions, in particular their parliaments. Most people are not that interested in politics. Many are far from convinced that their countries are democratic in practice; only a third appear certain. Three-quarters are not satisfied at all, or not very satisfied, with the way that democracy works in their country (for comparison, the figure for the more established democracies of western Europe ranges between a third and a half in terms of dissatisfaction).

Latin America

A United Nations (UN) report on *Democracy in Latin America*[39] paints a picture of dissatisfaction similar to that found in the new democracies of central and eastern Europe, although it notes that this discontent with politics is framed by evidence of considerable progress. Of the eighteen Latin American countries considered in the report, only three were democracies in 1975. Since then, relatively free and fair elections have been held in all eighteen countries. The human rights situation has improved, although significant problems remain. The role of the judiciary and the strength of other constitutional checks and balances have improved but there remains considerable room for further improvement. Yet despite these advances, the report concludes: 'The reality is that politics . . . has major limitations and is in crisis. It lacks the capacity to address the problems to which citizens demand answers.'[40] Governments find it difficult to deliver because economic and international pressures constrain them from providing the social conditions that their populations would like to see, and because there are groups within their own societies that are able to use their economic and latent political power to constrain political choices.

The governance indicators from Global Barometer surveys do not make happy reading.[41] Only a third of those surveyed in Latin America stated that they were interested in politics. Trust in political institutions – the parliament and president – runs at around 30 per cent, and trust in political parties dips below 30 per cent. Political parties as agents of representation are in severe crisis, manifest in 'people's increasing loss of confidence in them'.[42] Only 1 per cent of those surveyed think that corruption is not a serious problem.

As noted in Chapter 1, you can get a comfortable majority in most Latin American countries in response to the 'Churchill test' – namely that democracy is the preferred form of governance to all others. The non-democrats tend to come from less well-educated groups whose socialization developed in a period of authoritarian regimes that encouraged a strong distrust of democratic institutions and politicians. The democrats are found across all social groups, but they are more likely to express themselves through non-traditional means than through mainstream parties. But according to the UN report, 'preference for democracy does not imply strong support'.[43]

Surveys at the start of the twenty-first century show that throughout Latin America[44] nearly half those who believe that democracy is the best available form of governance also think that economic development is more important than democracy; nearly half would support authoritarian government if it resolved economic problems. Many appear to have doubts about some of the basic rules of democracy: around a third of the group who favour democracy think that it could operate without political parties or a national legislature and that the president should impose order by force and control the media. The UN report goes on to identify three broad categories of Latin American attitudes towards democracy. It found that 43 per cent of the sample in the 2002 survey fell into the 'democrats' group, 30.5 per cent into the 'ambivalent' group and 26.5 per cent into the 'non-democrat' group. The democrats thus need the ambivalent group on board to get a majority, and the figures indicate the thinness of the support for democracy.

It would be a mistake to describe the citizens of the countries of Latin America as apathetic. Unmobilized citizens perhaps amount to a quarter of the total, but so do a very active group of citizens: 'In addition to voting, they contact public authorities when there are problems that affect their community, they take part in public demonstrations, and they donate their time, labour or money to initiatives to resolve community problems.'[45]

This group of the highly active is joined by wider groups of people who are more occasionally active beyond voting, dipping in and out of politics as circumstances demand.

Africa

The Global Barometer figures on governance indicators for Africa show a mix of support for, and disenchantment with, the political process.[46] However, nearly half say that they trust the president a lot or a very great deal. Nearly three-quarters are very or somewhat interested in politics and over half express satisfaction with the way democracy works in their country. On the other hand, only 10 per cent say they trust their parliaments a lot; 3 in 10 think that most or all public officials are corrupt and a further 4 in 10 think that some public officials are corrupt.

However, support for democracy remains at high levels. After two survey rounds in 1999–2001 and 2002–3, the Afrobarometer *Briefing Paper* comes to the clear view that Africans have grown weary of military and authoritarian rule and remain overwhelmingly supportive of democracy. Yet, the *Briefing Paper* also found evidence that commitment to democracy may be relatively shallow, with people willing to consider one-party rule as an acceptable 'authoritarian' form of governance. Behind the satisfaction with democratic governance across the continent, there are some big differences in individual countries. Ghana saw a big increase in the way democracy was perceived to work at the turn of the twentieth century, whereas public opinion in Nigeria headed in the opposite direction. In terms of the standing of democracy in various African countries, the survey reveals half where it is perceived to be advancing and half where deficits and concerns are becoming more prominent over time. The authors of the *Briefing Paper* conclude:

> The bad news . . . is that these democratic commitments decay, often in response to disappointing government performance or to ruling parties that overstay their welcome. But the good news is that democratic legitimacy can be renewed, either by improved performance or, in its absence, by replacement of an under-performing government at the polls.[47]

It would appear that the basic commitment to democracy in Africa is strong, but fragile. The core idea of democracy retains high support, even if the practice leaves something to be desired.

East Asia

Figures from the Global Barometer[48] for East Asia – including Japan, China, South Korea, Mongolia, the Philippines, Taiwan and Thailand – show a concern about corruption in government, with nearly half of those surveyed saying that corruption is present among almost all or most public officials and the vast bulk of the remainder of the sample taking the view that corruption is present, but among just a few officials. About half the population describe themselves as not very interested or not interested at all in politics. Trust in political institutions is modest, with again about half of those surveyed having not much or having no trust in their parliaments. On the other hand, around two-thirds – excluding those in China – said that they were very, or fairly, satisfied with the way that democracy works in their country.

India

India stands out as a beacon, with over fifty years of democracy in conditions of significant social inequalities and ethic division. Indians appear to be attached to the idea of democracy not because it has solved the country's economic and social problems but because it expresses a real sense of equal citizenship in a divided society. Nearly two-thirds think that their vote has an effect on decisions and there is strong support for the basic institutions and processes of democracy. This support is for the *system*, rather than for the politicians who populate it: nearly two-thirds think that politicians do not care what ordinary people think, and less than a quarter rate their politicians as effective. 'It is quite obvious that though people value the system of representation, they do not find the representatives elected by them as worthy of high regard.'[49] Not the least of the complaints is about the endemic levels of corruption among public officials. In the everyday construction of people's experience of the state, corruption is just a given.[50]

Should Disenchantment be a Matter of Concern?

The chapter has explored the range, variety and magnitude of our discontents with the democratic system. In many respects, given evidence of its global presence and long-running nature, it could be argued that a certain degree of discontent with politics is normal. These discontents show a degree of difference – between a lack of confidence, disenchantment, cynicism and an outright hatred of politics. The range of feelings and attitudes towards the way that politics is practised in both the new and old democracies straddles that range but it is difficult not to conclude – given the spread and scale of the evidence – that globally people in democracies are negative about their formal political institutions and politicians.

Does this matter? There could be something cyclical about general public attitudes to politics. An optimist could argue that what has gone down might come back up again. 'Yes', would be my reply, but what is going to turn things around? Change happens in human societies in complex ways but the actions and intentions of humans are certainly part of the story. Who is going to lead the move back to political engagement, and how are they going to do it? Political parties and various civic associations provided the base for mobilization and engagement in many of the advanced industrial societies. Can we find similar organizations to replace them, or can they be revived?

Some argue that formal politics is not dead, it is just sleeping. If there is something important at stake, people will return to the polls and politicians. The Bush–Kerry US presidential campaign in 2004 saw turnout rise to 60 per cent, having been around the 50 per cent mark in the three previous elections. But such a turnout took presidential election voting only to the levels achieved in the early 1960s. Upward shifts in voting are to be welcomed, but it would be wise not to conclude that all is well with the state of US politics. The disquiet about politics goes much deeper than turnout rates can reveal. Certainly people can be mobilized back into voting, and perhaps politics in general,[51] but in the light of the evidence presented in this chapter it appears that there is a deeper malaise about the way politics is both practised and understood in new and established democracies.

There can be little doubt that a degree of scepticism about politics is healthy. When you look back to the 1950s and early 1960s in some of the established democracies, it is difficult not to think that people were too deferential or trusting. In the newer democracies, it could be argued that people just gained a healthy disrespect for politics more quickly.

These discontents could be explained away by a rise in *expectations* on the part of citizens, and a greater willingness on their part to complain. Yet satisfaction with government and politics is down virtually everywhere and it is hard to give advice to policy makers about what could change this, beyond turning back the clock to a time when people were more deferential, more polite and less sophisticated about politics.[52] In short, there may not be a problem that can be addressed, it is just that citizens have become more critical. There is, however, a dividing between healthy scepticism and outright non-belief in the value and efficacy of politics in democratic governance.

It is difficult to get away from the idea that a general and widespread disengagement from, and disenchantment with, formal politics does not sit comfortably with the long-term health of democracy. Indeed, a pessimistic reading of the degree of disenchantment from formal politics is that it will in the end undermine support for both democracy and democratic decision making. That is the explicit fear expressed in the UN report on Latin America, referred to earlier, and plainly it is a concern in some of the other newer sites for democratic governance where the concern is, as Pippa Norris puts it, that 'a disillusioned public will not function as a check on authoritarianism'.[53] If democracy is seen to fail, then other forms of governance may win popular endorsement.

This fear is the one that stalks many of the commentaries about the state of politics in democracies in advanced industrial societies. Russell Dalton makes the point very clearly:

> The political culture literature argues that citizens must be supportive of the political system if it is to endure – and this seems especially relevant to democratic politics. In addition, democracy is at least partially based on public endorsement of the political decision-making process; it is not to be measured primarily by the efficiency of its outputs. Democracy is a process and a set of political expectations that elevate democracy above other political forms.[54]

In short, the universal appeal of democratic governance that was celebrated in Chapter 1 might prove to be short-lived if the practice of democracy fails to be seen to be making a decent go of fulfilling those ideals.

What could be severely damaging to democracy as a set of procedures for making collective decisions in society is if people perceive that the formal system of politics is no longer worth engaging with. The trouble with disenchantment at the beginning of the twenty-first century is that it might be undermining the processes of formal politics that make democracy work and offering no viable alternative. The danger is that people will come to regard the formal political system as not worth bothering with and yet also find that the new politics of campaigns and protests – a minority interest, in any case – fails to satisfy because it cannot ultimately by-pass the formal political system or overthrow its power. Because of these concerns, it should be clear that we should not be sanguine about the scale of discontent with formal democratic politics, and that we need to understand in greater depth what is driving the disengagement from political activity.

3

Explanations for Political Disenchantment

> Declines in political trust may reflect a convergence of causes rather than a single explanation. Recognition of these multiple influences may be a first step in understanding why political support is changing in contemporary publics.[1]
>
> Russell Dalton, *Democratic Challenges, Democratic Choices*

In this chapter, I turn from description to analysis. I begin by exploring six explanations for the growth in disenchantment with the way that politics is practised in democracies. These explanations are grouped in pairs. The first two basically blame *politicians* – it is their behaviour and their incompetence which is at fault. The second pair point rather to the changing nature of *citizens*: they have got harder to govern because they are more critical, or just more individualistic and fragmented. The third pair – and the one to which I give most attention because I think it has the most going for it – rests on the argument that the *environment* for democratic politics has got harder and more out of control at the beginning of the twenty-first century. Globalization and technological challenges have meant that people no longer believe that politicians and politics are able to deliver any real opportunities for collective choice. Events are moving beyond their control, and as a result the capacity for collective action is diminishing. Politics – the construction of collective decisions – has lost its grip and that is why people no longer think it matters.

Is Politics Failing because Politicians are More Venal or Incompetent?

Corruption

It is clear that in the eyes of many people politicians are not the best advertisement for politics. Politics is often viewed as a rather grubby and unpleasant feature of modern life. People who take up politics as a trade or a vocation tend to attract more derision than admiration. Politics is something you apologize for, rather than being proud about. A political career is for the sad and desperate: for those who seek glory and personal gain, but are too ugly to be pop or film stars!

But does a rising tide of corruption among politicians explain the rise of political disenchantment? In the case of the advanced industrial societies, there is no evidence to suggest that people are disenchanted with politics because politicians have in the last twenty years become more corrupt and venal. Chapter 2 gave extensive evidence of twenty or more years of declining confidence in politics and disengagement in these countries from formal systems of representation. However, you would search in vain for evidence that corruption – defined as politicians and officials using their public position for private gain[2] – has grown in these countries. On the contrary, the available information suggests that corruption remains at comparatively low levels. In the authoritative Corruption Perceptions Index, the lowest ranked – and therefore least clean – advanced industrial democracy is Italy, as Table 3.1 indicates. Transparency International (TI), a non-governmental organization (NGO), draws on a wide range of surveys and evidence to produce the index, and is well regarded as an independent and comprehensive judge. The index score relates to perceptions of corruption from business people and country analysts. The nearer a country scores to 10, the closer a country is considered to be corruption-free. Even though it was the lowest-ranked advanced industrial country, Italy was nevertheless 40th out of over 150 countries ranked by TI.

In many advanced industrial countries, there have been some high-profile cases of corruption among politicians. These cases may well confirm the impression for some that the political system as a whole is corrupt. Corruption may well be a perceived problem with some popular resonance in, for example, Italy or the UN, Canada and perhaps, too, in the UK, where allegations of 'sleaze', if not outright corruption, has become part of the language of political debate since the Thatcher governments of the 1980s. Yet in the UK at least nearly 80 per cent of citizens are of the view that ministers and members of parliament (MPs) in general do not take bribes.[3] People's direct experience of corruption remains at very low levels in the majority of the advanced industrial democracies. A global survey for TI conducted in 2005 found that when asked directly if they or anyone in their household had paid a bribe in the last twelve months, fewer than 5 per cent of the citizens of the established democracies in Europe and North America responded that they had.[4] For the advanced industrial democracies, evidence of extensive direct corruption, let alone evidence to show it has increased, is

Table 3.1   Corruption perceptions index: top forty least corrupt countries

Country rank	Country	2005 CPI score[a]
1	Iceland	9.7
2	Finland	9.6
	New Zealand	9.6
4	Denmark	9.5
5	Singapore	9.4
6	Sweden	9.2
7	Switzerland	9.1
8	Norway	8.8
9	Australia	8.8
10	Austria	8.7
11	Netherlands	8.6
	UK	8.6
13	Luxembourg	8.5
14	Canada	8.4
15	Hong Kong	8.3
16	Germany	8.2
17	USA	7.6
18	France	7.5
19	Belgium	7.4
	Ireland	7.4
21	Chile	7.3
	Japan	7.3
23	Spain	7.0
24	Barbados	6.9
25	Malta	6.6
26	Portugal	6.5
27	Estonia	6.4
28	Israel	6.3
	Oman	6.3
30	United Arab Emirates (UAE)	6.2
31	Slovenia	6.1
32	Botswana	5.9
	Qatar	5.9
	Taiwan	5.9
	Uruguay	5.9
36	Bahrain	5.8
37	Cyprus	5.7
	Jordan	5.7
39	Malaysia	5.1
40	Hungary	5.0
	Italy	5.0
	South Korea	5.0

Note: [a]CPI = Corruption perceptions index.
Source: Data from Transparency International website www.transparency.org.

not really there. There can be little doubt that many feel in a general sense that politicians use power for their own gain and are prone to doing deals with 'big interests', but these are best seen as part of the expression of the disenchantment identified in Chapter 2, rather than a powerful explanation of that disenchantment.

There can be little doubt, as our review in Chapter 2 shows, that in many of the newer democracies corruption is considered to be a significant issue. Yet – as the case of India perhaps shows – people appear to be able to live with corruption and yet still want to make democratic politics work. Plainly corruption is undesirable, but it offers only a partial explanation of why politics is held in disdain. Moreover, as Table 3.1 indicates, some developing countries and new democracies are relatively free from corruption. Ten such countries make it into TI's top forty of least-corrupt states. Where it does exist, it is likely that distaste for corruption is real, and is perhaps more keenly felt by citizens in the ideological context of rhetoric about democracy. It may be that politicians are no more corrupt than under earlier authoritarian regimes – it would be a difficult thing to show – but the reality of corruption is bound to undermine people's hopes stimulated by the arrival of democratic governance. It may be that corrupt activity by politicians has a part to play, but it hardly seems an overwhelmingly explanatory factor.

Economic Incompetence

Is disenchantment perhaps explained by governments' economic incompetence? It seems logical to expect that democratic politicians would lose public confidence if they proved themselves to be economically incompetent, and that their credibility would be undermined as a result. There is no doubt that political leadership, if judged as failing to deliver economic success, can find its hold on office threatened at elections. But I am interested in those cases where disenchantment is not directed solely at individual leaders, but at the *political system* as a whole. Here, the evidence is that poor economic performance cannot be an explanation because, at least as measured by gross domestic product (GDP), the economic performance of advanced industrial economies has been relatively strong; yet political confidence has still declined. In North America and most of western Europe, a period of extended economic growth has accompanied a decline in political confidence. In many of the newer democracies in central and eastern Europe relatively successful economic performance has again accompanied evidence of political distrust. Fast-developing democratic countries such as India, too, have seen a lack of confidence in the political system. If governments are making any contribution to the economic success of their countries, it would appear that the political system as a whole is not getting any credit for it.

In some parts of Africa and Latin America, commentators fear that economic failure will undermine basic support for democracy, as we have noted in Chapter 2. But economic performance varies greatly in the democracies, with some in Europe and Asia proving to be economically highly successful. The spread of discontent in these countries appears to be unconnected in any clear way with their relative economic performance.

To summarize: it is difficult to establish that the behaviour of politicians or the performance of political systems have somehow declined compared to some past 'golden era' and that these shifts explain the loss of legitimacy for the politics of democratic governance. Problems with corruption or incompetence might help us to explain variations between and within countries over time, but cannot really give us an explanation of the global phenomenon of political disenchantment.

Truth and Power

There is one further element in the behaviour of politicians that might be an explanation of popular distrust. Playwright Harold Pinter, in a lecture accepting his Nobel Prize for the Arts in 2005, expressed a strong view that is probably quite widely shared about politicians:

> [T]he majority of politicians, on the evidence available to us, are interested not in truth but in power and in the maintenance of that power. To maintain that power it is essential that people remain in ignorance, that they live in ignorance of the truth, even the truth of their own lives. What surrounds us therefore is a vast tapestry of lies, upon which we feed.[5]

This sense that politicians are power-hungry liars has, as the survey evidence identified in Chapter 2 has shown, become part of the common currency of our age. Worldwide politicians are the least-trusted occupation, and many people think that politicians lie most of the time. But do they lie now more than in the past? That would be difficult to establish, and these issues are returned to in Chapter 7. What is clear is that fewer people trust both politics and politicians than in the past. Might the explanation for the change of perception be something that has happened to *citizens* to make them less trusting, rather than a shift in the behaviour pattern of politicians?

Does Disenchantment Reflect the Emergence of a More Critical or Fragmented Citizenry?

One thing to emerge from Chapter 2 was the widely expressed view that citizens are becoming more critical and challenging. The evidence certainly does not support the idea that citizens are simply now much less interested in the world around them, and therefore less engaged in politics as a result. Political scientist Pippa Norris argues that:

> We have seen the growth of more critical citizens, who value democracy as an ideal yet who remain dissatisfied with the performance of their political systems, and particularly the core institutions of representative government.[6]

As part of a wider pattern of change in both the mature democracies and the rest of the world, the communications revolution has challenged old hierarchies with the free flow of information. Sociologist Tony Giddens sees disenchantment with politics as part of a wider pattern of change in society:

> In a world based upon active communication, hard power – power that comes only from the top down – loses its edge. The economic conditions that the Soviet Union couldn't handle – the need for decentralisation and flexibility – were mirrored in politics. Information monopoly, upon which the political system was based, has no future in an intrinsically open framework of global communications . . . The communications revolution has produced more active, reflexive citizenries than existed before. It is these very developments that are at the same time producing disaffection in the long-established democracies. In a detraditionalising world, politicians can't rely upon the old forms of pomp and circumstance to justify what they do. Orthodox parliamentary politics becomes remote from the flood of change sweeping through people's lives.[7]

One of the most sophisticated versions of this line of argument is provided by Ronald Inglehart. Economic development and growth, he argues, 'reduces the tendency for mass publics to defer to authority',[8] as people feel more secure in their position and material wellbeing. When people are insecure, they favour authoritarian policies and strong leaders – that is a common pattern found in the developing world or in countries that have experienced a period of massive social and economic change. But in more secure and wealthy nations, people shift from a narrow focus on survival to a more expansive set of concerns about their quality of life. As a result post-materialists:

- Have a more demanding evaluative standard for politics
- Are more likely to challenge societal leaders
- See less need for self-denial and discipline and place greater value on self-expression and self-realization.

The growth in these values and attitudes, in turn, lead Inglehart to conclude that:

> The rise in postmodern values brings declining respect for authority and growing emphasis on participation and self-expression. These two trends are conducive to democratization (in authoritarian societies) and to more participatory democracy, issue-oriented democracy (in already democratic societies). But they are making the position of governing elites more difficult.[9]

As Inglehart admits, it is difficult to get the evidence to back up this thesis, because the quality of opinion data we have is limited and we lack a full set of 'before-and-after' figures in a range of countries. In part, too, we know that culture tends to change gradually and incrementally, so it may be that the change process, as described, is only some of the way through.

But how convincing is the idea that we are all becoming critical, post-materialist citizens? It is certainly not the case that everyone in mass democracies is moving from a focus of survival to a wider focus on quality of life. Nor is every citizen the kind of self-confident information-savvy individual that appears to be in Tony Giddens' mind's eye. Moreover, the assumption that affluence brings greater propensity to engage in politics may be true in the sense that people in that position are more likely to have the skills and resources for political engagement, still a classic and dominant explanation for levels of participation. But there is a counter argument, along the lines that contentment breeds apathy or that individual purchasing power enables people to buy their way out of collective problems in protected or gated communities – for example, through private schooling, transport and medical care. These new critical post-materialists may be moving into participatory and issue-based politics only in very small numbers (see evidence presented in Table 5.1, pp. 90–1).

I shall be following up these issues of how people engage in politics in more detail in Chapter 5, but for the present I shall argue that I do not think that the rise of critical citizenship explains political discontent to any great degree. It is a factor for a minority of citizens, but for many others 'critical' is not the right adjective to explain the dynamics of citizenship that they experience. They are not confident or assertive about politics, and are more alienated and confused. The argument to be developed in the rest of this book is that something less straightforward and benign is happening to the citizens of democracies and their relationship to politics. The explanation for the growth of disenchantment rests much more on other more substantial and deeply rooted changes.

Social Cohesion

What about the idea that a lack of social cohesiveness limits the scope for collective decision making? As Jean Grugel[10] argues, it is now common for people to invoke the importance of 'civil society' for the establishment and maintenance of effective democracy. It is not always entirely clear what the term refers to, but in a broad sense it appears to be about the network of community organizations, associations and voluntary organizations that are not part of government, nor do they operate as private companies in the market. Michael Edwards comments that:

> In their political role, voluntary associations are seen as a crucial coun-
> terweight to states and corporate power . . . especially when formal citi-
> zenship rights are not well entrenched, it is civil society that provides the
> channels through which most people can make their voices heard in
> government decision-making.[11]

Weaknesses and faults in civil society are sometimes used to explain failings in the process of democracy, and in particular the capacity of people to engage.

In countries that have gone through a transition to democracy, civil groups have often played a major part in mobilizing opposition to the previous, usually authoritarian, regimes. But with the arrival of democracy, fatigue among activists can set in, and in any case their reach may have been limited. Government bodies may seek to coopt and work with key groups of activists that in turn may remove further energy from civil society. As a result, there can be a lack of capacity in civil society to support the everyday activism that is a common feature, as we have seen, of more mature democracies. Grugel suggests that a similar pattern of concern about the viability of civil society organizations also applies to the newer democracies of Africa, Latin America and Asia. The implications for democracy are potentially grave: 'A strong civil society matters because it helps determine the *quality* of democracy. Civil society organizations . . . are a means for checking and controlling the state and a tool to push the state towards deeper reforms. A weak civil society implies a thin democracy, where patterns of participation are low.'[12]

This concern about the state of civil society and the willingness for citizens to engage is, however, not just restricted to new democracies. The social base for democracy has also become a major focus of discussion in more mature democracies, based on the idea that we may be faced with a decline in *social capital* – the networks of trust, mutual assistance and reciprocity that help connect us. Social capital is a concept that tries to capture how the relationships and connections between people are important in building mutual understanding and commitment. Much of the research on social capital has been dominated by the work and approach of Robert Putnam,[13] whose central thesis is that the associational life of mature democracies, and in particular the USA, has declined. Colloquially, as Robert Putnam puts it, people are 'bowling alone', engaging in ten-pin bowling and other sports and leisure activities in fragmented small groups rather than through larger groups and organized leagues. Generational and social trends in terms of increased TV watching means that more people have lost the habit of association, and that habit is vital for building social networks, trust and a shared sense of norms. Social capital, in turn, is seen as central to the practice of democratic politics because it gives people the capacity and willingness to work together cooperatively to solve problems.

There has been a lot of discussion and debate about the evidence for Putnam's thesis. Some people have argued that the decline in associational engagement is not the key thing, but rather the increasingly uneven distribution of the time and capacity to engage.[14] Others argue that although some formal groups may have declined, others have risen to take their place. Have women gained more on the associational front through increased freedom from home ties, and men lost out? Still others doubt whether trust has declined in all countries to the same degree and in the same way as in the USA.

Among researchers examining associational membership in Britain, there is little support for a general decline in social capital (see Table 3.2).[15].On the other hand, associational membership is hardly in a robust state of health, given that in 1999 nearly half of all men and women reported no associational ties. This may, of course, be a misleading figure as people may not be remembering their associational ties, but it is consistent with the finding of Pattie, Seyd and Whiteley's Citizens' Audit, that concluded that 55 per cent of Britons are not members of any group.[16] These figures,

Table 3.2   Participation in voluntary associations, England and Wales, 1972, 1992 and 1999

	Men			Women	
	1972	1992	1999	1992	1999
Membership in organizations (%)					
Trade unions	39.5	26.4	22.3	15.7	16.3
Sports/hobby clubs	25.0	25.6	26.1	11.1	14.0
Working men's clubs or Social clubs	27.6	21.2	17.9	7.6	7.0
Professional associations	11.2	–	13.8	–	7.7
Church or religious groups	9.5	8.1	7.0	12.4	11.1
Tenants'/Residents' groups	3.5	6.8	7.0	8.2	9.0
Parent–teacher associations	5.4	3.5	2.4	7.2	6.5
Political party	7.4	3.5	3.1	2.5	2.0
Voluntary services groups	–	3.1	2.5	5.3	4.5
Environmental group	–	4.5	3.8	4.2	3.2
Other community/civic groups	–	2.9	1.7	3.3	1.9
Women's institutes/groups	–	–	–	4.3	3.6
Scouts/Guides organizations	–	–	1.1	–	1.7
Pensioners' group	–	–	0.7	–	0.4
Other	15.1	12.2	7.9	9.1	7.2
Mean number of organizations					
All listed organizations	1.44	1.18	1.17	0.91	0.96
Seven common organizations	1.18	0.95	0.86	0.65	0.66
% non-participants	22.6	36.3	40.6	46.9	48.6
N	10,309	3,248	4,206	3,478	4,701

Note: – = not applicable or not available.
Source: Reproduced with minor corrections from Yaojun Li *et al.*, 'Dynamics of social capital: trends and turnover in associational membership in England and Wales, 1972–1999' *Sociological Research Online*, 7 (3) (2002) (available at http://www.socresonline.org.uk/7/3/li.html).

however, record membership only in any one year. If one looks at data over a decade the picture is more positive, in the sense that people move in and out of memberships, and fewer than 15.6 per cent of the population were never members of any association during the 1990s. This figure has led Alan Warde and his fellow researchers to conclude that: 'in the light of the large numbers of people who move in and out of organizations from year to year, Britain appears to be a more participatory and active society than might otherwise be imagined'.[17]

Some groups are clearly losing out on associational ties to a much greater degree than others. Table 3.2 shows associational memberships in England and Wales, drawing on data from a range of surveys. The first survey in 1972 covers only men but the surveys in 1992 and 1999 include women. The results show a complex set of 'up and downs' in associational memberships, although there is a general picture of decline. There are also difficulties in drawing comparisons because the same organizations are not brought to the attention of respondents to the survey on each occasion, though seven types of organizations – trade unions, sports/hobby clubs, working men's or social clubs, church or religious groups, tenants'/residents' groups, parent–teacher associations and political parties – were referred to in each survey. In these surveys there is no big change for women, but for men the mean number of the seven organizations in which they are involved drops from 1.18 in 1972 to 0.86 in 1999. Moreover, almost that entire male decline in membership is due to the reduced numbers involved in trade unions and working men's clubs. Indeed, as Table 3.2 shows, the mean number of voluntary organizational engagements for women went up during the 1990s. But the major point is not about growth or decline in associational activity. It is working-class men that have lost out on associational contacts. Women still lag behind men slightly. Middle-class professional and managerial workers seem best placed in terms of associational memberships, the benefits of which are 'increasingly going to professional and managerial workers relative to other social class groups'.[18] The positive experiences, skills, networks and capacities gained from membership of associations in civil society may be increasing the prospects for political engagement for some much more than others.

A detailed comparative study by Robert Putnam and other researchers leads Putnam to concede that the pattern of change in social capital in a range of advanced industrial democracies is far from universal. Indeed, he argues that in other countries the evidence of social engagement and cohesion suggests 'the simple thesis that citizens everywhere are increasingly "bowling alone" '[19] may be mistaken. He goes on to argue that *patterns* of social cohesion and networking are changing their form. In an important restatement of his original argument, he suggests that:

> the new individualistic forms of civic engagement may be less conducive to the pursuit of collective goals. The older forms that are now fading combined individual fun with collective purpose, and they were multi-stranded, as in Catholic unions or party sports leagues. The newer forms of social participation are narrower, less bridging, and less focused on collective or public-regarding purpose. An important hypothesis that

emerges . . . is that the newer forms may be more liberating but less soli-daristic – representing a kind of privatization of social capital.[20]

Robert Putnam argues that with the decline of trade unions and more formal associations run through churches, the impact of a downturn in social connectedness is most strongly felt by those who are *already disad-vantaged*. These civic and voluntary organizations mixed social groups and classes, and in particular expressed solidarity across social groups. Putnam concludes that the overall decline in social capital may not be the key shared experience of advanced industrial societies but rather that social capital has become more unevenly distributed, accumulated most among those who need it least. The new social groups and organizations – envi-ronmental groups, newer-style churches, gender-based support groups – are more class-specific and more directly appealing to various elements of the middle class and professionals. The comparative ease of access to the internet for these groups further accentuates the social divide over the tools of connectedness.

The claim of a general decline in social cohesion and connectedness across advanced industrial societies cannot, however, be seen as a key explanatory factor in the scale of political disenchantment identified in Chapter 2. The idea that social capital might be becoming more individual-ized and more narrowly focused and less able to deliver 'bridging' between social groups is an intriguing one. As Putnam is at pains to point out, the evidence is far from clear cut, but it does hint at an issue that will be explored again in Chapter 4. For the present, it can be concluded that a decline in social capital does not provide the 'magic bullet' for explaining the overall decline in political engagement and confidence in most indus-trial democracies.

Is Politics in Trouble because Issues are Moving beyond its Control?

Politics makes sense only if it is part of a dynamic to change the world through our collective will. As Andrew Gamble suggests:

> In the modern era politics has promised to give human societies control over their fate, by creating a space, a political realm, in which to seek answers to the fundamental questions of politics – who we are, what we should get, how we should live . . . Underpinning all these notions, however, is the belief that what becomes of us and our societies is in our hands.[21]

But if the world is beyond our collective control or beyond the control of our political institutions, then politics runs the danger of becoming irrelevant. Are there forces at play in the twenty-first century making our current practice of politics pointless? Some finger globalization and the rise of the global economy dominated by multinational corporations (MNCs) as great forces that sweep away politics because the economic power they express is so overwhelming that political organizations have no power to resist. Some see the irrelevance of politics as driven by the impact of technological advancement and change, such that human activity supported by that technology is seen as dangerously out of control, threatening the human condition and our environment in a way that no politics can influence. This concluding section of this chapter reviews these arguments and suggests that these factors make politics more challenging, but not impossible. They feed into a new spirit of critical scepticism that means that doing politics has got tougher.

Globalization

Let us start with the issue of *globalization*. There are a very complex set of debates about what globalization means, but for now I will take the definition offered by Jan Aart Scholte: globalization is 'respatialization with the spread of transplanetary social connections'.[22] You may not find this definition a model of clarity, but what I think it means it that globalization brings in its wake substantial changes in the way that economies and societies work, driven by a more rapid communication and a stronger set of connections between different peoples and organizations across the world.

Some writers suggest that the forces of globalization are so powerful that they are sweeping away nation states and making the democracy embedded within them irrelevant. A turbocharged global economic market is moving the power of decision away from nation states towards powerful global corporations, and vast swathes of the population of the world are caught up in economic forces they cannot control.[23] There is no point denying that globalization presents us with challenges, but there are reasons to doubt the extremely pessimistic line of argument that our collective capacity to influence the processes of globalization has totally evaporated.

We live in a world where there is a significant further development towards a global market in which patterns of production and consumption are organized by transnational companies (TNCs) and other related organizations, operating across national boundaries, creating global finance markets and patterns of international trade which in turn influence the shape of national economies. In the industrialized countries, these forces are experienced in terms of sweeping changes, with old-style industrial jobs declining and new-style service and high-technological jobs emerging. Consumers in these countries observe an increasing amount of goods coming from outside their national boundaries as their economies are brought into the ambit of a global market to a greater degree than ever before. The non-industrialized parts of the world have faced new economic demands and some new opportunities, but so far, at least, the impacts of globalization have done little to redress the disparity between rich and poor countries, and may indeed have worsened the situation.

The *hyper-globalist position*[24] is that globalization is an unstoppable force that is driving the world economy into an integrated, borderless whole, in which MNCs can move freely to locate where it best suits them and in which innovation and changes in production and consumption are fuelled by avaricious companies and fashion-obsessed consumers and enabled by spectacular technological advance. The degree and intensity with which the world is being tied into a single market makes national resistance pointless; those governments that try to control the process will suffer from the withdrawal of global companies and investment, currency depreciation and low economic performance. The rise of the global market means that governments will lose their autonomy, the universal policy prescription being to break down barriers and allow the free play of competition and exchange. Associated with this understanding of global capitalism there is an implicit or explicit acceptance of an ideology of *neo-liberalism* that argues for free trade and economic freedoms and against state regulation and control; together, these forces provide the only game available for countries to join. Politics becomes doubly irrelevant as its main instrument, nation states, have no power and people in such states have no choice but to run their affairs according to the demands of the neo-liberal project.

There is no point denying that globalization has changed our world, but there are good reasons for doubting the position taken by the hyper-globalists. First, the existence of global trade is not a new phenomenon and although its depth, intensity and global coverage may have increased it does not have the overwhelmingly dominant impact implied by the hyper-globalist thesis. As Peter Dicken puts it, after a careful review of the evidence: 'although there are undoubtedly globalizing forces at work, we do not have a fully globalized world economy'.[25] The complex processes of production have become more globalized, but the location of clusters of specialized industries in many countries suggests that physical proximity of certain firms, industrial networks and skilled personnel remain important. Production cannot simply be moved around the world as the advantages of operating in certain locations are deeply embedded and not easy to forgo. Most MNCs still have significant national connections and much economic activity remains in the hands of small and medium-sized businesses (SMEs). Moreover, there is a distinctive regional dimension to most trade: Europe trades mostly with Europe, and so on. The global economy appears to have a considerable number of embedded localized features and factors that the hyper-globalists overlook.

The hyper-globalists are also too negative about the capacity of the state. Again to quote from Peter Dicken: 'the state remains a most significant force in shaping the world economy. It has, whether explicitly or implicitly, played an extremely important role in the economic development of *all* countries'.[26] According to Dicken, nation states play at least four key roles in the current global era. First, the *traditions* and ways of doing things help to shape the nature of the economies that operate in their territory. There are significant national differences in the extent to which individualism is the dominant cultural force, as against collectivism based around the family or a wider social group. There are disparities in the way that authority is viewed, and in the attitude to *risk* and its management within societies. There are different understandings of the proper *social* division between men and women. A member of one of the Nordic states may see the world differently from that of a Latin American one. The global society does not exist, and significant cultural differences remain, and are played out through the policies of nation states. More explicitly on the economic front, there are several forms of advanced capitalism:[27] for example, a distinction can be drawn between a broadly free-enterprise liberal version that finds its most obvious expression in the USA, a social partnership model that dominates the thinking of many European nations and a state developmental form that is practised most widely in Japan, South Korea and other East Asian countries. It is not sensible here to dwell on the complexities, overlaps and multiple variations between types of capitalism as the main point is just to establish that there are limits to the universality created by globalization.

Nation states and their cultures not only influence the forms of capitalism in their territories in a general way, they also intervene to regulate and control capitalist enterprises and forces. They seek to exercise control over trade, foreign investment and industry-level policies, covering issues such as health and safety, wages, training, taxation, merger and environmental impacts. '[A] nation's "degrees of freedom" depend very much on its relative position in the world economy and, in particular, on the extent of its dependence on external trade and investment'.[28] So policy interventions are not always open to all, and they are by no means always successful, but they are extensive. Moreover, most nation states take a third broader role – to try to make their economies and their countries more competitive; a considerable amount of effort is put into supporting and developing industrial and service clusters within countries. Finally and in their fourth role, states have organized into regional blocs to shape and direct trade and other policies with their near neighbours. The most integrated and advanced of those blocs is the EU, but there are free-trade agreements (FTAs) in regional blocs covering the Americas and East Asia.

Some of these interventions by nation states, individually or through collective blocs, are sometimes accused of creating the conditions for globalization and the neo-liberal project. For some, of course, the state is by definition in cahoots with capitalism and is therefore going to be pushed down a different course only by large-scale popular action. This is the position of some at least in the anti-global capitalist alliance that saw the battle on the streets of Seattle during the 1999 World Trade Organization (WTO) meeting there as a key point in an ongoing conflict.[29] Others see the issue in less stark terms but still argue that governments can trap themselves into sleepwalking into a neo-liberal version of globalization. Thus, for example much of the recent debate about the proposed EU constitution has been driven by a claim by opponents that the Union is a plot by neo-liberalizers to wreak havoc with the more traditional social partnership approach of European capitalism. The opposition has been such that the future development of the constitution is unclear. However for the purposes of this book, these debates simply illustrate that politics is alive and kicking. Globalization has made politics harder; but as Andrew Gamble points out:

> Acceptance that there is something called globalization, or at least that there are certain trends towards a global market, is not the end of the argument but the beginning of it, since there are so many ways in which states and groups can adjust to these changes.[30]

Nonetheless, globalization does provide a very tough challenge for politics. Politics needs to define interests and organize their expression. It needs to ensure that collective decisions are binding; that their authority and legitimacy is accepted; and that they can be effectively enacted. With the best will in the world, it would not be possible to say that current international institutions such as the UN, the World Bank, or the WTO have offered a fully operational engagement of interests that proffers the prospect of some substantial capacity for tackling global poverty and environmental issues. Although some people in those organizations are aware of the issues, and do see the need for reform[31], finding a way forward is not going to be easy (some of the potential solutions are reviewed in Chapter 10). But, as Andrew Gamble argues, the only way to resolve these issues is to construct a politics that works: 'These are political problems; they will not be solved by any other means, and they dwarf most problems that have been faced in the past. In these circumstances the idea that politics is at an end seems a little premature'.[32]

Science and Technology

If globalization has not rendered democratic politics redundant, are there other issues that suggest that the world is so out of control that politics no longer has any point? Technology, and its uses in providing economic growth and expansion, bring with it enormous potential benefits. But it also can create acute political challenges, especially if the speed of the developments that are taking place seems to be running ahead of the capacity of political institutions to deal with them. The issue of the sustainability of the environment in the light of economic growth is one that stretches the capacity of our political institutions. Fears about population growth, the management of waste, maintaining biodiversity and coping with global warming have been central to political debate since the 1990s, and there have been many warnings of potential ecological disaster if these issues are not addressed.

These developments create major challenges for politics. First, international cooperation is often required if effective solutions are to be found and that cooperation is difficult to achieve given conflicting interests between industrialized and developing countries and because monitoring behaviour with respect to any agreements is likely to be a time-consuming and challenging task. Second, the deal to be struck in any sustainability debate is between the current generation – demanding benefits here and now – and future generations – that are by definition not here and not demanding. Politics in mass democracies is likely to find deal making in these circumstances lop-sided and oriented towards the here-and-now.

Nor should it be assumed that science can provide the answers.[33] Science can provide much insight, but in the end environmental issues involve value judgements and debates about what to do collectively and therefore have an irreducible political element. First, there are political issues about what we should do to *sustain* the environment. What should be the trigger for an intervention when the borderline between a sustainable and unsustainable threshold has been passed? How do we know when to stop people doing something or to take some action to preserve something that should not be lost? Scientists can answer the question only if prior issues about who or what is affected by the threshold being breached have been resolved. Responding to the question – what matters? – is a political as well as a scientific matter. Normative issues about what we should do remain at the heart of environmental debates. Second, political issues raise their head over how any *intervention* should be undertaken. Interventions that restrict people's liberties or unfairly constrain their freedom need to be justified in a mass democracy. There is sometimes an authoritarian streak in some environmentalist rhetoric that sits uncomfortably with the norms and values of liberal, mass democracy. Many environmentalists, recognizing this concern, argue for citizenship education on environmental matters and better forms of political deliberation so that the values associated with environmental issues can be debated and win support. We are left with the conclusion that issues of environmental sustainability may present enormous challenges to politics, but still need the input and dynamic of politics if they are to be tackled.

Science and Politics

Science and technology cannot fix things on their own. In some areas, science has part of the answer, but not all of it. In other areas, science presents answers that require political responses. The genetic modification of food and plants, the prospects for human cloning and various medical advances are among a number of issues where the progress of technology runs the risk of developing at a faster pace than we are able to cope with. In part this is because science is no longer viewed as a separate technical activity, but is funded and supported by major corporate and professional interests. People are not as sure as they once were about the expertise of all scientists and, if the debate over genetically modified (GM) foods is anything to go by, many suspect the validity of some of their knowledge claims. Technological developments, such as cloning, stem cell research and studies connecting genetics and behaviour throw up ethical and moral issues with which we have only just begun to engage. According to Dr Alan Leshner,[34] the chief executive officer (CEO) of the American Association for the Advancement of Science (AAAS), the implications of recent scientific developments have changed the relationship to the public such that 'we can't just educate our way out of the divide between science and society, because the problem is not people's lack of understanding of scientific issues – but the very fact that they don't like some advances of science'. Leshner goes on to argue for a new type of dialogue between science and the public that constitutes a part of a wider democratic politics. The key is the need to move beyond communicating science *to* the public and moving to communicating science *with* the public: 'We need to change the nature of science communication from a monologue to a dialogue and listen to the public and their concerns.'

Joining policy debates poses hard challenges for scientists. Their caution about the state of knowledge can be taken as indecisiveness. On the other hand scientists, believing that they have a special contribution because of their expertise, can display a level of arrogance that leads them to treat the political process with contempt. Politicians and members of the public find it difficult to verify what scientists tell them and, where there are differences among scientists, to judge which view is the right one. Yet scientists often find it infuriating when some maverick view is given as much credence as the peer- and evidence-backed consensus of the scientific community. Scientists value reason above all, but in political debate reason, rhetoric and emotion are all justifiable factors to put into the mix.

Above all science, and politics are about different things. Science is about discovering 'a truth', and being willing to share that truth and provide evidence to support the contention, while recognizing all along the contingent, or at least limited, nature of any claim and the possibility of alternative explanations. Politics asks what, if anything, can and should be done in the light of a perceived concern or problem. That judgement is coloured by an assessment of who might win or lose, and by wider value considerations about what kinds of interventions are right or wrong. Science is about *discovering*, politics is about *doing*, even if sometimes scientists don't discover anything and politicians don't do anything.

We need ways of 'making expertise legitimate in political terms'[35] by establishing its impartiality, independence and accountability; and at the same time allowing for a public debate that can deal with the normative choices thrown up by science and work through systematically the social, economic and environmental issues at stake.

Yet we have to remain hopeful that political process can bring the runaway society under control. In the past, technological developments have seemed threatening but they have been managed and brought benefit to humankind. With the right framework of decision making, driven by the right style of politics, there is no need to assume that the benefits of technology cannot be enjoyed again. One of the big challenges facing politics is how to construct an exchange between science and democracy:[36] a demanding and daunting set of challenges created by growth and technological advance mean that we need more effective politics, rather than less of it.

Conclusions: Politics in Hard Times

The disenchantment with politics identified in Chapter 2 in both established and newer democracies is not down to a demonstrable increase in corrupt or venal behaviour on the part of politicians. It may be that people's sensitivity to corruption has increased, but that may reflect only a symptom of political disenchantment rather than its cause. Individual politicians, and perhaps even political systems, are damaged by gaining a reputation for economic incompetence, but the last decades have not been by any means a universal story of economic disaster – on the contrary, there has been sustained growth in many countries that have at the same time seen increases in political disenchantment. The idea that disenchantment is wholly explained by the rise of critical citizenship or the collapse of social capital is again not supported by the evidence; neither factor is universal enough in its operation to be anything other than part of the explanation of political disenchantment.

What is clear when looking at the impact of globalization and the technological challenges we face is that doing politics in the twenty-first century is hard, and people's sense of doubt that politics can cope with the big issues that matter may have fuelled a sense of disenchantment. Yet, I still want to hold that effective delivery by politics and the government system remains a viable prospect, although it is the case that 'compared to the problems of the planet and the human species, the capacities of politics seem woefully inadequate'.[37]

The toughness of the challenges we face has had significant knock-on implications, making politics seem more remote. In responding to the challenges it has faced, politics has inevitably become more technocratic and bureaucratic. The complexity of what politicians try to do through their interventions, policy programmes, spending plans and services means that their actions are mediated through a complex web of institutions both inside and outside government at local, national and supranational level. Moreover, a certain element of under-performance against the scale of the challenges appears to be built into the system.

There is one other factor in explaining political disenchantment that has not been raised so far, but is worth putting into the mix. Our world has become less certain in its divisions and less confident in its utopian visions. We are less certain about what the 'right solutions' are, and less confident in our ability to meet the challenges we face. The collapse of the Soviet Union has been enormously significant, but we have not entered a period where history has ended and the ideology of liberal capitalist democracy has simply triumphed. Rather we have entered a period of greater uncertainty and diversity: socialists have lost some of their old certainties and are searching for a new social democratic or more radical ways forward. For social democrats and progressives there has been a rather inconclusive and as yet unresolved debate about a 'third way'.[38] Conservatives have been 'torn between their enthusiasm for global markets and liberalization on the one hand and their attachment to the nation-state and nationalism on the other'.[39] The world of ideology is diversifying rather than ending, with new ideologies emerging around nationalism, ethnicity, environmentalism and religion. Our politics has become more complex in its mix of big *ideological* issues of freedom, equality, religious belief and ecological sustainability and more *managerial* issues about organizing our security, welfare and quality of life. In most mass democracies politicians can no longer say: 'Vote for me because I am socialist red, conservative blue or a green environmentalist.' They have to demonstrate competence and performance alongside the espousal of values.

The need to understand multiple ideologies and yet demonstrate management capacity simply adds to the litany of challenges faced by politics and explored in this chapter. The challenges are made worse by the tendency in mass democracy to hold myths about the way the system is supposed to work that bear little relation to reality. For politicians, the world is not controllable in the direct simple way that some of the myths of democracy imply that it should be. We (the citizens) tell them (the politicians) what we want, and they deliver it, and if they succeed we reward them with our support again; if they fail, we kick them out. Democracy as a working model of governance hardly ever matches this vote–deliver–judge process that dominates our thinking about the way it is supposed to work.

Governments can rarely exercise direct control; rather they can steer. Political and other social scientists have developed a whole new body of work to capture the challenges of governing in an increasingly complex environment.[40] The 'governance approach', as it is called, recognizes that what can be achieved by politicians – and, more broadly, governments, is mediated through a complex web of *institutions* and a dispersed range of *networks*. Politicians do not sit, as some media commentary implies, at the top of one consolidated, bureaucratic machinery of government with all the levers of control just sitting in front of them. Nor are the only conversations they have about what to do conducted through periodic elections. Rather, a multitude of special interests and lobbies both inside and outside the government machine put up ideas and projects for their consideration. Moreover, in the world of modern governance achieving many desired changes requires that governments do not simply act on their own but instead in concert with other governments or with citizens or specialist and sectional interests. Environmental issues again provide a good example of these complex processes of governance in action. They often require a mixture of global and local action; interventions around energy saving or recycling need the active support of businesses, community groups and citizens in general. Modern politics takes place through the medium of governance. But constructing clear and effective intervention in that medium is not straightforward. Politics, as the theme of this chapter makes clear, is a tough business.

4

The Politics of Mass Democracies: Designed-In Disappointment?

> Why is politics so consistently disappointing? . . . Few factors
> have more causal force in politics (do more to determine what in
> fact occurs) than how well we understand what we are doing.
> Disappointment is a mixture of dismay and surprise. If we
> understood politics better we would certainly be less surprised
> by its outcomes, as well as surprised much less often.[1]
>
> John Dunn, *The Cunning of Unreason*

Introduction

This chapter explores a different explanation of the global rise of political disenchantment to those examined so far. It takes up the theme suggested by John Dunn, that people are disappointed by politics because they do not understand it. This chapter argues that the increased discontent with formal politics can, at least in part, be explained by a number of misunderstandings of the political process that have taken hold in the discourse of democracies. As a result, many citizens fail fully to appreciate that politics in the end involves the collective imposition of decisions, demands a complex communication process and generally produces messy compromises.

Individualism

What is more, the chapter suggests that this problem has been compounded by the spread of market-based consumerism and the nature of *individualism*.

Making decisions through markets relies on individuals choosing what suits them. The 'lionization' of our role as active choosers leaves the political processes that steer government struggling to deliver against that ideal.

Democracy means that you can be involved in the decision, but the final decision is not necessarily the one of your choice, and yet you are expected to follow it. Politics is, even in a democracy, a very centralized form of collective decision making compared to market-based alternatives.

Voice and Communication

Second, politics as a form of collective decision making relies on *voice* rather than the market mechanism of exit to enable you make your views known. If you don't like something you see in a shop you can go elsewhere, but in politics the only way to get something is to use *voice*, and that carries far more costs than exit (see p. 74 for a definition of these terms). But expressing your interest or opinion is only the start of a more general challenge in politics: that of *communication*. Voice is not the key mechanism in politics. You have not only to make your views known, you also have to listen. Politics is not about individual choice, it is about collective debate; it is about the mutual taking into account of diverse opinions and interests. As a result, communication within politics is often a difficult, time-consuming and problematic business. Knowing what you want, and knowing how to get it from the political system, is both testing and complex.

A Stumbling Search

Politics often involves a stumbling search for solutions to particular problems. It is not the most edifying human experience: it is rarely an experience of self-actualization and more often an experience of accepting second-best. It works through a complex process of mutual adjustment as politicians, officials and others directly involved in government develop coping or manipulative modifications to their behaviour in the hope of inducing the right response from others. The results tend to be messy, contingent and inevitably involve a mix of winners and losers.

A propensity to disappoint is thus an inherent feature of governance, even in democratic societies. I think that a substantial part of the discontent with politics is because the discourse and practice of collective decision making sits very uncomfortably alongside the discourse and practice of individual choice, self-expression and market-based fulfilment of needs and wants. As a result, too many citizens fail to appreciate these inherent contradictions and limitations of the political process in a democratic setting.

More often than not in popular discourse, people are asked to contrast the ideal of democracy with its rather grubby current practice. Michael Moore[2] sells books with the central thesis that the 'great' democracy of our times, the USA, is run by stupid white men who manipulate election results and make decisions in tune with the interests of their 'big business' backers rather than the people. David Beetham[3] offers a more erudite version of the same thesis. He argues that politics has become tied too closely to 'big business' and that this closeness makes the general public in mature democracies increasingly alienated from the political process because they are no longer in control of it.

I do not dispute that business interests have special advantages that can challenge democratic politics or that globalization creates significant new challenges for the political process. The power of business and the values of democratic politics have throughout the history of mass democracies sat rather uneasily alongside one another. But even in the absence of these constraints, I would argue that politics would still struggle to achieve all that people hope from it.

I now examine three propositions about politics which I think have been largely overlooked in the search for explanations of our current discontent.

Proposition 1: Politics is an Inherently Centralized Form of Collective Decision Making

Market-Based Allocation

Let us imagine there is some collective event and we have to decide who should attend. We could all turn up to watch our local team play football on a particular Saturday, or all decide to go to the same cinema on a Friday night to watch a film. We don't, because of a set of individual decisions made by ourselves and by the sellers of football and cinema tickets. Some of us choose to go to a see a film or football match and some do not. The sellers price the tickets according to the expected demand and the capacity they have available in their cinema or football stadium. That price makes the option of going to the cinema or football match more or less attractive to us. If we really think the film is going to be good we might be prepared to pay quite a lot; if we are not sure, we might baulk at a high price and change our minds and do something else. We might, for example, decide not to go to the cinema, but go to the football match. The *rationing process is internalized.* We make our own choices within the constraints of our income and according to our preferences.

The above is an example of *market-based allocation* and an illustration of an everyday process we are all familiar with. As Adam Przeworski explains:

Decentralized mechanisms generate allocations by each individual choosing actions designed to maximise his or her objectives given the actions of other individuals. The resulting allocation is associated with a combination of actions in which no one wants to act differently given the actions of others. Hence, the outcomes of decentralized mechanisms are self-enforcing.[4]

Such is the genius of the market. Free exchange produces efficient matching of demand and supply. But we are all familiar with another way of getting involved in collective decisions.

Centralized Allocation

The main alternative to allocation by markets is allocation by *centralized authority*. That is the way of allocating that we associate with government or the state:

> Centralized mechanisms operate by one, some or all individuals deciding the allocation to all. Such allocations may not be in the best interest of everyone. Hence, their implementation may necessitate coercion. The distinguishing feature of centralized mechanisms . . . is that they can and do force individuals to do what they do not want to do and prevent them from doing what they want to do.[5]

Going back to our earlier example, we could think of the decision about whether to go to the match or the cinema being made for us by a central committee of elected citizens. They would face a rationing challenge and might decide that all citizens with names beginning with the letter 'S' should go to the football on that Saturday and that all citizens with names beginning with 'Z' should to the cinema that Friday. Apart from the likelihood that the cinema might be relatively under-used, it is probable that to enforce the decision the citizens' committee would have to have 'name' police out checking that you qualified under the rules to get in and it would have to be clear that if you tried to break the rules, you would be punished.

As a way of allocating tickets, democratic collective decision making appears to be inherently controlling and bureaucratic. Moreover, it is far from certain that even if you had the right name for one of the days, you would want to go to that particular football match or see that film in the cinema on that day! Even in a democratic system collective decision making through politics is, at its heart, a centralized form of decision making and one that could appear to be quite careless with your interests or concerns as an individual. It is becoming clearer now, I hope, why we might not automatically like it as a decision making system.

So why do we put up with it at all? Generally, we do not look to centralized mechanisms to work in allocating football or cinema tickets. We think that those allocations are best left to the market. But centralized systems for deciding collective allocations make a lot more sense in a whole lot of arenas. Without getting too involved in the debate about what the role and extent of government should be – something that is a regular area of dispute in our democracies – it is clear that collective decision making using centralized structures has an important role to play in a range of contexts.

First, we might support a centralized decision making system when we are trying to allocate public goods that cannot be efficiently divided up and where there is a danger that people would free-ride on their provision if they were not forced to contribute. So, for example, defence could be seen self-evidently as a public good, assuming that everyone in a nation wants to avoid a foreign invasion. We can only do defence together, and we all need to make a contribution in kind or by paying for others to do the job. The same applies to many other public goods, including clean air, open spaces and street lighting. Another argument for centralized collective decision making is where the decisions freely taken by individuals would lead to an inferior outcome. Sometimes, the issue is simply one of establishing certainty: as we drive around in our vehicles, it is important that there is a general rule that we all drive on either the left or right. It doesn't matter which, but it does matter that we stick to one or the other rather than all decide for ourselves. On other occasions, we need centralized decision making because if we left it to individuals they would shirk an action that is in all of our interests for them to take. So, for example, many countries require that drivers have an annual check on their vehicle to make sure that it is roadworthy. Plainly it is in their interests that their vehicle is safe to drive, but it is also in ours since we do not want them careering off the road as we are walking by because the steering wheel has come off in their hands.

Public action is also often needed when it comes to some goods and services in order to license certain providers or make sure that consumers have access to appropriate information. On other occasions there might be common goods – for example, fish stocks – that if over-exploited will be depleted to the detriment of us all, and we need to agree how to share them out. Generally, some broadly and centrally agreed mechanism for allocating those resources would need to be decided upon, although the mechanism itself might not be centralized or top-down: it could involve market credits or quotas for fishing that could be traded.

Finally, we accept some centralized decision making because we, or at least many of us, share certain values which we want to see enshrined in the societies in which we live. We may think that some relief should be given to the poorest members of our society; we may think that children deserve a good education, and therefore support government provision of free schooling; we may, rather more controversially, think that people should be encouraged to be good parents and obey certain moral strictures.

Centralized decision making is a core part of our societies, and *politics provides the mechanism for deciding what those decisions should be.* We accept the prospect of coercion in order to live our lives more efficiently and in a way that meets our needs and interests. In many respects, such a deal would be a 'no-brainer' if all our interests were harmonious. Indeed this form of collective decision would, like the market form, be self-enforcing. But politics is a tough process to live with precisely because it – and the coercion that goes with centralized decision making – makes sense only because our interests are in conflict with those of others.

We need to allocate public goods through such mechanisms because we have *different claims on them.* We need certainty in some areas, but we may well disagree about what the best course of action is in any particular case: although we may all agree that traffic rules are a good idea, we may not all agree about how pedestrians should be made to cross the road. In some cities, there has been a big move to break down barriers to pedestrians and limit the number of designated pedestrian crossing points, in order to give them greater freedom to cross roads where they want and so signal to drivers that they need to drive more slowly and carefully in urban areas. In other areas, such as the allocation of scarce goods or the imposition of value judgements, the fact that conflicts are inherent in the political process is self-evident.

So *politics exists to manage conflicts.* It leads to a process of centralized decision making following which a collective decision is then imposed. Politics is premised on all or some of us deciding the allocation and access to desired outcomes for everyone. The promise of democracy is, of course, that you can be involved in the decision process, but nothing can take away its centralized dynamic. You are not guaranteed what you want even in a system of democratic governance. The genius of the market is in part that rationing is internalized – you calculate knowing what you can and cannot afford – but in the case of politics rationing is imposed and external: you get what the system gives you. Little wonder that it is not automatically popular.

Proposition 2: Politics is Driven by Complex Communication That is Demanding and Prone to Failure

'Exit' and 'Voice'

If you don't like something in a shop, you walk out and go somewhere else until you find what you do like – the 'exit' mechanism. You don't have to bargain your way out of the shop – except perhaps in some automobile or car showrooms with particularly aggressive sales personnel! The system works because if enough people walk out then the shop gets the message that what it is selling is not what people want, and it changes its stock (or prices) accordingly.

When it comes to the world of government, the 'exit' mechanism does not work and we have instead to rely on what Albert Hirschman refers to as 'voice'.[6] 'Exit' refers to the act of leaving by the consumer and implies the existence of a market with competition and various suppliers: it is a classic *economic* mechanism. 'Voice' is the act of complaining or protesting, with the intention of achieving an ameliorating response from the organization under a challenge: it is a classic *political* mechanism.

Voice can come in different forms. All the common forms of participation – such as campaigning, writing letters, approaching an official, protesting – are ways to express voice. Even boycotting products – a form of participation that has also grown in recent years – makes sense only if it is accompanied by voice so that the focus of the sanction is aware of the reason why you want its behaviour to change. But whether it is through voting, individual contacting and complaining or more collective forms of organizing and protest, voice is a key mechanism for transmission in politics.

Voice, especially in its more developed collective forms, carries more costs for the individual than exit. It is time-consuming to engage in individual complaints and protests but collective action raises a whole host of further problems. Is the action likely to be successful? Is the effort in joining or even coordinating a campaign likely to be rewarded? Will a collective campaign emerge without my participation, on whose success I will be able to hitch a 'free-ride'?

Yet, voice is not enough in politics. Politics also requires that you *listen*: communication rather than voice is the top political activity. This observation is true no matter what your image is of people and how they approach politics. Whether we engage in politics as other-regarding citizens, self-interested individuals seeking to fulfil our private desires, or as problem solvers searching for understanding and a way forward, communication is the key.

Politics in the Public Realm

Some see politics as a process that takes place in the public realm where together as citizens we decide what is right for ourselves. In order to do that, we must exchange views and come to a collective judgement. This way of understanding rests on a rather noble image of the way that politics works. It is central to Bernard Crick's well-known book, *In Defence of Politics*, where he argues that politics is about taking into account the views of others:

> The political method of rule is to listen to these other groups so as to conciliate them as far as possible, and to give them a legal position, a sense of security, some clear and reasonably safe means of articulation, by which these other groups can and will speak freely. Ideally politics draws all these groups into each other so that they each and together can make a positive contribution towards the general business of government, the maintaining of order.[7]

Many of those writing in recent years and trying to diagnose why politics seems to be going wrong have argued that we have lost this special sense of the 'public realm'.[8] The public domain in this discourse has its own culture and codes; it provides a framework of norms which guides behaviour where citizenship trumps market power or the bonds of clan and kinship. A sense of service and civic duty are the driving forces of this world – a gift of history – and they are in danger of being fatally undermined by aggressive and negative forces. Others have advocated reforms that call for much greater deliberation in the way we make decisions. Indeed, 'the deliberative model of democracy has been the dominant new strand in democratic theory over the last ten to fifteen years'.[9] These theorists argue that politics must involve discussion and more of it, and that deliberation must be on an equal and inclusive footing so that people can move beyond their starting positions to develop a deepened awareness and a confidence to engage in public affairs. We shall return to these arguments again later in the book, but for now we have established the point that from this perspective on politics, communication is vital.

But what if we take a rather more hard-nosed approach to what politics is about? You may already be thinking that the idea of politics being noble is a bit difficult to take. You may be thinking instead that politics is about people trying to bring to fruition their private desires in a public arena. If you hold such opinions, you may be glad to know that many of those who study politics agree with you; indeed, there are whole schools of thought that start with 'the assumption that people get involved in politics in order to further their own personal objectives'.[10] *Rational choice* or *strategic action* approaches to the study of politics are highly favoured by many analysts.[11]

The 'Calculus Approach'

The idea that people are involved in politics for their own purposes is often associated with what has been termed the 'calculus approach' to politics.[12] The idea of strategic calculation dominates many fictional accounts of plotting and scheming politicians and, of course, famously underlies much of the advice provided to a ruler by Machiavelli, in his primer on government, called *The Prince*.[13] However, the point of this way of thinking about politics really hits home if you assume that everyone engaged in politics behaves strategically, instead of just a few leaders manipulating the rest of us. The calculus approach relies on reasoning similar to that practised in much of economics; it assumes that those engaged in politics have fixed preferences or tastes. They are seen as acting instrumentally to maximize the attainment of their preferences, and that in doing so they behave in a highly strategic manner, calculating a range of options before selecting the one that delivers the most benefits.

Crucially, in order to engage in a calculus approach to politics people need a lot of information and certainty, in so far as it is possible, about the actions of others. The central insight of much rational choice work is that politics requires good *institutions* to frame the process of strategic interaction between different interests.[14] What any actor does depends a lot on what they think that others will do. Political institutions can favour effective communication to a greater or lesser degree. More communication – so that people can know what is on the agenda, what are the most likely range of choices, what others are likely to do and can see that effective enforcement will occur if a decision is made – is likely to lead to better decision outcomes, according the rational choice institutionalists. For those who see politics as about individuals pursuing their private desires, as well as those who see politics as noble, communication is the key to politics.

The 'Cultural Approach'

Communication is also central to a third way of looking at politics. This perspective, sometimes referred to as the 'cultural approach' to politics,[15] does not want to assume that people will behave differently as citizens in the way that the 'politics as a public discourse' school tends to, but is equally not convinced that people are capable of the kind of strategic calculation favoured by the rational choice school. It rests on the view that human behaviour is not fully strategic, but is bounded by an individual's world-view: the choice of what to do depends on the interpretation of the situation rather than purely strategic calculation. Communication is central to this way of understanding politics, because it rests on a view that people are constantly struggling to understand their world and are looking to frame their responses to problems by reference to a 'mental map', an understanding of the way that life works that makes sense to them. But they also need cues from others in order to frame their responses.

This way of thinking about human behaviour, some argue, applies well not only to the world of politics, but also to the world of economics.[16] Claiming to be closer to the experimental evidence from psychology about the way that people actually make decisions, it favours an understanding of people as *problem solvers*. Humans, it is argued, perceive and learn only in regard to a problem: they observe a situation and try to define it and categorize it – if it displays such-and-such characteristics then it must be so-and-so. These judgements are in turn developed into broad clusters of rules, and eventually into default hierarchies that help to simplify the decision about what the most appropriate response in any given circumstances is. People develop mental models or 'maps' that enable them to make coherent predictions about their environment. These maps are not employed in a rigid manner and are subject to challenge – people do not have perfectly ordered frameworks for understanding; they are seen by some as a myriad of rules of thumb and by others as broad perceptions of ways of life or understandings of how things work. Crucially, people try out action choices and learn from the responses of their environment. Different ways of defining a problem and different understandings of the repertoire of feasible responses are the stuff of politics, and central to this approach is the notion that people can learn to resolve conflicts and cooperate as they develop shared mental models.

Communication and Dialogue

No matter which way of understanding politics and people's behaviour you adopt, communication is a key activity. We have seen that voice is a crucial political weapon, but politics is about more than that. Getting others to understand what you want, and listening to what others want, are central to the process, but communication of this type is notoriously difficult in complex situations. Expressing what you want may be easy enough if you are confident about a situation or are clear what the options are and how to respond, but even if you reach that step, it is only the start. Engaging in politics is a tough and demanding road.

Politics as an expression of citizenship demands sustained dialogue: politics as the pursuit of self-interest requires a deep understanding of the responses of others. Politics as problem solving involves a complex process of testing, learning and adjusting, and is time-consuming and demanding. Buying a major product or service – such as a home – can involve hours of research, thought and debate with any codecision makers; politics is potentially like that for every decision. The level of information about what should and can be done is often unclear, there is often limited certainty about outcomes and the range of interests to be taken into account is often inexhaustible. No wonder politicians often look tired!

Communication is central to every step in the political process – politics is about much more than shouting about what you want, although for some people social or economic barriers limit their capacity to even articulate their interests. Politics is also about searching for solutions that will stick because they treat the problem and have sustainable support. Communication starts with the gathering of opinions and interests to form coalitions; it continues to be central to establishing a legitimate process for coming to a judgement about what should be done, and it underlies the successful implementation of any choice made. Communication failure is possible at any point in the process: little wonder we often find politics disappointing.

Proposition 3: Political Decisions usually Involve Mutual Adjustment among Governing Elites and Result in Messy Outcomes and a Complex Distribution of Costs and Benefits

It is important not to move from the claim that the government is a centralized form of decision making to the claim that politics works by the imposition of central direction or the establishment of a common purpose. Both tactics are often tried in democratic governance, but they are accompanied by bargaining, or persuasion, or what Charles Lindblom calls 'mutual adjustment' among senior politicians, bureaucrats, representatives and organized interests[17] – the elite activists of the policy process. We often experience, as citizens, the outcomes of politics as controlling and occasionally arbitrary impositions, but the outputs of governance we experience are often driven by complex decentralized bargaining and negotiation. The results tend to be messy and contingent, but nevertheless do keep things moving. However, at the receiving end politics can appear to produce the worst of all worlds: directions about what to do that appear to have no guiding hand or logic.

Complexity and Coordination

One of the most common complaints about government is that it is not coordinated – one department is not aware what another is doing or, worse, that policies appear to contradict one another. As Lindblom points, out in democratic societies government is hardly ever entirely coordinated in the sense that it is subject to a central direction held together by a unified common purpose. Indeed, in most democracies we design in checks and balances and a division of power in order to make such coordination more difficult to achieve, as a brake on the danger of arbitrary use of power. The complexity of what modern governments try to do inevitably leads to a plethora of agencies, departments, sections and units. Coordinated ('joined-up') government should mean that policy decisions and activities are responsive and can adapt to each other. Coordinated politics is most often achieved through mutual adjustment among politicians, officials and groups. Crucially, from our point of view, citizens generally 'do not directly participate'[18] in this process, but are central to what emerges (see Figure 4.1).

Figures 4.1a and 4.1b provide contrasting representations of the way that government works. In the centrally regulated system (Figure 4.1a), everything flows from actor *A*. If that person was elected or appointed to oversee a government process we might see that attempt to give central direction as an expression of democracy. Indeed, in public presentation of government

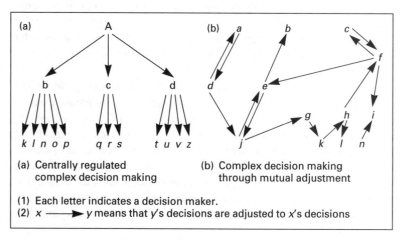

(a) Centrally regulated complex decision making

(b) Complex decision making through mutual adjustment

(1) Each letter indicates a decision maker.
(2) *x* ——▶ *y* means that *y*'s decisions are adjusted to *x*'s decisions

Figure 4.1   How government works

Source: Adapted from Charles Lindblom, *The Intelligence of Democracy: Decision Making through Mutual Adjustment* (New York: Free Press, 1965).

decision making systems, these sorts of hierarchical depictions are often used precisely to reassure the public that the person that they put in charge is in charge of the system. However, in practice, most government systems are much closer to the representation provided in Figure 4.1b. The process works through mutual adjustment but even then not every decision maker is adjusted directly to each other decision maker. To make the picture even more complicated, we could then introduce at various points some central supervisors – or as the British government and media have dubbed them 'tsars' – who are asked to bring the different parts of the government machine together to tackle particular problems. In the UK, we have 'drugs tsars' and 'transport tsars', a lot of debate and initiatives are currently aimed at trying to make government more 'joined-up'.[19]

Lindblom[20] identifies a dozen types of mutual adjustment. First there are the forms of adaptive behaviour undertaken by decision makers in which they respond to the *decisions of others*. Broadly, they can carry on doing what they are doing and not worry about the consequences for the other actor, or they can change their behaviour in order to avoid some or all of the adverse consequences that their actions might have. Second, there are forms of manipulated behaviour whereby actors look for accommodation with each other through *bargaining*, *negotiation*, or *influence*. In addition, they may seek to strike a deal through offering compensation or some form of reciprocity. They can try to cut off other options by getting authoritative backing for their decision, by changing the incentives for another actor, or by getting in there first, with a prior decision, and hoping that as a *fait accompli* other actors will modify and adjust their behaviour appropriately. Finally of course, they may seek *allies* in order to use third parties to support their position and persuade others of its rightness.

Sometimes people say to elected leaders: 'You are in charge, why don't you decide and then make it happen?' The process of mutual adjustment that is central to decision making in any complex system of democratic governance means that it is difficult and often close to impossible to deliver on that request. The making of policy inevitably involves compromise and lacks the coherence that might be given by over-arching central direction. Politicians with limited time and limited spans of control can make a difference, but they have to choose the issues over which to intervene and where to make an impact. Indeed, one of the real arts of political leadership is to get and then sustain such a focus.

In short, there is a contradiction between the naïve concept of democracy that is often in our heads and the reality of the way that the governmental process works. That reality is not the product of some grand conspiracy but rather of the division of power built deliberately into our systems of democratic governance and the sheer complexity of what is being attempted.

Policy and Implementation

I have not even so far mentioned the process of *implementation* – the process by which policies get put into place on the ground. If mutual adjustment drives a complex policy formulation process, then a similar set of relationships drives the process of turning a policy into practice. Pressman and Wildavsky[21] show that because implementation usually relies on joint decision making through a range of agencies the probability of the policy failing – that is, of it not being carried out according to the objectives of the policy maker – increases according to the number of decision points. Failure may occur for a whole host of reasons – poor communication of the policy, lack of resources, skill or will on the part of the implementers, and inappropriateness of the policy to local conditions. Given multiple decision points within individual agencies and many senior managers and even junior staff – or what are sometimes termed 'street-level bureaucrats' – the difficulties of successful implementation become immense. The problems may, however, not be as great as Pressman and Wildavsky portray; in particular, hurdles can be overcome the second or third time that a process of policy implementation is tried.[22] This may, in part, explain another well-recognized feature of government – the tendency to try the same policies again despite their previous failure – and it certainly confirms that there are no easy solutions to the challenges of implementation: no amount of performance targets and information gathering can resolve some problems at a stroke.

Distributional Consequences

Policy and implementation have, because of the complex and closed processes that determine them, a somewhat unsatisfactory and arbitrary feel from the viewpoint of the citizen. So, too, can the distributional consequences of government decisions. As Przeworski explains:

> Public decisions invariably entail distributional consequences. Even the purportedly universalistic legislation differentially affects people who have different resources and different values. As Marx noted, the law that prohibits everyone sleeping under bridges in fact concerns only those who have nowhere else to sleep.[23]

In a whole host of ways, governments create a situation where someone gets more and someone gets less; the problem is that a lot of the time its not clear to us why that should be so. We are aware of a range of benefits and subsidies that are provided to people, and their distribution is often explained by reference to their need or the centrality of what they do. In that sense, they can be legitimized, although arguments still arise about giving money to, for example, the elderly (shouldn't they have saved earlier in their lives?) or to farmers as subsidies (to get rich producing food that no one wants?). But every service, every regulation and every intervention by government – even those that are formally universal in character and available to all – has a *distributional consequence* because access and utility vary according to our circumstances. Schools enhance the capability of some, but can fail others; building a road helps some vehicle drivers more than others and helps drivers in general more than pedestrians or those who enjoyed the open space on which the road was built. Government decisions have a complex range of distributional consequences that are difficult to understand and certainly not always easy to justify. Naturally enough, many people tend to like activities that favour them but dislike those that don't. Even the most public spirited and other-regarding citizen finds it difficult not be jaundiced about some elements of public spending or activity: everyone has their own favourite examples of waste. Even before we get into the argument about the 'size' of government and the opportunity cost of money handed over in taxes that is not available for private consumption, it is clear that government decisions lead to distributional outcomes that provide another reason why politics can tend to disappoint.

Conclusions

Politics disappoints in part because of the way it is designed. As a centralized form of decision making it is inherently controlling. To take part in politics is time-consuming and challenging given the scale and quality of communication that is required. The outcomes of the political process are seldom clear cut and are often messy compromises.

We might wish it were otherwise, but politics is not the most heroic of human endeavours. Its minimum claim is that it is better to decide things by politics than by arbitrary acts of violence. A stronger claim is that in a democracy politics can protect your interests, engage your community commitment and help find solutions to significant social problems. We should care enough about both claims to worry about whether politics works, and to that extent keep our disappointments with politics in perspective: too great an alienation from the system makes it unworkable.

A certain level of credibility is central to the operation of politics, as I suggested at the end of Chapter 2. A degree of *legitimacy* needs to surround the process. Legitimacy is not an all-or-nothing issue;[24] it requires clear rules about how decisions should be made, a sense that those rules can be justified in public debate and a clear demonstration of some element of consent having been granted, either by the people as a whole or by their representatives.

The second element that gives political systems credibility is *loyalty*, premised on the view that in the long run the citizens regard the system as worth maintaining. As Hirschman points out, loyalty influences the dynamics of the political system. Initially, it may delay the use of 'voice' because it is hoped that the organization will correct itself; if dissatisfaction remains, the loyalists may begin to use voice and ultimately the threat of exit. After the threat of exit, loyalist voice may become particularly demanding. Loyalty, in part because of the barrier to exit it provides and in part because of the sense of investment on which it rests, encourages voice and 'the discovery of new ways of exerting influence and pressure toward recovery'.[25] Loyalty may in certain circumstances act as a stimulus to a powerful form of loyalist voice. Above all, it gives the government and other organizations time and opportunity to respond and improve.

The third element that provides credibility is *resilience*, especially among representatives and active citizens – the ability to come back and fight another day. The distributional outcomes of decision making – the complex patterns of winners and losers – need to be accepted in the short run, although they can be challenged again later: politics relies on losers having the determination to come back and try again.[26] Losers need to stay mobilized, at least to a degree, and view the prospect of change to their advantage as possible in the future: short-term disappointment needs to be tempered by long-term hope.

Understanding politics – its dynamics and its limitations – can limit the disappointment that citizens appear to display in both mature and newer democracies. How we understand what we are doing matters in politics because it can determine our actions and behaviour. There are worrying signs in contemporary democracies that all may not be well in the way that citizens are engaging in politics. Part II of the book examines this argument in detail, in particular in relation to mature rather than newer democracies, for which less information is as yet available.

Part II

The Pathologies of
Political Practice

Part II

The Pathologies of Political Freedom

5

The Decline of Citizen Engagement?

> Most people have strong feelings on few if any of the issues the
> government needs to address and would much prefer to spend
> their time in non-political pursuits . . . The people want to be
> able to make democracy visible and accountable on those rare
> occasions when they are motivated to be involved. They want to
> know that the opportunity will be there for them even though
> they probably have no intention of getting involved in govern-
> ment or even paying attention to it.[1]
>
> John Hibbing and Elizabeth Theiss-Morse, *Stealth Democracy*

This chapter examines the activism of ordinary citizens in democracies and
their engagement in politics. It explores evidence that suggests a propensity
for engagement that is widely but thinly spread, and is unevenly distributed.
It further argues that the dominant form of engagement is moving from
collective and intensive involvement towards more individualistic and
'woolly' political acts that have an episodic character. Systems of democratic governance are not so much groaning from the pressure of critical citizens but creaking from the impact of semi-detached but occasional assertive
citizens. As John Hibbing and Elizabeth Theiss-Morse argue, people want to
be involved, but on their terms and on an intermittent, piecemeal and
sporadic basis.

There are substantial numbers of people that politically engage at least
occasionally beyond the act of voting, and in many democracies a healthy
variety of options are open for that engagement. This chapter adopts a fairly
broad definition of what constitutes 'political acts' undertaken by citizens,
and shows how political activism constitutes a significant feature of many
democracies. On small-scale issues, and by means that generally involve
only a limited commitment of time and effort, we can say that many are
politically active. However some people are politically inactive even on the

basis of a fairly broad and generous definition like this. The base for citizen activism is also stronger in some countries than in others: some democracies, perhaps especially the newer democracies, lack the *civic base* (the practice of forming groups and associations that foster skills and create networks) that can help to support or sustain democracy. There are also concerns about the decline of an associational habit in the mature democracies.

It is also clear that the propensity to engage in politics is not equally distributed even within countries. The more educated you are, the higher your social and economic position, then, generally, the more likely you are to engage in everyday politics. A range of other factors also influence people's willingness and propensity to engage: people have to feel part of something to want to participate in it, and they often have to be mobilized. Even in those countries with a very active citizen base, engagement tends to be something that is done to a greater degree by the better-educated, middle-class sections of society. Some groups appear to be significantly more prone to disengagement: the poor in general, ethnic monitories and, most worryingly, young people. Whatever else it is, the world of everyday activism is not socially representative and the limited numbers and range of those engaged should be a cause for concern.

People make an input, identifying what they want, but they do not engage in a wider analysis of the issues. The growth of boycotting, complaints and other forms of activism appears to have a 'consumer' feel, and activism could be in danger of becoming more of a lifestyle statement than a serious engagement. Campaigns and protests are engaged in as part of a portfolio of work and leisure activities that can express your ethical identity, but not a grappling with the underlying complex issues. Activism in fact too often seems to be little more than a sophisticated form of consumerism for the well-resourced, that enables them to get better access to public resources and decisions and gives relatively cost-free expression to their identity and favoured causes.

How Do Most Citizens Engage?

In Chapter 1, I celebrated democracy because, as a system of governance, it provides citizens at large with a 'voice' in the processes and institutions that determine how power is exercised and how decisions are made in their societies. In the eyes of most observers, activism and engagement are central to the very rationale of democratic politics.

What kinds of activities do people engage in when it comes to everyday democratic politics? Certainly many people discuss and debate political issues on a regular basis with family or friends. Many conversations involve some reflection on politics and political choices, but beyond talking, what do people do? How do they act politically? We have already seen in Chapter 2 some evidence of a declining but still very substantial willingness to engage in voting. But voting is something to do maybe once a year, depending on the number of national or local elections in each particular country. But what about more everyday activism: are there political acts that are undertaken on a more regular basis? Insofar as there are, they are most likely to involve attempts to influence government representatives to sort out a repair on a house, do something about the local school, or make sure that a hospital does not close. Everyday politics is not, however, always driven by the immediate and self-interested concerns of participants; it can be about a cause that people believe in, or a challenge to the behaviour of powerful institutions – government agencies or multinational companies. Everyday activism can involve signing petitions, boycotting certain products, or even going on a march to protest against a war or in favour of debt relief for developing nations. We need to adopt a wide definition of 'everyday activism'.

Table 5.1 reports the response of a range of citizens throughout Europe to questions about their political activism over a period of twelve months. The surveys were undertaken in the early part of the twenty-first century, so they give a fairly up-to-date picture of how people engage in politics on an everyday basis beyond the act of voting.

Looking at the figures contained in Table 5.1 reveals several things. First, political engagement is not something that people do all the time. On average[2] the most popular forms – signing a petition or buying a product to make a political or ethical point – had been undertaken by only a quarter of the participants in the survey in the previous twelve months. Second, it is perhaps surprising how many and various the forms of political activism are. People may not all be active all the time, but there are lots of ways in any twelve-month period that they are trying to make their voices heard. In the UK, drawing on the range of political activities listed in Table 5.1, it is estimated that in a twelve-month period eight out of ten citizens had participated in politics.[3] People, as we argued in Chapter 2, are not simply disengaging from politics: they are trying to make a difference in a variety of ways.

Overall levels of activism suggest that it is a mistake to see people as apathetic. However, the evidence from Table 5.1 indicates that many people are cut off from the world of formal politics – for them it is an alien world – and this is reflected in the relatively low membership and engagement with political parties. Intensive forms of engagement through working for action groups or other organizations draw in only a modest number of individuals.

Table 5.1 Patterns of activism, various European nations

| | Western Europe | | | Eastern Europe | | | | Southern Europe | | | Nordics | | | | |
Activity	UK	France	Germany	Poland	Hungary	Slovenia	Czech Rep.	Spain	Greece	Italy	Sweden	Norway	Denmark	Finland	Average
								Per cent of involvement							
Contacted politician or government official, last 12 months	18.1	17.6	12.8	9.5	14.7	12.2	22.7	12.0	14.5	12.0	16.5	23.8	17.9	24.4	**14.7**
Worked in political party or action group, last 12 months	3.4	4.9	3.9	2.9	2.9	3.5	4.6	6.1	4.8	3.0	5.0	9.3	4.1	3.4	**4.2**
Worked in another organization or association, last 12 months	9.2	17.6	17.8	5.8	2.9	2.3	15.1	16.7	5.7	7.5	24.6	28.1	17.3	30.7	**13.7**
Worn or displayed campaign badge/ sticker, last 12 months	9.8	11.4	5.8	2.9	3.2	2.1	5.0	9.8	2.7	7.3	10.7	22.8	5.1	15.7	**7.7**
Signed petition, last 12 months	40.0	34.8	30.5	6.9	4.2	11.8	16.1	24.2	4.7	17.4	40.8	37.3	28.2	24.0	**25.8**
Taken part in lawful public demonstration, last 12 months	4.4	17.9	10.6	1.3	3.7	2.7	4.5	17.5	4.5	10.9	6.4	8.9	8.3	2.0	**9.3**

Boycotted certain products, last 12 months	26.1	26.6	26.1	3.6	4.8	5.1	10.8	8.0	8.5	7.5	32.5	20.2	22.9	26.8	**17.4**
Bought product for political/ethical/environment reason, last 12 months	32.2	28.0	39.2	9.8	10.5	9.6	22.6	11.6	6.6	6.5	55.1	36.6	43.8	41.8	**24.4**
Donated money to political organization or group, last 12 months	7.8	2.9	9.2	9.2	1.7	6.5	11.6	5.3	2.3	3.0	6.5	11.5	9.1	6.9	**6.8**
Participation in illegal protest activities, last 12 months	0.8	2.6	1.1	0.2	0.8	0.8	1.3	1.7	1.4	1.8	0.8	0.8	1.1	0.3	**1.3**
Member of political party	2.7	2.3	3.6	1.7	1.6	5.0	4.1	3.2	4.8	3.9	8.2	8.8	5.9	7.3	**3.8**

Sources: Data from European Social Survey (ESS) (2002).

When people do engage it mostly takes the form of low key acts, such as signing a petition, boycotting some product or buying some product for political or ethical reasons. Contacting someone in authority or who might influence those in authority is another core feature of our politics. Demonstrations and protests remain a form of political activism that is popular to some degree in some countries. But plainly it would be a mistake to conclude that politics had taken to the streets to replace the decline in formal engagement. People are engaged but in a relatively thin and sporadic way with the political system.

It is not possible to report for the whole of Europe a comparison between forms of political activity now and in the past. However, it is possible to examine the case of the UK, where the results of a survey undertaken in the early part of the twenty-first century can be compared to one undertaken in the 1980s. The evidence suggests that more *collectivistic* forms of participation have declined and that more *individualist* forms have come to the fore. The figures are not completely comprehensive or convincing but, compared to the mid-1980s, signing a petition or contacting a politician has declined while contacting the media has increased, as has the boycotting of products to express political views.[4] It is not clear that there has been a big shift from the mid-1980s to the beginning of the twenty-first century; collective forms still have a role, as there are many willing to join groups, protests and rallies, but political activity has tended to centre more on such activities as contacting a public official, boycotting something, or donating money. There is also a lot of what has been termed 'micro participation' which 'refers to actions designed to influence indirect agents of the state in the day-to-day world'.[5] Individualistic activity can be focused on getting something done that is close to a citizen's immediate interest, such as better treatment in a hospital or access to a school, but it can also involve attempts to change environmental or foreign policy.

Table 5.1 shows some consistent differences between European countries, as well as some interesting oddities. When it comes to illegal protests, France appears to be well ahead of the field, with Italy its nearest rival, although in all countries the numbers engaged in such activity is very low. The practice of lawful public demonstrations is relatively popular in France, Germany, Spain and Italy. The rather more humdrum signing of a petition is most popular in the UK, Sweden and Norway, but not something you do in Greece or Hungary.

The most activist countries appear to be the Nordics, and then those of 'mainstream' western Europe such as the UK, France and Germany. The southern European countries show more diversity, with Spain appearing to have relatively buoyant levels of activism and Greece having relatively low ones. Everyday activism appears to be at its lowest in the newly democratized eastern European countries – Poland, Hungary, Slovenia and the Czech Republic – who all appear to have levels below the average for European countries. Compare Poland to Sweden, for example, and on every measure of activity apart, somewhat surprisingly, from donating money to a political cause, the Swedes appear to be more active than the Poles, often by quite a large factor.

Uneven Capacity to Participate: Exploring and Addressing the Issues

We now explore the factors that drive people's response to activism, and look at how barriers to engagement may be understood. The conventional approach to explaining differences in political participation rests on what is called the social and economic status (SES) factor. A detailed and definitive study of the USA concluded that:

> The central tenet of the SES model is that people of higher socio-economic status – those with higher education, higher income and higher status jobs – are more active in politics . . . SES has been found in many contexts to be a powerful predictor of political activity.[6]

The Citizens' Audit in Britain confirmed in 2004 that this link between socio-economic status and political participation still endures: 'political engagement is very much dominated by the already well-resourced; in other words, the most highly educated, the rich, and those from the top educational echelons'.[7] Some very graphic confirmation of the impact of SES factors is provided in Table 5.2, that compares the responses from European citizens in different countries against evidence about the level of education they received. It shows clearly that for all types of political activity those with higher levels of education are more likely to engage and get involved: those reaching the tertiary stage reach consistently higher levels of engagement than those whose schooling finished primary or secondary school. Even when it comes to illegal protest activities and legal demonstrations, it is the better educated that are more likely to engage. The differences are often quite substantial: everyday activism is a more everyday activity for some social groups than others.

The figures in Table 5.2 suggest that the skills and personal capacities associated with higher education – and, more broadly, higher SES – are vital in driving the propensity to participate. But other factors can influence participation. The CLEAR model that I have developed with my colleagues draws on a range of research into participation to identify five factors that can drive the uneven response to participation by citizens:[8]

Table 5.2 Political activism linked to educational attainment across a range of European countries

Measures of activism	Not completed primary education per cent	Primary or first stage of basic per cent	Lower secondary or second stage of basic per cent	Upper secondary per cent	Post secondary, non-tertiary per cent	First stage of tertiary per cent	Second stage of tertiary per cent
Contacted politician or government official, last 12 months	5.6	10.7	10.2	14.6	19.7	23.5	29.0
Worked in political party or action group, last 12 months	1.4	2.7	2.3	4.4	6.5	7.0	9.2
Worked in another organization or association, last 12 months	4.0	7.1	8.4	14.7	18.5	24.2	28.2
Worn or displayed campaign badge/sticker, last 12 months	1.8	3.9	6.1	7.6	11.4	11.6	15.9
Signed petition, last 12 months	6.7	10.6	22.1	26.9	34.7	40.0	45.2

Taken part in lawful public demonstration, last 12 months	3.0	4.7	7.3	9.4	11.6	14.2	22.2
Boycotted certain products, last 12 months	3.5	5.2	12.2	18.4	25.5	30.3	38.5
Bought product for political/ethical/environment reason, last 12 months	5.6	8.0	15.1	27.2	31.8	46.0	48.4
Donated money to political organization or group, last 12 months	2.1	3.3	4.3	8.0	8.3	11.5	12.0
Participated in illegal protest activities, last 12 months	0.4	0.8	1.5	1.0	1.7	1.6	3.1
Member of political party	2.3	3.7	2.3	4.5	4.4	5.5	5.4

Source: Data from European Social Survey (ESS) (2002).

- Can do – the resources and knowledge to participate
- Like to – a sense of attachment that reinforces participation
- Enabled to – a set of supporting civic institutions that makes participation possible
- Asked to – mobilized through direct invitation from public authorities or the efforts of a range of non-governmental, voluntary and community organizations
- Responded to – seen evidence that their views had been considered by public authorities and those engaged more regularly in the political process.

The five factors are examined in more detail below, and in each case I argue they are capable of overcoming some of the inequalities built into the participation world. CLEAR can be used as a diagnostic tool to examine the particular constraints and prospects for participation in any setting where the basic trappings of democratic governance have already been established.

Can do

When people have the appropriate skills and resources, they are more able to participate. These skills range from the ability and confidence to speak in public or write letters to the capacity to organize events and encourage others of similar mind to support initiatives. They also include access to resources that facilitate such activities (ranging from photocopying facilities through to internet access, etc.). These skills and resources are much more commonly found among the better-educated and better-employed sections of the population: those of higher socio-economic status. However, none of the requisite skills and resources is exclusively the property of high SES, some skills rest more on an individual's resources: their education or, more broadly, their *capacity for engagement*. The resources available to communities are also affected by the facilities and capacities available, but it is possible for public, voluntary, or community bodies to intervene to make up for any socio-economic limitations. Capacity building efforts are aimed at ensuring that citizens are given the support to develop the skills and resources needed for them to engage.

Like to

'Like to' rests on the idea that people's felt sense of being part of something encourages them to engage. If you feel a part of something, then you are more willing to engage; if you feel excluded or sense that you are not welcome, you may decide not to participate. If participation is seen as just for old people or for men, then others may not feel comfortable or able to join in. A sense of trust, connection and linked networks can, according to the social capital argument (Chapter 3), enable people to work together and cooperate more effectively. Sense of community can be a strong motivator for participation, but given the inherent diversity in many communities then, conversely, an absence of identity or a sense of being an outsider can militate against participation.

This factor can again be addressed by policy makers and non-governmental practitioners. The most important initial step in diagnosis is to gain an understanding of the sense of loyalties and identities held in various communities. It is not easy to manipulate or change these feelings, but it is possible to give people the opportunity to believe that they are part of a wider civic identity built around their locality or some sense of equal and shared citizenship. Recognizing and promoting such a sense can help develop the positive environment of community engagement that means that people want to participate. However, even if people feel engaged with that wider community, they may still choose not to participate: people may prefer to let others do the work of participation for them or feel that their elected representatives are already doing a good job. The choice about whether to participate remains with the individual citizen; the point of the diagnosis is to understand what needs to be done to ensure that citizens have a choice.

Enabled to

'Enabled to', as a factor in participation, is premised on the research observation that most participation is facilitated by groups or organizations. Political participation in isolation is more difficult and less sustainable (unless an individual is highly motivated) than the mutually reinforcing engagement of contact through groups and networks. Collective participation provides continuous reassurance and feedback that the cause of engagement is relevant, and that participation is having some value. Indeed, for some, such engagement is more important than the outcome of the participation. Research shows that the existence of networks, groups and civic infrastructure which can support participation and provide a route to decision makers is therefore vital to the vibrancy of participation, and can actually facilitate or inhibit it. Where the right range and variety of groups exists, there tends to be more participation: 'umbrella' organizations that can support civic, community and voluntary groups can play a particularly important role. They can help groups and 'participation platforms' to become established, provide networks of contacts and information, explain how to campaign and engage and facilitate access to the relevant decision makers.

Asked to

'Asked to' builds on the findings of research that mobilization matters: people tend to become engaged more often, and more regularly, when they are asked to engage, and often depends upon how they are approached. Mobilization can come from a range of sources, but the most powerful form is when those responsible for a decision ask others to engage with them in making the decision. Case studies have demonstrated how open political and managerial systems in local municipalities can also have a significant effect by extending invitations to participate to their citizens.[9] The variety of participation options is important, because some people are more comfortable with some forms of engagement (such as a public meeting) while others would prefer, for example, to engage through on-line discussions. Some people want to talk about the experiences of their community or neighbourhood while others want to engage based on their knowledge as a user of a particular service. The nature of the 'ask' is important. Participation can be mobilized by the use of *incentives* (e.g. honoraria for service), through establishing a sense of *obligation* (as in the case of jury duty), or by offering *bargains/exchanges* (where participation is accompanied by action in response). The focus of the 'ask' is vital; it could be directed at a particular neighbourhood, or a larger cross-authority population. The sustainability of participation is also relevant: can the 'ask' be sustained, and will citizens keep responding? Who is being asked is another issue. There is a dilemma between developing 'expert citizens' and rotating/sampling involvement to get at 'ordinary citizens'. The 'asked to' factor asks policy-makers to address the range and the repertoire of their initiatives: how do they appeal to different citizen groups?

Responded to

'Responded to' captures the idea that for people to participate on a sustainable basis they have to believe that their involvement is making a difference, that it is achieving positive benefits. This factor is both the most obvious, but also the most difficult, factor in enhancing political participation. For people to participate they have to believe that they are going to be listened to and, if not always agreed with, will at least be in a position to see that their views have been taken into account. Meeting the challenge of the 'responded to' factor means asking public authorities how they weigh messages from various consultation or participation events against other inputs to the decision making process: how are the different or conflicting views of various participants and stakeholders to be prioritized? Responsiveness is about ensuring feedback, even when this is not positive in the sense that the dominant view of participants has been accepted. Feedback involves explaining how the decision was made, and the role of participation within the decision process. Response is vital for citizen education, and thus has a bearing on the 'front end' of the process as well. Citizens need to learn to live with disappointment: participation will not always 'deliver' on immediate concerns, but remains important, and citizens' confidence in the participation process cannot be premised upon 'getting their own way'. Ideas of natural justice are important here: participation is necessary to ensure that citizens get their case heard, and that it receives impartial judgement. If something affects you, you should be able to make your case and have it listened to, but you cannot be guaranteed a positive outcome.

The CLEAR model is about recognizing that a variety of factors can drive participation. Its aim is to provide a diagnostic tool so that the factors constraining engagement among some groups and sections of society can be addressed.

Concerns about the Quality of Participation

'Atomised Citizenship'

Even for those who do engage, there are questions to be asked about the quality of their engagement. The ordinary activism of citizens too often amounts to little more than a thin and individually focused involvement: people say what they want, maybe get something they want or at least get their concern expressed, but do not have any wider engagement with the political system, or with each other.

Participation can often amount to little more than being a more effective customer of public services. This kind of 'activism citizenship' is not necessarily a bad thing – indeed, given the complexity of the organizational arrangements of public bodies and the central importance of public services to many of our lives, it plainly has a positive role in ensuring that the people's paper rights to good-quality public services are translated into practice. Lobbying for better access to schools, or to block a proposed development in the neighbourhood, to get a better water supply, or to obtain improved street lighting are all laudable – and, indeed, an appropriate expression of democratic rights – but there is cause for concern if all the engagement amounts to is what some writers call 'atomised citizenship'[10] and others refer to as 'personal democracy'.[11] At the end of their detailed study of civic participation in the UK, Charles Pattie and his colleagues warn that:

> The growth of atomised citizenship runs the risk of a growth of policy fragmentation and failure. The best example of this process is in relation to NIMBYists.[12] Whether it is car owners who want faster travel times but oppose local motorway construction, or holiday-makers who regularly fly into Europe while bitterly opposing local airport expansion schemes, or newly-weds who turn into staunch opponents of local building projects once they have bought their first house[:] all illustrate the problem. If the institutions of civil society become weak, then it becomes harder to counteract these tendencies, and individuals will not have to face the logic of their own choices in a fragmented individualistic political system.[13]

In a review of the state of democratic engagement in the USA, Matthew Crenson and Benjamin Ginsberg identify a similar concern:

> American democracy is not dead. It has, however, undergone a transfiguration, and so has citizenship. These changes do not come from some vast conspiracy to deprive the general public of its place in politics. In fact, twentieth-century political reforms have given citizens unprecedented access to the political process . . . But the new opportunities for citizen involvement have changed the nature of citizenship itself. The proliferation of opportunities for individual access to government has substantially reduced the incentives for collective mobilization. For ordinary Americans, this means that it has become standard practice to deal with government as individuals rather than as members of a mobilized public.[14]

If we leave aside a possible charge of creating a romantic image of a (perhaps mythical) era of active citizens and collective action, all these writers point to a contradiction built in to today's everyday activism in mature democracies. It provides better democratic access to government decisions that immediately affect you, but it does not offer a wider framework for that engagement. Giving freedom of information rights, adopting a multitude of consultation procedures, providing hotline contact points, empowering a range of people to serve on public boards, community committees and government agencies are all valuable forms of granting access, but they all allow people 'to play politics alone'.[15] If all the engagement is directed towards personal gain or privileged access to public services, it fits in with a culture of immediate gratification and in turn, as argued in Chapter 4, feeds into a constant sense of disappointment with the political process. This is not to argue against rights to such access, etc. but it is to suggest that, as a formula for a healthy democracy, it may not be enough. Politics requires that people face 'the logic of their own choices'; it also requires people to engage in wider issues.

Professional Lobbyists and Protest

When individuals do fight for wider causes, it is also clear that the terms of their engagement are also changing, and moving towards an attenuated form of involvement. As Chapter 6 suggests, people in mature democracies have increasingly been able to hive off their cause commitments to professional lobbyists and protest organizations. A narrow group of high-intensity activists with only a token relationship with the members of the organizations they head can engage in elite-level policy battles, a form of lobby engagement that may provide a way of checking the power of business in the lobbying process. But the implications for wider citizenship are perhaps more negative than positive: people are not mobilized collectively except for the occasional mass rally or media stunt, they are approached and managed by professional lobbyists as individual supporters or sponsors. Supporting causes can just become part of a wider identity statement expressed through the sending of an occasional cheque and attendance at a pop concert-based rally. It is a form of engagement that perhaps tells us more about such individuals than it does address the issues or problems that are supposed to be the focus of attention.

Conclusions

The argument of this chapter is that in both mature and newer democracies the existence of a wider cadre of citizen activists cannot be taken for granted. In newer democracies, the enthusiasm of the reform period has given way to the practicalities of getting by in a vast changing global economy. In more mature democracies, a combination of new opportunities for individualistic access and shifts in the pattern of lobbying has created an environment that seems capable of supporting only the most individualized and privatized forms of engagement. We are not so much critical as erratic citizens when it comes to engagement, and while our erratic engagement may do the job for us it puts burdens on the political system and does little to build a wider sense of engagement in, or understanding of, a political process.

It is also clear that the propensity to engage is unevenly distributed. Should we ensure that the barriers that can block access to the system are lowered still further to allow a wider range of people to engage in politics? How far can we go to deliver on the dream of active citizens that appears central to the democratic ideal? There is certainly enough activism around to suggest that people can engage. The problem is how to construct a political system to cope with the kind of engagement people want and to enable the political system to be both sustainable and effective.

6

The Professionalization of Activism?

> High-intensity political participation . . . takes a lot of time and
> effort on the part of those who are involved in it . . . Highly
> active participants are much more important to democratic poli-
> tics than is often recognized . . . Indeed democratic politics is
> impossible without them.[1]

Paul Whiteley and Patrick Seyd, *High-Intensity Participation*

> There are perhaps no more than 100,000 really committed
> activists in Britain – by which I mean people for whom, beyond
> work and the immediate demands of family life, politics is a
> really time-consuming activity. By contrast, surveys tell us that
> apparently marginal activities such as dressmaking and knitting
> are actually engaged in by 3 per cent of all British men over the
> age of 16 – about 700,000 in all.[2]

Michael Moran, *Politics and Governance in the UK*

High-Intensity Activism

Politics is done in detail and with intensity by a small group of semi-profes-
sionalized and specialist actors. As Paul Whiteley and Patrick Seyd argue,
politics would be impossible without that input. This world of high-intensity activism and its wider hinterland is examined below. It is a small world
with, as Mick Moran points out, relatively few actors engaged in it
compared to many other activities. Attention is focused, initially, on party
activists and concentration is then directed towards the rise of lobby organizations that represent the interests of a vast array of citizens and seek
influence on their behalf. Interest is also focused on protest activism: the
movements, radical NGOs and protest politics groups that give spark and

103

challenge to the political world. These various forms of activism overlap to some degree, and sometimes provide recruits from one to the other; in some cases, individual citizens may be engaged in all these forms of activism.

The common issue with all these forms of activism is that they have become increasingly the domain of 'professionalized' actors and, as a result, restricted as forms of citizen expression. Political parties have not only lost members in droves, but those members that remain have a limited role in decision making and campaigning. Powerful party leaderships dominate their parties and experts organize campaigns. Members retain some importance as foot soldiers at election time and provide a shallow pool from which party candidates and representatives for governance agencies at various levels can be selected. Parties have seen a decline in their roots in civil society and become more creatures of the formal system of governance.

In contrast to parties, lobby groups have seen a vast increase in membership on paper but, for the most part, their only involvement is via their credit card; such groups too are largely run for and by professional politicos. The approach of such experts is, by definition, one that emphasizes their special knowledge and capacities and again is dominated by elite actors at the top of various professional institutes and organizations. Strange as it may seem, protest activism also displays similar tendencies, even in this 'alternative' world the professionalization of protest activism and the role of the media have to an extent created a world of spin-doctoring and manipulation to rival that of the formal electoral and representative politics that protest activists so often purport to despise.

Party Activists

Decline in Membership and Activism

Political parties perform a range of vital functions in a political system. They support the recruitment, selection and development of political leaders for government. They enable the expression of citizens' interests. They bring together a range of perspectives and positions into effective coalitions. They also express broad values and ideological positions to capture the wider concerns of citizens. Increasingly, though, parties appear to be performing these functions without much in the way of direct input from members and with less public legitimacy for their activities.

A detailed study of party politics in advanced liberal democracies[3] concludes that most political parties have seen a decline in membership and a greater degree of public scepticism about their role, which in turn is reflected in greater electoral volatility and less partisanship (strong identification with a particular party). The researchers conclude it is 'undeniable that [the] popular standing [of political parties] has been weakened in most Western democracies'.[4] Chapter 2 recorded some of the evidence about the substantial decline in membership; Wainer Lusoli and Stephen Ward note that:

> Even where parties can recruit members, they are increasingly from restricted social groups within society. Party members are increasingly middle class, with left-of-centre parties especially dependent on professionals from the public sector. Correspondingly, there is an under-representation of women, young people and ethnic minorities.[5]

Parties do not have the depth of connections into their communities that they once had and as a result they cannot act so easily as a 'transmission belt' of citizen concerns and interests to government. The issue is not just that they have struggled to recruit members; there is evidence of a long-term decline in activism within parties. Parties find it difficult to recruit officers for their branches and, in many cases, candidates for elections. Many members are willing to pay their dues but do little else. Those that might be more actively inclined to engage are constrained by party decision making structures that give them restricted influence.

Parties are more vehicles for leaders than carriers of members' views. As Lusoli and Ward put it:

> In part, the changes in party membership and activism are reflections of broader external changes in the political landscape and internal structural changes within parties themselves. These have arguably strengthened the position of party elites whilst eroding the collective power of activists.[6]

Professionalization of Parties

Leaders have found their position enhanced by the role of the modern media, and the way that TV and print coverage is given to leaders and their positions rather than to those of parties. Changes in the electorate and the issues confronting politics have encouraged a process whereby the more ideological preferences of party members have in many cases given way to a search for the middle-ground and broader electoral appeal by party leaders. Many if not most parties are becoming more 'catch-all' seekers of votes so that their value as vehicles for those looking to push or express a particular set of values or preferences has therefore declined. Internally, parties are much less reliant on members than they were; party members are increasingly not even the most important resource available to party organizations. Despite declining membership, the organizational strength of political parties in most mature democracies, in the sense of income and central party staffing levels, has increased.[7] Parties rely more on large private sponsors or state funding and less on the membership. The ability of leaders to operate with a greater degree of autonomy from members reflects 'the transformation of political parties from labour-intensive to capital-intensive organizations, controlled by professionalized campaigners directed from party HQ'.[8] Elections are increasingly fought, and the strategies decided upon, with advice from professional managers and advisors;[9] parties are now run for and by professionals and although party members remain important, they are not as central as they once were.

The general dynamic of the professionalization of parties and their reliance on state and other non-membership sources of funding is known in political science as the 'cartel party thesis'.[10] Broadly, instead of being rooted in civil society and taking citizens' views to government, parties have increasingly become part of the *machinery of governance*, an indispensable mechanism for arranging elections and choosing political leaders, and in many instances funded and supported by government.

As Peter Mair argues:

> On the ground, and in terms of their representative role, parties appear to be less relevant and to be losing some of their key functions. In public office, on the other hand, and in terms of their linkage to the state, they appear to be more privileged than ever.[11]

Activists are fewer, and those that remain involved are often on the margins of party decision making. For many, activism remains based around a role as volunteers supporting others and a cause, but parties are also a recruitment agency for those that want to serve as elected politicians or be appointed as party representatives on various local and regional government boards and agencies. Parties remain central to the operation of democracies, but their role is more as a 'feeder school' for the formal institutions of governance rather than a training ground or base for active citizenship.

Disenchantment with Politics

The gap between parties' weakening capacity to reach into communities and the tightening grip on the formal institutions of governance contributes to the crisis in legitimacy of the political system that has been a major theme of this book. Parties run not only the most formal elected agencies of governance but their appointees are also to be found on various quasi-governmental bodies and organizations. The tension created in the political system between weak informal linkages and strong formal power is reflected in the disaffection that parties attract in many mature democracies. On the basis of a wide-ranging survey of the position of parties in advanced industrial democracies, Paul Webb concludes:

> there is evidence of a significant level of disaffection with, or cynicism towards, parties; what is more (although not all of our authors have managed to track this in a systematic fashion because of the unavailability of measuring instruments which are consistent across time), in some cases this dissatisfaction seems to have grown.[12]

The scale of disenchantment with parties in Italy and Belgium in 2002 was such that Webb argued that their systems were at the stage of full-blown crisis. The only major exception to the overall picture identified by Webb is Spain, where parties are still admired for their role in establishing democracy after the Franco dictatorship. It is possible that in other newly established democracies parties enjoy support on a similar basis. But, overall, while parties do valuable things for democracy, they do them in the context of declining public respect and engagement. 'Parties without partisans' is the dominant theme of the studies in this area.[13]

The Rise of the Citizen Lobby

Professional Advocates

When it comes to the world of citizens' groups, we find many of the same trends we have observed in relation to parties. What is emerging is a pattern of campaigning groups run by professional staffers – effectively advocates without active members.[14] Again, just as with parties, it is difficult to think of a democratic system running without their input, but that input is not providing a channel for large-scale citizen engagement.

The idea that organized groups participate to represent people's views and interests in democratic systems has been dominant in the study of politics since the 1950s.[15] Groups provide a way for individuals more effectively to represent their particular or specialized concerns; by banding together and joining forces, people can make a bigger impact on the setting of the policy agenda, the making of government decisions and the practices of decision making. Groups are needed given the complexity and multiple challenges of the policy agenda in democracies, and they have become central to our governance processes. They lobby and campaign to protect people's immediate interests or express their support for a cause, idea or standpoint.

Governments need groups because they are 'repositories of expertise; they can help make a policy legitimate, and their cooperation can ensure the successful implementation of policy'.[16] The connection between government officials and politicians and groups is often very close: complex patterns of alliances can build up and groups expect to be, and often are, regularly consulted by government. Government officials may try to exclude groups they do not agree with, and promote support groups that share their position. In the 1990s in the UK for example, Amnesty International was simultaneously courted by the Foreign Office because it was critical of China over human rights issues, and criticized by the Home Office because it was also unhappy about the UK's own human rights record. Different factions inside government may even wage a 'policy war' through competing interest groups.

Representation through lobby groups makes for efficient promotion of a cause or stakeholder concern that a group of citizens may share, and the evidence suggests that the number of citizens' lobby groups has increased substantially in recent decades. Jeffery Berry provides a detailed analysis of this development in the USA, arguing that these groups 'profit from tailoring their appeals to narrow audiences with bold, emphatic, and unyielding policy stands'.[17] 'Citizens' groups' can be defined as lobbying organizations that mobilize members and donors around interests other than their professional or narrow sectional concerns; they focus on campaigning across a full range of issues from the environment, through social matters, to religious and moral concerns. Many of these groups have seen huge increases in membership: Greenpeace USA had 800,000 members in 1985 and 1,800,000 in 1992; Greenpeace UK had 30,000 members in 1981 and 410,000 by 1993; the World Wildlife Fund had only 12,000 members in 1971 and 207,000 by 1993. The more traditional environmental lobby group, the Sierra Club, had 113,000 members in 1970 and 650,000 in 1992.[18]

Citizen Lobbying

The US lobby world is traditionally seen as dominated by 'big business' and the professions. Berry suggests that the main increase has been in citizens' groups' participation in the politics of Congress. As a proportion of all groups participating in active lobbying, corporations and professional associations stayed in roughly the same position; labour unions and trade associations saw some tailing off in their activity. Citizens' groups, in contrast, saw increased participation – from 23.5 per cent of total lobbying activity in 1963 to 31.8 per cent in 1991.[19] The press coverage of citizens' groups also increased from 28.9 per cent of that of all lobby groups in 1963 to 40.2 in 1991.[20] The lobby world is no longer the preserve of a tight-knit network of industrial lobby groups and expert professional associations: in the USA, at least, 'citizen groups have become prolific and enduring participants in legislative policy-making'.[21]

The USA may be considered a particularly fertile ground, as the two main-catch all parties and a long tradition of associational activity have created the space for multiple factions to push their particular concerns or interests. Yet studies in other countries suggest that there has been a similar explosion of citizen groups able to lobby and influence policy makers. In the UK, for example, a range of environmental groups has seen a large increase in membership. Many of these organizations also raise substantial sums of money through sponsorship and other arrangements and each has annual expenditures of substantially over £1 million.[22]

The citizen lobby groups, even those with a strong anti-establishment image, are in most cases professionally run and managed, staffed by professionals, with policy and legal expertise in the areas on which they focus, and have a capacity for fund-raising, marketing and financial management that ensures that the organization works as a business as well as a focal point for campaigning and lobbying. Critics complain about the 'bureaucratization' of these organizations, but given the scale of operations and the level of funding involved this is probably inevitable.[23]

The contribution of these citizen groups to the democratic process is substantial. They have proved extremely skilful in identifying and organizing 'constituencies', they run and manage complex organizations and campaigns. They can, however, offer only limited selective incentives or benefits and 'the only return most members of [such] groups will get is the ideological satisfaction that they are fighting some injustice'.[24] These groups have, according to Jeffery Berry,[25] had some successes in challenging and checking the power and privileged position of business. In outright conflicts with business, citizen groups have not always won, but they have won enough battles to be considered a significant force. They have used the traditional tools of lobbying to give what might have otherwise been unorganized voices a say in the policy debate. Their contribution to democracy is considerable; if they did not exist, then a democrat would want to invent them.

'Checkbook' Participation

Citizen groups are *for* citizens, but not necessarily *of* citizens. The standard form of group lacks a large-scale active membership; they ask people for money; they campaign on the behalf of citizens, but they do not draw great numbers into direct political activity. This kind of participation ('checkbook' (US) or 'cheque book' (UK)) is characteristic of that achieved by the citizens' lobby groups. As Grant Jordan and William Maloney comment, the large citizen organizations such as Greenpeace or Amnesty International 'are best seen as organizations with financial supporters rather than membership bodies'.[26]

Theda Skocpol explains that in the US case, at least, the rise of a new form of 'checkbook' membership reflects a significant shift in the attitude and approach of high-intensity activists, or what Skocpol calls 'civic entrepreneurs':

> Classic American association-builders took it for granted that the best way to gain national influence, moral or political, was to knit together national, state, and local groups that met regularly and engaged in a degree of representative governance. Leaders who desired to speak on behalf of masses of Americans found it natural to proceed by recruiting self-renewing mass memberships and spreading a network of interactive groups . . . Today nationally ambitious civic entrepreneurs proceed in quite different ways [using] . . . new routes to civic influence opened up in late-twentieth-century America. Patron grants, direct-mail techniques, and the capacity to convey images and messages through the mass media [have] all changed the realities of organization-building and maintenance.[27]

Changing Pattern of Compaigning and its Implications

What has emerged are groups that are advocates without active, large-scale memberships, run by professional staffers. A new cadre of civic professionals has emerged, a class of high-intensity activists that do the job of campaigning for others. 'Cause-oriented advocacy groups offer busy privileged Americans a rich menu of opportunities to, in effect, hire other professionals and managers to represent their values and interests in public life'.[28]

This depiction of the changing pattern of citizen group campaigning certainly rings true for the UK,[29] and given the shared contextual forces behind the changes identified by Skocpol – growing affluence, changing work patterns, different roles and opportunities for women and men, and the increasing dominance of the media – there is every reason to expect that the pattern of change described by Skocpol can be to some extent observed in most industrialized democracies.

The implications can generally be seen as positive, these groups can often help give a 'voice' to causes and concerns that would not otherwise be heard. However, as Skocpol points out, there are also potentially negative impacts of this style of advocacy.[30] First, it is not engaging directly many citizens – its way of operating is through staff-heavy organizations and media-based campaigns. Most 'members' hand over their money and are then left on the sidelines. Second, the new-style groups may have opened up opportunities for representing neglected interests, but many of these interests reflect the concerns of the already privileged educated and professional classes. Third, the style of advocacy of citizens groups tends to magnify polarized voices; the professional campaigners tend to fear that their members may be fickle and try continually to carve out a niche for themselves and keep their activities in the public eye. They thus have every incentive to go for drama, controversy and conflict with government or other groups in order to keep themselves and their chosen issues in the media spotlight.

The way that citizen groups are working may in fact be contributing to the sense of 'disconnect' that is the main theme of this book. As Skocpol argues, 'both the artificial polarization and the elitism of today's organized civic universe may help to explain why increasing numbers of Americans are turned off and pulling back from public life'.[31] Citizen groups, by their very mode of operation, may contribute to a general malaise in politics, offering only a thin, narrow and conflict-laden engagement. In the language of Chapter 4 they may offer people 'voice', but they do not offer them the opportunity to listen to the demands of others or make a case for compromise.

Insiders and Outsiders

One dilemma well recognized both by groups and within the academic literature is the tension between insider and outsider strategies.[32] Citizen groups can be drawn into an 'insider' technical and consultative role with policy makers in government and perhaps neglect the wider and more demanding challenge of reaching out to and engaging members of the public, the 'outsider' campaigning strategy. In practice, many groups do a bit of both: they operate on the 'inside track' and then seek to mobilize support for their cause by media-focused campaigning. This way of working can lead to negative public perceptions about politics. In order to emphasize that they are not part of the political establishment – the 'them' of politics – citizen groups oscillate between 'insider' and 'outsider' politics and in 'outsider' mode tend to heap all kinds of blame on government, bureaucracy, 'big business' or other easy targets to explain failures and to reinforce their image as part of the 'us', and the media is often very happy to support this conflict-laden form of politics. This is not to argue that governments or business should not be criticized, far from it, but it is to suggest that the style of attack used by today's citizen groups may have the unintended consequence of making people's understanding of politics more negative and limited.

Citizen groups can thus offer a great deal to politics, but they may be in part to blame for a negative culture by contributing to a political lobby aimed at getting 'the government' to do more without having the depth and roots to reach out to the public. From the perspective of this book, the growth of the citizens' lobby has two drawbacks. First, no matter what else these groups do they are not stimulators of any substantial participation or engagement process among citizens; they often have little in the way of explicit direct democratic relationships with their supporters. But although internal democracy may be limited, leaders remain concerned to keep the hearts and minds of their supporters with them, so they are attentive and responsive, which leads to the second issue of concern. Demands to keep sponsors 'on side' leads to citizen groups too often taking a populist line in politics in which they blame the government or politicians for their failures and difficulties. No matter how much the government has done to respond to issues and concerns is it never enough, because the priority is to persuade their own supporters that they are 'on the case' and 'battling against the odds' to deliver for them and their cause and need their continued support. A by-product of this is an impression of a cycle of seemingly never ending 'non-delivery' by politics.

Protest and Dissent

Protest and Democracy

If parties and citizens groups are central to modern democracy, then so is protest. Without dissent and its willingness to challenge authority it is difficult to see how democracy could have been called into existence. As Professors Skocpol and Fiorina argue:

> Democracy, after all, grew up historically out of century-long struggles among social groups and between state authorities and their subjects. In a very real sense, first liberal-parliamentary regimes and then democracies were a product of organized conflict and distrust. The energy to forge

liberal and democratic regimes came when people crystallized their misgivings about concentrated or arbitrary power. What is more, middling and subordinate groups in society had to organize, amass resources and assert themselves.[33]

The spirit of challenge to be found in the first wave of democracies was also a vital ingredient in establishing democracy in other countries more recently. The organized dispute and challenge of citizens can claim a part in other victories, including the formal abolition of slavery, the promotion of women's rights and the challenge to race discrimination. Protest is not just a part of democracy, it is its beginning.[34] Radical activism through civil society can come in a range of patterns and is often described in a variety of ways.[35] There is often reference to *movements* such as 'the peace movement' or 'the anti-globalization movement', or more social movements such as 'the women's movement' or 'the gay liberation movement'. The term 'movement' implies a broadly based informal, or at least only loosely organized, activism that does not rely on a single organization to provide structure and direction to its development. It is clear that these movements have made a contribution to change and new thinking in many democracies. More formal but still relatively non-institutionalized forms of engagement are sometimes labelled as *grassroots activist networks* or *Do it Yourself (DIY) politics*, where perhaps a more tightly knit group of activists will organize campaigns and protests. We are all familiar with campaigns organized by such groups against motorway building plans, airport expansions or rainforest logging. At the most formal end of the spectrum, such movements in turn fade into protest-oriented non-governmental organizations (NGOs), such as Greenpeace. The impact of NGOs, across a whole spectrum of issues in both older and newer democracies, is considerable.

These various types of activity are connected. The loosest and most general form of network-driven social movement often provides the inspiration behind DIY politics and protest-oriented NGOs. Both DIY groups and NGOs are distinguished by a commitment to more direct action and a more focused concern on single clearly defined goals, such as stopping the construction of a particular road or supermarket; but in the case of NGOs, this may just be a part of a range of other activities to influence government policy or public opinion.[36]

Global Activism

Radical activism is often local but it can also be seen as increasingly global in its outlook. Civil society networks and groups bring citizens together to challenge, protest and to try and bring about change. In recent decades, as Jan Aart Scholte puts it, 'contemporary civil society has gone global'.[37] First and most obviously, much protest has been addressed at the perceived injustices of the process of globalization concerning debt relief, trade restrictions, human rights and so on. Second, many radical activists have directly challenged and sought to engage with global institutions such as the G8 of world leaders or the World Bank and other global organizations. Third, global activists have used global communications to coordinate and organize campaigns. The very process of globalization has thus in part supported the development of global protest. Formal global organizations, through coordinating committees and internationally oriented funding arrangements (from trusts and funds or individual benefactors such as George Soros), have begun to be part of the furniture in the world of global protest: activists claim that they are promoting 'transplanetary' solidarity. The impact of globalization is also felt in a more informal way by large gatherings and protests that enable activists to recognize and construct a shared sense of purpose and identity around the cause or campaign that is the focus of their action.

Limitations and Criticisms

There can be little doubt that the democratic world would be less rich and less open without the impact of this activism. However, there are a number of limitations to both its nature and scale. Although there is evidence of activists' influence and capacity to hold governments and business to account, the scale of activists' activities should not be overplayed; they are too few in number and restricted in membership to have the resources to achieve all their objectives. Two criticisms may also be made of the way they bring citizens into the political process. First, as Jan Aart Scholte argues, civil society institutions 'often fall short on democratic credentials in their own behaviour' and some 'have been run with top-down managerial authoritarianism that stifles internal debate dissent':[38]

> Some advocates who have claimed to speak for the grass roots have actu-
> ally rarely ventured into the field. On the contrary, a number of jet-setting
> staff have lost touch with their notional beneficiaries as they fly from one
> global conference to the next.[39]

Some of the organizations involved are fronts for governments, or corporations, families, political parties and foundations. Even those which are properly autonomous are often not clear about how their leaders emerged and

where their policy positions came from: the democratic credentials of these civil society organizations or networks cannot always be taken for granted. Global civil society in particular is often the preserve of professional activists.

Second, these organizations rely on the mass media – TV, radio and the press – to get their message out into the wider political world, and are prone to offer a rather simplistic understanding of political issues. As protest has got more global so the media appears to play a bigger and bigger part in getting the protesters out on the street and keeping the protest going. Protest as such has become as much a part of the world of spin and media manipulation as the more traditional practices of politics. The priorities of mobilization demand simple, easy messages, not an in-depth understanding of complex issues. As Martin Shaw points out, the argument over the Iraq War in 2003 showed how millions could respond in support of the simple demand to 'Stop the War', but had little to say about what to do in the aftermath or whether leaving Saddam in power would have been better. We can draw the conclusion that

> [A] mass demonstration is a blunt instrument. In an intense crisis, which poses one seemingly simple question above all others, such a movement allows large numbers of people to offer an answer and influence the more conventional political process . . . but when issues become more complex . . . this kind of movement becomes less relevant.

The mass mobilization runs out of steam, and a more specialized politics takes over once the energy and commitment of protesters can no longer be sustained. The problem with this kind of engagement is that it offers only an 'over-simplified politics':[40] the engagement stops precisely at the moment that politics is designed to deal with, when conflicts are not clear cut and solutions are not obvious.

Protest movement politics can degenerate into a form of *identity politics*. People protest as a lifestyle statement because it tells us something about them rather than making any sustained contribution to the political process. Marilyn Taylor is right to argue that 'wearing the "t" shirt and identifying with campaigning organizations can still be an important form of political expression and identity', but it is a limited and constrained form of engagement. Protest politics has an important place, and for a small group of activists it can provide an intense and extensive base for engagement. For most citizens, however, it provides just another opportunity to say what they care about and reinforce a sense of identity – one that they can take up or leave as they please.

Concluding Comment: Participation by and through Experts

Activists and the institutions through which they work – parties, lobby organizations or protest movements – all provide vital elements of the political process in our democracies: they all have the task of giving citizens a way into politics. However, all are failing to varying degrees in their ambitions to bring large-scale collective engagement to the political process. Parties are struggling to deliver the political functions of aggregating and cohering interests. Lobby-style organizations may be winning small victories but are less successful in addressing bigger issues and audiences in a sustained and effective way. Protest organizations provide channels for dissent, but have not established a substantial pool of critical and active citizens, let alone a global civil society.

What they have created is a large pool of activist experts who jointly inhabit with technical, professional and business experts a world of high-intensity engagement. Not all of us want or need to be involved in detailed discussions about what is the appropriate regulatory framework for the drugs industry – a topic that takes one of my neighbours to Brussels, Washington and Tokyo on a regular basis. The complexity of what governments does and the range of issues on which they need to decide means that much of the practice of policy making and implementation inevitably has to be the work of experts with technical/specialist knowledge and interests. The challenge is to find ways for the public to engage on terms that they find palatable. These challenges are considered further in Part 3 of this book.

The message from researchers who study parties, lobby groups and protest campaigns is consistent even if they often present it with different terminology. Students of parties talk of the 'cartel party' thesis that sees parties as creatures of government rather than civil society, those who study lobbying refer to the rise of 'checkbook' groups – powerful but with disengaged memberships – and those who study protest refer to its professional-ization in a media-dominated world.

Parties, citizen groups, and protest organizations have all been neglecting the role of talking directly to the public. The issue becomes one of getting 'the government' to do something rather than asking whether their organization is playing a great enough role in enabling the public to understand and engage with issues, and, where appropriate, change their own behaviour.

One particular illustration can be used to highlight what we may be missing through the professionalization of activism. In a pamphlet titled 'The death of environmentalism',[41] two long-standing environmental campaigners, Michael Shellenberger and Ted Nordhaus suggest that the well-funded and organized US environmental lobby has neglected the challenge of winning over public opinion over issues such as global warming. It has found it easier to blame the government rather than challenge the public to change their behaviour if environmental challenges are to be met. The lobby has taken the easier route of focusing on technical issues, and blaming politicians for not being brave enough in the stance that they are taking. The issue of citizens themselves needing to accept the need for change in their lifestyles has not been addressed.

A considerable debate followed the publication of this pamphlet and echoes of the debate can be observed in other countries. Lobby organizations can focus too much on scoring 'debating points' by drawing on their detailed expert evidence and making loud claims about the failings of the political system to respond. This overlooks their responsibility to win arguments and actually change public opinion and behaviour.

Parties, citizens groups and protest organizations offer an accessible route into politics for the few rather than the many. But many of the forms of engagement they offer may inadvertently undermine the political process. The way that they construct their linkages between policy making and citizens can help reinforce 'the disconnect' between citizens and the political process. Parties can turn people off politics through their posturing and rigidities; the lobby groups can make easy political points by blaming government for any problems or difficulties and so increase people's disillusion. Protest organizations can mobilize through simple slogans, but fail to engage people in facing up to serious political choices.

The institutions of parties, the lobby and protest bring opportunities for cohesion, diversity and dissent to the political process. We need them, but we need them to work better.

7

The Dangers of Cynicism

> Politics is the art of looking for trouble, finding it every-
> where, diagnosing it incorrectly and applying the wrong
> remedies.[1]
>
> Groucho Marx

Groucho Marx, the US humourist, probably now has more followers who share his understanding of politics than Karl Marx, the father of modern communism. This chapter looks at the roots of the cynicism that character-izes the attitudes of many to the world of democratic politics. It begins by identifying an influential academic school of thought – public choice theory – that presents government and politics as always prone to failure because of the self-interested actions of politicians, officials and lobbyists. There is nothing illogical about this theory but its application can have perverse and unfortunate consequences. Attention is then turned to a less highbrow but perhaps more direct case for cynicism: the view that politi-cians lie more now than ever before. The evidence and arguments for this position are reviewed, and found wanting. This is not to deny that politi-cians lie, but it is to dispute the idea that they are lying more than ever before and to point out that 'lying' is often too blunt and crude a description of their communication practices. There is a difference between presenting yourself and your arguments in the best light, and lying. As citizens, we should be more aware of our own tendencies not always to tell the unvar-nished truth.

Consideration is then given to the role of the media, and here I find some considerable support for the idea that the media, both in its message and manner of coverage, has encouraged a style of communication between politicians and citizens that feeds cynicism. The point here is not to blame the media because both politicians and we, as citizens, are complicit in the dominant form of political communication in our societies. The power of the media is considerable – it provides the main means of communication between politicians and the public. The challenge is to sustain, and indeed encourage, free reporting, at the same time as to create a media that supports rather than distorts the democratic process. Few, if any, democracies today have got the balance between these two objectives absolutely right.

The chapter concludes by arguing that many politicians are more honourable than we might think, and that on the whole there is evidence that they keep their promises. A degree of healthy scepticism about politicians and the political process is prudent for a citizen, but the final section of this chapter points out the dangers when this tips over into corrosive and excessive cynicism.

A Cynicism Index?

'Political cynicism' can be defined as a deep scepticism and pessimism about politicians and a suspicion about their motives that stretches into scorn or disparagement of their actual role. Lots of people today are pretty cynical about the way that politics works though it is hard to be specific about how many. It is, however, clear from the evidence presented in Chapter 2 that cynicism about politics is a characteristic of the citizens of democracies worldwide.

To examine this issue in more detail, we could develop a sort of 'cynicism index' to run along side the corruption and democratic audits that are undertaken to measure the standing of politicians and civil servants in various countries. Using only European data, I offer below the beginnings of such an analysis. Figure 7.1 shows that, with little observable difference between men and women, a quarter of citizens from a range of European countries think that hardly any politicians care what they think, and a further third hold the view that very few politicians care. There is some variation by country, but overall there appears to be a substantial number of people who think this way.

It is therefore unsurprising that substantial numbers of Europeans do not trust politicians. Over 1 in 10 has no trust in politicians, and less than half of 1 per cent has complete trust. Compared to trust in the legal system, or the police, politicians fare badly (Table 7.1). Taking the lowest four ratings in Table 7.1 as a combined low-trust ranking, nearly half of all those European citizens asked put politicians in this category, while the legal system is given this low-trust rating by just over a third of those asked and the police by only 15 per cent. Again there are differences between countries and different groups within countries, but the message is clear: from a 'cynicism index' viewpoint, many people don't trust politicians. Basically,

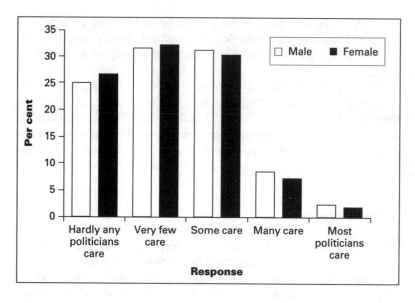

Figure 7.1   Do politicians care what you think? Responses from European citizens

Source: Data from European Social Survey (ESS) (2002).

they see politicians as self-serving: as Table 7.2 shows, 3 in 10 people think that nearly all politicians are simply concerned to get votes and uninterested in the opinions of the people, while a further 3 in 10 think that this applies to most politicians.

The evidence in Tables 7.1–7.2 and Figure 7.1 points, without doubt, to quite widespread cynicism about the way politics works. We can now combine responses to produce a 'cynicism index'. Of citizens surveyed across Europe at the beginning of the twenty-first century, roughly half (49.1 per cent to be more exact) thought nearly all or most politicians are just interested in votes rather than their opinion, while also thinking that hardly any (or very few) politicians care what they think. So we could say that Europe has a 'cynicism index' of 49 out of 100. The evidence from around the world presented in Chapter 2 already suggests that the cynicism index elsewhere is likely to be as high.[2]

Table 7.1 Europeans' trust in the legal system, police and politicians

View	Trust in the legal system	Trust in the police	Trust in politicians
No trust at all	5.6	3.0	11.8
1	3.6	2.1	7.5
2	7.1	3.8	12.6
3	9.7	6.0	15.8
4	10.4	7.2	13.5
5	18.4	15.4	19.6
6	12.3	13.0	9.8
7	13.5	17.5	6.0
8	12.0	17.8	2.6
9	4.6	8.1	0.6
Complete trust	2.8	6.1	0.3

Source: Data from European Social Survey (ESS) (2002).

Table 7.2 Politicians interested in votes rather than opinions of people: evidence from Europe

Interest	Total
Nearly all just interested in votes	29.9
Most just interested in votes	30.5
Some just interested in votes	28.2
Most interested in opinions	9.9
Nearly all interested in opinions	1.5
Total	100.0
N =	41,579

Source: Data from European Social Survey (ESS) (2002).

Public Choice Theory: An Academic Framing for Cynicism

Self-Serving and Selfish Motivations

Cynicism has a long tradition in thinking about politics. One reading of Machiavelli's *The Prince* is to see it as a cynical take on politics, to assume the worst in others and use strategy to dupe and trick them:

> For there is such a distance from how one lives to how one ought to live that he who abandons what is done for what ought to be done learns what will ruin him rather than what will save him, since a man who would wish

to make a career of being good in every detail must come to ruin among so many who are not good. Hence it is necessary for a prince, if he wishes to maintain himself, to learn to be able to be not good, and to use this faculty and not use it according to necessity.[3]

In modern political science the mantle of cynicism is best expressed through public choice theory. James Buchanan, who in 1986 won a Nobel Prize in part for his work in developing the theory; defines public choice as 'the science of political failure',[4] and this way of thinking about how politics works has had a major impact on public policy.

The theorists of public choice have been highly influential and have seen their ideas promoted through a range of think tanks. They are deeply sceptical of the ability of government to achieve positive goals through their interventions, they recognize that markets can fail but for them government intervention is much more prone to failure. The ideas of public choice were a crucial element in the ideological make-up of the New Right and of politicians like Margaret Thatcher and Ronald Reagan, who wanted to rein in the power of the state. More generally these ideas have become part of the commonsense of late twentieth and early twenty-first century thinking. They have played a significant role in the formulation of reform measures aimed at public services and more generally have fed into thinking about what is 'good governance', as promoted by international bodies such as the World Bank and International Monetary Fund (IMF). This is not to suggest that public choice ideas have been dominant or all-conquering, but rather that echoes of these ideas have found substantial resonance in recent debates about government and politics.

Does public choice theory provide a good guide for politicians and citizens to follow? We first outline the public choice perspective, and then identify some criticisms and limitations of the approach. Borrowing from economic modelling, public choice theorists assume that people are rational and self-interested and primarily interested in any exchange in getting the best they can out of it for themselves. They do not deny that people can be motivated by a sense of solidarity or love, but they argue that when looking at politics as well as economics it is best to assume that most behaviour is narrowly self-interested. They present a world of politics dominated by favour-seeking interest or pressure groups that try to force a good deal for themselves out of governments. In addition, they argue that politicians manipulate and distort priorities in order to get voted back in and bureaucrats and public sector workers line their pockets and advance their careers by trying to maximize the budget and resources they receive.

Public choice literature is deeply pessimistic about the capacity for effective collective action, believing that the self-serving and selfish motivations of those engaged in politics will undermine any good intentions or ideals. If the government tries, for example, to support agriculture to ensure the availability of food for its citizens, that good intention soon gets distorted by the behaviour of farmers and others who are the beneficiaries of the policy, who will back the election only of political parties that will maintain or enhance the subsidies provided. This search for special privileges is called 'rent-seeking behaviour' by public choice theorists, and they appear to regard it as an inevitable and ubiquitous part of government–interest group relationships. Farmers get subsidized not because we all benefit from the availability of food and other produce but because farmers pay for the election of politicians that favour their interests.

If politicians are not getting into bed with special interests then they are being held prisoner by their government's bureaucrats who demand larger and larger budgets for their departments and agencies. In much of the public choice literature, bureaucrats always want a bigger budget because it means they get bigger salaries, more power, greater patronage and more prestige. They control the information supplied to politicians and are in a monopoly position to say how much it costs to do certain things and how much demand or need there is out there for their service.

Neglect of the Public Interest

Politicians themselves, according to public choice theory, are prone to adopting highly manipulative strategies in their dealing with their electors. First they stage-manage economic cycles: they bribe electors in the run-up to elections and levy taxes after elections, and as a result public indebtedness grows. One politician supports another's pet scheme and in return that politician receives support for their own pet scheme: special or minority interests get what they want out of the system and the silent majority loses out.

The fundamental message of public choice theory is that democratic politics frequently leads to a neglect of the public interest. The promise and processes of collective decision making are pretty much guaranteed to be derailed because people – politicians, bureaucrats and lobbyists – behave in an opportunistic manner in order to look after themselves.

Criticisms and Limitations

So cynicism has an academic foundation, and it would be foolish to deny that the behaviour identified by public choice theory can sometimes be observed. But for the critics of public choice theory the world is not as simple as public choice theorists suggest and whatever insights public choice has discovered it, is not a science of political failure. Politics is contingent and depends on *context* and *institutional frameworks* that affect people's behaviour.

The critique of public choice has three main elements. First, people can decide within limits what to do. They might judge, even using self-interest as a guide, that a short-term benefit to them could be discounted in favour of a long-term return (indeed, many rational choice and game theorists recognize this point). Bureaucrats, politicians and lobbyists may all think, for example, that for the long-term health of the economy some cuts in spending might be justified. So the first point is that even self-interested behaviour does not have to be as stupid as cynics sometimes suggest. Public choice theorists are not the first to see politics as a battle of self-interests, many others take that position. The problem with public choice is that its ideas of what people would judge as in their self-interest are very myopic and limited.

Second, self-interest is not the sole motivational factor in politics. People do not have to be self-interested short-term maximizers. When they engage in politics, motivations other than self-interest can and frequently do come to the fore.[5] People can see norms not as sanctions but as commitments that reflect a way of understanding life. Action for individuals is not based on a weighing of costs and benefits but rather on their commitments (their beliefs and values) which often lead them to pursue a course of action and feel that they could not act in any other way. Other motivations that could be seen as highly relevant to the study of politics that are also ignored by public choice theory are such things as people's sense of *social identification*: how and to what extent they define themselves as members of a group. People are more likely to follow a rule if they regard themselves as members of a group from which the rule emanates. There is also *intrinsic motivation*; the reward for doing something is the doing of it. We know that the desire to do the right thing or care about others is not alien to the human condition, so why should we assume that people abandon such logics when they approach politics? Of course, most public choice theorists think of themselves as moral people who care for the public good. What gives them the right to deny the same feelings to everyone else?

The third line of criticism is that research findings coloured by public choice thinking are 'empirically dubious'.[6] We can reflect on a few points here. For every lobby asking for support there could be another lobby suggesting that an alternative approach would be better; both could win the support of politicians, the issue is which lobby will win. Democracy is not undermined by the presence of lobbies provided there is some balance in the system, and that less-well-resourced interests can get access to it. These are matters for empirical judgement, not theoretical assertion. For every bureaucrat looking to expand their empire there can be another trying to stop them in order to protect their own and another that makes their name from privatizations, contracting out and cost-cutting. Some might even be concerned with the public interest! The behaviour identified by public choice theory may be one of several practices that can be observed. Politicians do also sometimes do deals and manipulate tax breaks and economic cycles, but the public are not always dumb enough to fall for it. Prime Minister John Howard introduced a sales tax in Australia just before an election and London's Mayor Ken Livingstone brought in a congestion charge in the face of substantial initial public opposition; in the end, both comfortably won their re-election. In short, to quote Colin Hay:

> [Public choice theory] is an unduly pessimistic depiction of the human subject, a far from universal condition and a wild extrapolation from particular contexts and times in which the narrow pursuit of self-interest has (regrettably) become institutionalized as the dominant mode of conduct. In short, what is (thankfully) politically, institutionally and culturally contingent is presented as a trans-historical and universal necessity.[7]

Public choice theory captures the *potential* for a short-term, self-interest to infect politics; it can happen but it does not have to happen. I do not dispute the value of some public choice insights, but the theory has severe limitations when it comes to understanding the complexity of democratic politics.

Do Politicians Lie More Today?

A Post-Truth Environment?

For many people, their sense of cynicism comes from a sense that politicians lie all the time. One of the strongest recent statements of this line of argument comes from Peter Oborne, in *The Rise of Political Lying*, which suggests that politicians now lie systemically and often whereas before they lied only occasionally:

> Britain now lives in a post-truth environment. Public statements are no longer fact based, but operational. Realities and political narratives are constructed to serve a purpose, dismantled and the show moves on . . .

This is new. All governments have contained liars, and most politicians deceive each other as well as the public from time to time. But in recent years mendacity and deception have ceased to be abnormal and become an entrenched feature of the British system.[8]

New Labour and Tony Blair are the main empirical targets of Oborne's book, although he also appears to think that George Bush is also a liar. Much of the book comprises empirical evidence about examples of political lies, especially those of New Labour since 1997.

Some examples are powerful, but others do not make an overwhelming case. Thus we are told that the Prime Minister 'unblushingly contradicts himself as much as he likes' and the example to support that claim is that apparently in his 2002 party conference speech he said 'the test is to listen, adapt and move forward' but informed the same conference a year later 'I've not got a reverse gear'.[9] Looked at from a slightly more neutral perspective than Oborne's you could see the two statements as compatible – in the sense that going forward and not reversing are not in contradiction with one another. But you might also be wondering what there is at stake in these statements to make a fuss about.

Peter Oborne might have a more powerful point if he argued that politicians lied over big things even if they told the truth over smaller things. One of the biggest lies told in recent years, according to many, is the claim from Mr Blair and President George Bush, in the build-up to the 2003 Iraq War, that Saddam Hussein's regime had weapons of mass destruction when they knew that it did not. The counter-argument, of course, is that their failure was one of false or inadequate intelligence-gathering, rather than outright lying.

One problem with much of the debate in this area is that it neglects the gradations between lying at one end of the spectrum and full truth at the other end. As Oborne recognizes, a lie requires a clear falsehood and the intent to deceive. But you can deceive through a falsehood uttered in good faith that is not a lie, a distinction that goes to the heart of the debate over weapons of mass destruction in Iraq. A milder crime that Oborne recognizes is giving a misleading impression by stressing certain truths and omitting others.

We have already noted two shades of truth-telling that are not lies – unknowingly telling a falsehood and trying to accentuate the positive – and there are others. People tell 'white lies' in order not to hurt people's feelings – indeed, in some parts of our lives we celebrate such behaviour and sometimes call it being a good friend or partner. Telling a story or creating a narrative that puts you in a good light is not unique to politics. Doing what politicians do when they are campaigning and saying 'I see what you mean' and 'I see where you are coming from', etc. is lauded when practised by others as a form of empathy or good management. Of course the person might not mean it, but whether they are a vicar, a new age hippy, a social worker, a politician or a journalist, that judgement could apply.

The point is that 'lying' is a strong word, and in the current debate its scope is being pushed too far in order to bolster an attack on politicians. There is also a sense in which the attack on politicians is a little two-faced. Journalist Libby Purves presents evidence on the amount of small-scale petty cheating that there is in society.[10] Is our beef with politicians that we are small liars and they are big ones? Or is that we want them to be better than us? If this is all there is to the charges of the cynics, then they are blatantly ridiculous.

Not telling the whole truth is not necessarily cheating; it can be a way of getting on in a complex society. If we think that the world is divided into truth-tellers and liars, we have forgotten some of the rules of communication that we use every day: we all fudge, dissemble and pretend we are listening when we are not. We all present ourselves in a way that makes it more likely that people will be persuaded to do what we want them to do if we need their cooperation. In this sense, we, like politicians, are all liars.

The thesis that politicians are now systematically lying, whereas in the past they did not does not convince. The reality is surely that all politicians do tend to tell some half-truths and the occasional outright lie. They always have, and they always will. You could make a case to counter the thesis that all politicians are liars by looking at whether if they win power they follow through on their promises. One detailed study of whether the different political parties in Britain acted on their manifesto commitments when in power found that 'they do the majority of things to which they pledge themselves in their opposition manifestos'.[11] Now there is a challenge for some PhD student out there, if that is they can face the idea of reading through what are often long and turgid documents and then trying to make sense of them and see if they had any impact. Come to think of it, that is what most PhDs are about.

The Role of the Media: Defender of Democracy or Creator of Corrosive Cynicism?

There can be little doubt about the importance of the media in the political process in democratic societies. The written and, in particular, broadcast media enter our lives in a pervasive manner. The TV is watched for many hours, radio is part of the background to our lives, newspapers continue to be read in large numbers and the internet provides a whole range of new ways of receiving information. Many conversations about politics take as their reference points what was said or written in some media report; most of our knowledge about what politicians say and what they are doing (or not doing) is filtered through the mass media. Our understanding of the key issues that face our societies are substantially influenced by the concerns, focus or even the obsessions of the media. Politics without a free media is impossible to imagine in a democratic society, but there are a number of concerns about the role the media plays.

Charges Against the Media

Four specific charges can be identified. The first is made in most mature democracies and in many of the newer democracies, and it is that the media has 'dumbed down' the coverage of news and political issues because of the fierce battle for audience that is a focal point of media operations. The battle for attention means that reporting focuses on the immediate, the scandalous and the negative. Reporting of serious issues gets reduced to sound bites or conflicts between opposing views: what is produced is heat, but not much light. Media people become stars because of the impact they make with their speed of reporting, their scoop, or because they expose where wrongdoing has occurred. The simple and the dramatic is preferred to a story that establishes complex shades of grey about an issue and tries to analyse it in depth. In almost all democracies you can find concern about this trend in media coverage because of the fear that it creates a poorer and less fertile terrain for political exchange and debate. People become cynical about politics because most issues are just too difficult to understand and politics and politicians become, as a result, the equivalent of hapless participants in a reality TV show.

The second criticism is that there is now a fusing of reporting and comment in a way that is unhelpful to political debate. The emergence of 24-hour news available through the TV, radio and internet has meant that comment is needed more than ever before, and has encouraged the printed media to be more editorializing and provocative in its coverage in an attempt to compensate for no longer being first with the news. The emergence of free newspapers that spend less time and money on journalists and reporters again encourages a mix of reporting and comment. Round-the-clock broadcasting has led to the emergence of talk radio shows that 'use abuse, exaggeration, accusations and character assignation to build their audiences'.[12] Internet blogs add to the available stream of combined commentary and information. Politics can quickly become a matter of opinions with no resort to evidence or coherent argument. This in turn builds a sense that politics is all rather pointless, a sort of background jabbering while people get on with their lives.

A third claim about the role of the media is much bolder: that media coverage has actively spread a culture of contempt for politics. This claim is most prominently made in the UK, but might be thought to apply, too, in Australia, Canada, and the USA.[13] The media – both print and broadcasting – are said to have used their power to denigrate both politicians and the political process. According to Meg Russell:

> Media outlets rarely miss the opportunity to imply that politicians are corrupt, hypocritical or simply inept. To some extent similar cynicism pertains to all professions, but this is by far the most extreme case.[14]

This line of attack may reflect market pressure and the desire to keep the public happy but the media are then not really to blame, since all they are doing is pandering to the tastes of the public. John Lloyd, however, puts the blame fairly and squarely on a culture that has developed in media reporting, a style that has not been driven by market pressures alone since for Lloyd it is the BBC – a UK broadcaster funded directly by a compulsory fee provided by the public – that is the king of the cynics.

Lloyd argues that you cannot understand the argument that led to the 2003–4 Hutton Inquiry into the claim made by the BBC that the government had lied in the build-up to the 2003 Iraq War unless you recognize that a proper journalistic desire to be challenging and critical has got out of hand. Within the BBC and among other media, he argues, there was a culture that encouraged reporters to be adversarial, basically to ask all the time: why is this politician lying to me and to you, the viewers and listeners? Journalists see themselves as the holders and definers of the truth and in the case of the BBC a whole organization came to believe this position. This in turn leads to a fourth accusation against the media – that they place themselves above politics and, in the end, above democracy, claiming the position of supreme arbiter and judge.

Countering Criticism

What can we make of these four claims? The 'dumbing down' accusation is probably fair in terms of the way that news is produced for mass audiences, although a great deal of serious reporting and analysis is available to people if they are prepared to look for it. The thinness of mainstream media offerings do perhaps therefore encourage a rather naïve understanding of politics and ultimately encourage cynicism given that politics can never deliver against the simplistic framework that is set up. The mixing of reporting and comment probably also encourages a skewed debate in which there is no evidence or facts, just opinions, and that in turn has led to a culture of cynicism as the whole world is portrayed as a battle of prejudices.

The last two claims are, I think, less easy to justify. One can think of times when the media or some journalists in particular do appear to have behaved like that, but not all reporting follows that approach, even on the BBC! My family may regard this last judgement as suspect given the amount of times they catch me shouting at some news reporter or analyst on the TV or radio. However in the cold light of writing I can accept that someone saying something I disagree with is not necessarily mad or a liar (also I am aware the reporters can't hear me when I shout at them). In so far as a culture of contempt is a deliberate product, it should be possible to correct it by changing editorial standards and not deifying those journalists that make their reputation by being constantly cynical about politics and politicians. Dumbing down and the cross-over between reporting and commenting are, however, much more deeply rooted in market pressures in the media industry, and are thus much harder to address.

Conclusions

The problem with cynicism is that it is ultimately a fatalist creed: in its eyes, everything is done for base reasons and individual benefit and is prone, if not actually guaranteed, to deliver collective disbenefit. In the worldview of many cynics, he or she can see the right solution and cares for others; everyone else is either dumb or in it for themselves, or both. Journalists, comedians, satirists, citizens (and, of course, politicians) that take that stance – without at least a hint of self-doubt – claim a status for themselves that cannot be justified and make a contribution to democratic political process that has few positives and a lot of negatives. Cynicism that is too strong and too deeply held is a recipe for inaction: what is the point if everything is going to be undone by the selfishness and mendacity of others?

As I have argued in Chapter 4, some system loyalty is central to the operation of politics; without it, the likelihood is that people will not engage. They need to believe they can make a difference and the system needs to be given time to adjust to their demands. But too much loyalty would be a bad thing: one should not trust politicians or the political system without qualification. In many respects, there would be no need for democracy if we could always trust our leaders: we have democratic checks in place precisely so that we can hold our leaders to account. The paradox here is that a little cynicism is healthy, but too much a corrosive force.

Politicians have, to some extent, failed us. Too often they seem to fall into one of three categories – the dishonest, the time-serving compromisers, or the ideologues. Dishonest politicians promise and then don't deliver. If they ever had principles they have long since compromised them. They make decisions for reasons of expediency or to benefit themselves or their cronies. Honest but time-serving politicians are hardly much better. They fudge rather than act, and are not addressing the issues of pollution, poverty or ecological decay that confront our world. Worse still for many are ideologue politicians, who seem hell bent on manipulating division, creating simplistic 'enemies' or sowing the seeds of disunity and sectarian divide.

But politicians are not as venial, incompetent or divisive as we sometimes think. A certain scepticism is a healthy attribute in a democracy, but an unchecked cynicism can, as we have seen, undermine democracy itself. Democracy needs people to engage, not to stand on the sidelines as carping cynics.

8

The Perils of Populism

The British electorate are fed up with being taken for granted
and talked down to. They are fed up to the back teeth with being
told what they should think and say. They are fed up with the
yah-boo politics and name-calling which passes for political
debate. They are bitter about the politicians not attending to
their anxieties, not addressing their aspirations.[1]

Robert Kilroy-Silk on the launch of Veritas, a new party in the
UK, February 2005

The People and the Truth

'*Veritas*' is Latin for the truth, and it is in many ways an archetypal name for
a populist political movement. Unlike all the rest, populists claim to call it as
it is. The political world is divided into antagonistic groups: the people
versus the corrupt elite; the people versus those who don't belong. The perils
posed by modern populism come from its tendency to demonize opponents
and the political environment in general, and from its failure to appreciate
the complexities of democratic practice and the communities in which we
live. Populism too often collapses into the politics of blame and simplistic
solutions.

In the past, populism has been associated with the oppressive and intolerant political ideologies or creeds such as Nazism that were blatantly anti-
democratic. But populism today finds its most common expression inside
democracies and has in some cases forged an accommodation with democratic institutions. These modern forms of populism do not propose to abolish
free elections or install dictatorship: on the contrary, their demand is for a
democracy that 'delivers what the people want'. To that extent populism has
a positive function inside democracy – it can at least highlight for the political establishment issues it may have neglected or overlooked. In some cases
it may offer a platform from which to build a refreshed democracy. But there
are threats to sustainable democracy posed by this form of politics. The

132

threats revolve around what was described in Chapter 1 as the 'dark side' of democracy where power for the people comes to mean power for a particular section or part of the population. Populism tends to be illiberal: for a populist being the holder of the truth means that you know that others are liars and incompetents, it can't just be that they disagree with you.

Populists have emerged with both left-wing and right-wing agendas. Some, such as those of the *Front National* in France or the Austrian Freedom Party, espouse racism and chauvinism. Populism is not an inherently pathological form of engagement that is supported by people who are uneducated, unskilled, inadequate, or weak. Modern-day populism draws in people from all walks of life and with a varied background in skills and education. It exists in modern-day democracies as an ever-present potential challenge.

This chapter explores the dynamics of populism, opening with an analysis of its expression in a variety of settings. The discussion then moves on to explore the fundamental character of populism as a form of politics. The next section offers an assessment of the contribution of populism to modern-day democratic politics, a flawed and limited offering. The final section asks how populism stands with respect to democratic theory: its practice may feed popular naïvety – and, worse, intolerance – but does its existence remind us of something important about the nature and promise of democracy?

Populism Today: Its Range and Variety

The 'populism' that is of concern in this chapter is something more than politicians using the rhetorical device of claiming to speak for the people. Politicians talk about their values and their competences but there is an inherent tendency in democracies where popular support is the route to power for politicians to claim that their values are those of the people, and their competences exactly what the public want.

This populism is about more than opportunism, in the sense of stating your position in a way that maximizes your chances of support. Chapter 7 argued that the form of expression is an integral element in the way democratic politics works. We should not be surprised by this, and should have some faith that we can use a wide array of judgement criteria to decide whether to support particular politicians, despite the implausibility of their promises. Politicians can make promises both to cut taxes and also to provide wide-ranging and excellent public services that they know don't stack up. They can offer knee-jerk responses to problems, unsure whether they will work but clear that they want to be seen to be on the right side of the argument and above all that they want to be seen to be doing something. This is the charge that is often levelled at the UK's New Labour Government during Prime Minister Blair's leadership after 1997, with its penchant for newsworthy initiatives. Mainstream populists can often 'wrap the flag' around themselves and call themselves patriots, servants of the people; they claim to speak for the people (the good folks, the little guy, the silent majority) who have been overlooked. Ross Perot's and Pat Buchanan's US presidential campaigns, or much of the rhetoric employed by US President George W. Bush are all examples.

Modern-Day Populists

The populism borne out of the opportunism of mainstream politics is not the main focus of attention in this chapter. The focus here is on those politicians that use a populist rhetoric to challenge mainstream politics and seek to create a new political force by riding on a wave of public protest and anger. In the UK, former MP and TV star Robert Kilroy-Silk had a brief flirtation in 2004 with the UK Independence Party (UKIP) and then with his own rather boldly entitled Veritas Party, the leadership of which he in turn gave up after an ignominious failure to attract voters in the 2005 general election. He was, however, elected as an MEP in 2004 and will have that platform for a number of years.

Pauline Hanson in Australia had a longer run in her tilt at mainstream politics. Her One Nation party was founded in 1997,[2] claiming to speak for the people and suggesting that Australia was in danger of being swamped by immigrants and railing generally against the perceived 'political correctness' of the Australian political establishment. Her populist style is well captured by the following statement made at the launch of the One Nation federal election campaign in 2001:

> If I'm gone there will be someone else and someone else and someone else until we actually get democracy back in this country, to get the people we elect to parliament representing us and not overseas interests, multinationals and other organizations, the do-gooders, the bleeding hearts and the civil libertarians that are not interested in Australia.[3]

One Nation attracted nearly a quarter of the vote in the State elections in Queensland in 1998, but her popularity soon waned. Her positions and attitudes were attacked by opponents from the mainstream political parties and the controversial policy stances she adopted began to undermine her support. She blamed her declining popularity on Prime Minister John

Howard 'stealing her policies', but a number of personality disputes and rows within her party did not help. A further blow came in August 2003 when she and a party colleague were found guilty of electoral malpractice and financial fraud. In November 2003, the convictions were quashed, but her victim status did not help enough to get her elected when she stood as an independent in the Queensland State elections of 2004.

From New Zealand comes the case of Winston Peters. He was initially elected as a member of the mainstream National Party in 1978. He served that party in several positions but his maverick tendency and outspoken views – a 'no-nonsense' bloke who wanted to get problems sorted and tackle the issues that concern people – led eventually to a break-up. Shortly after the 1993 general elections he established the New Zealand First Party and in the 1996 elections it performed sufficiently well to be in a position to form a government coalition with the National Party. Peters became Deputy Prime Minister but with the arrival of a new leader of the National Party he was sacked from both the cabinet and the government. In opposition, Peters lost some of his former colleagues, who chose to join the National Party; his party's support waned in 1999 but revived in 2002. The Labour Party, however, refused to join in a coalition with Peters when he was in a position to form a government. However, elections in 2005 created a new opportunity for Peters to join a governing coalition.

Some populists have had a more major impact on the politics of their country. Jorg Haider[4] took over leadership of the Austrian Freedom Party and moved it much further to the right, but combined that platform with a populist critique of the established parties and the nature of the political system in Austria. At its height the Austrian Freedom Party under his leadership gained 28 per cent of the national vote and did sufficiently well in his home province of Carinthia to win him the governorship. The party waned in popularity after the controversy surrounding it joining a coalition government at the national level, when EU leaders threatened to boycott Austrian politics. Haider subsequently gave up the leadership of the party and formed his own new party in 2005. Other examples of European right-wing populists can be found in the case of Jean-Marie Le Pen's *Front National* in France or Umberto Bossi's Northern League in Italy.

Not all populists are right-wing – President Luiz Inacio Lula da Silva of Brazil was elected on a left-leaning populist platform. So too is Hugo Chávez, a former paratrooper and army lieutenant-colonel, who led an unsuccessful *coup* against the then Venezuelan government in 1992. Unusually, he achieved by the ballot box what force had failed to deliver, when he was elected president in 1998.[5] According to the Latin American political scientist Marta Harnecker, Chávez was brought to power on a wave of new hope about Latin American politics after years of economic weakness and political failure:

> The economic crisis brought with it a political crisis. Corruption reigned as scepticism about politics and politicians grew, and apathy was every-where. There appeared to be no way out. In this context Hugo Chávez won 56 percent of the vote in the presidential elections of December 6, 1998. The people, tired of corruption and increasingly sceptical about traditional politics, bet on a candidate who represented something new.[6]

This Chávez presidency has seen sweeping changes throughout the country, including new constitutional measures aimed at breaking the stranglehold of established elites, a range of significant welfare and educational programmes aimed at tackling poverty and a new foreign policy distancing Venezuela from the USA and more generally challenging neo-liberal ideas. President Chávez has attracted a lot of criticism from some US right-wing quarters, and is seen by some observers and fellow countrymen as anti-democratic. But equally he is widely seen as delivering on his promises to help the poor by exploiting Venezuela's oil revenues. His foreign policy efforts have attracted high-profile support from President Fidel Castro of Cuba and many other activists opposed to the neo-liberal globalization agenda.

Despite vigorous attempts by elements of the business community and trade union movement to unseat him, Chávez survived both an attempted *coup* in 2002 and a recall vote in 2004 that fell because the population decided to back Chávez rather than his opponents with its votes. He promotes a coalition of support around populist ideas derived from the nineteenth-century Latin America leader Simon Bolivar. His political style and substance is difficult to pin down, but according to Harnecker he relies heavily on his ability to communicate his ideas directly to many parts of society from the poor, through the middle classes to significant sections of the army. His political machine is increasingly composed of new activists and those attracted into engagement by his programmes and personality. But turning a commitment to popular involvement into a participatory practice is hard; Harnecker[7] argues that the major challenge facing Venezuelan politics is building up the scope for popular participation alongside Chávez's strong leadership style, a classic dilemma in the populist mode of organizing.

The Power of Populism

The real power of populism is its capacity to mobilize those who have previously not been engaged in the political process. Populism is a fragile ideology built on the axis of 'us' against 'them', and as such it can take a variety of diverse positions and platforms. It just depends how the 'us' is defined, and who exactly the 'them' is taken to be. It could be that the 'them' is the liberal establishment, or 'big business' or corporations. Populism finds expression as 'outsiders' mobilize waves of popular support that can in turn ebb away quite quickly. Sometimes those waves of support translate into long-term political programmes and keep their exponents in government for a considerable period of time. The dilemma is in finding a way of translating populism into something that can *accommodate* rather than *demonize* mainstream politics.

Exploring Populism

Populism seems to flow from a sense of resentment about the way that politics is working and relies on an attractive leader to exploit the situation and create a dynamic of engagement and support among the public. Often that activity is carried forward on a wave of emotion and high moral indignation. Populism is not normal politics: the mood has a 'revivalist flavour' and 'draws normally unpolitical people into the political arena'.[8]

The key dividing line in populist rhetoric is between 'the people', who are generally deemed as having sound sense and good judgement, and the elite or the establishment that are failing to respond to the people's wishes because they are selfishly making decisions to suit their own interests. Populism tends towards identifying a clear enemy – the establishment – and has a hazy but very positive view of the people. Populism does not call for the people to be educated or learn the skills of citizenship; rather, it is assumed that the people have those skills and the good sense to make wise decisions and that all that is required is an opportunity for them to express their views and leaders that will act on those views. The 'people' may need to be liberated and given the scope to have an impact; but they do not need to be changed. For populists, 'the consciousness of the people, generally referred to as *commonsense*, is the basis of all good [politics].[9]

The 'people', at a rhetorical level, appears to be everybody, but in practice distinctions are drawn between 'our people', and 'others'. Sometimes the dividing line is race, but it can be nationality or class. The idea of a great alliance of those who are excluded or kept out of power and influence over the current regime is a theme that runs through much populist discourse. For right-wingers, the enemy is often the liberal establishment; for left-wingers, it is often the business interests and more generally the neo-liberal project of globalization led by the USA. What populism promises to do is to listen to the 'silent majority' of citizens who have their interests and opinions overridden by corrupt politicians, self-interested political parties and well-connected establishment interests or strident minorities.[10]

Populism emphasizes the need for simple direct language and uncluttered communication. It often relies on a direct communication between the leader and citizen supporters through speeches, but also through TV and other media. Populists tend to dislike any institutions or people – bureaucrats, party officials, parliamentarians – that get in the way of communication between leader and followers. These institutions need to be carefully managed so that they do not usurp that direct line of communication between governed and governors: failure to communicate can lead to precisely the forms of political neglect and misunderstanding that originally drove the populist engagement with politics.

The relationship with the leader or leaders is central to the practice of populist politics. Populists do not necessarily want a leader like themselves in terms of social position or standing, but rather one who will deliver what they want and will deal with them directly and fairly.

Populism for citizens is a *reactive* form of political activity, mobilization at the behest of the leader. It is the leader that is followed and who, following the cues provided by 'the people', identifies and then expresses their wishes. Populism is not about direct democracy: referendums may be advocated but they are a means to an end and that end is what Cas Mudde calls 'responsive government':

> The heartland of contemporary populism is thus focused primarily on the output and not on the input of democracy. What [populism] demand[s] is responsive government, i.e. a government that implements policies that are in line with their wishes. However, they want the politicians to come up with these policies without bothering them, i.e. without much participation from them.[11]

What populism rests on, in all its forms, is the claim that it will make the 'grand project' of democracy work by creating a form of politics that is responsive to popular will.

Assessing Populism

On the surface, populism appears to be about popular sovereignty and giving power to the people and that is what, for many commentators, democracy is about. Much of the disenchantment about our political system is reflective of a sense that politics is not delivering – it is not giving us the results that we, the people, want. Populism today is the expression of the *politics of anti-politics*. Is populism an appropriate response? Surely one answer is to let the people govern. As Cas Mudde argues:

> More and more citizens think they have a good understanding of what politicians do, and think they can do it better. While this does not necessarily mean that many people also actually want to do it better, by actively participating in various aspects of political life . . . , it does mean that the relationship between the elites and the citizens has changed significantly, and possibly irrevocably, over the past decades.[12]

Politics and politicians are challenged now more than in the past, and that has opened up the field to populist outbursts that feed on the sense that the political system is not delivering.

Surely the political establishments of all countries need a good kick up the backside every now and then? I would not want to disagree with that. But a core theme of this book is not just that politicians and the political system need to change in order for us to have a sustainable democracy in the future: we, as citizens, need to engage with the political process more effectively and also in a more considered manner. As a form of short-term challenge, populism brings a certain dynamic to politics, but it also has some serious downsides.

My main difficulty with modern-day populism is that it keeps on asking the impossible of the political system: politics cannot work in the way that populists demand. Populism does not respect the core features of politics – the search for compromise between different interests, the need to understand another's position and the complexities of implementation – identified in Chapter 4. It fails to do this because it does not allow for the presence of differences between citizens. It posits that the people are one, and their voice, if properly understood, has a unified and unifying message. The people speak and the government should act to fulfil their wishes. Anything else that gets in the way of the delivery of that vision is a malfunction – or, worse, an act of deliberate sabotage – on the part of other political interests or actors. Yet, as I have already suggested, such an understanding of politics is naïve and mistakes the nature of politics in modern democracies.

Populism's tendency to demonize its opponents in political debate means that many populists do not like to listen and want instead to 'tell it like it is'. Populism can take deeply illiberal and intolerant forms. The narratives of populism often portray opponents as evil rather than simply people with different interests or values, often taking an emotive tone that can undermine the role of reason, evidence, respect and rules in the political process. It is important to be aware of populism's limitations as a form of democratic politics. Modern democracy is not about the will of the majority alone but also focuses on the needs of minorities, and populism runs the risk of neglecting this insight.

Populism offers a false recipe for resolving the problems of democracy. It feeds on the failings of democratic politics but also makes radical claims to deliver power to the people. The mobilization it encourages brings a short burst of energy to the political system, but it is opposed to the values and practices of mainstream politics. Populists rail against the compromises and complexity of modern politics, for them, the world is divided into the 'pure' people and the corrupt elite, and their politics is about breaking what they see as the domination of the latter over the former. For populists, the popular will must prevail: the 'people' know what they want, and a decent political system would deliver it.

Populism and Democratic Theory: A Minor Detour

At this point, I want to take a minor detour to explore how populism sits in the context of wider debates about the nature of democracy. How does populism stand in relation to democratic theory? As Margaret Canovan[13] points out, some theorists define democracy as 'liberal democracy', and say that populism fails to meet that standard because of its disrespect of minorities and lack of commitment to tolerance and compromise. A more intriguing line of criticism is that majority coalitions cannot fairly be constructed.

Riker's Claims

One of the most striking and well-known attacks on the idea of populism comes from William Riker, a key exponent of the public choice school in political science. In his *Liberalism against Populism*, Riker makes two main claims against the idea that democracy can find expression through establishment of the popular will.[14] Drawing on a wider 'impossibility theorem' Riker argues that even democratic voting systems cannot reveal the true interests of voters.[15]

First, Riker argues that individual preferences cannot be aggregated in a way that is consistently fair and logical. He starts with the idea that people have multiple and different preferences, and that they can rank their preferences against each other and according to the circumstances they find themselves in. Almost all social choices involve a situation where individuals rank their preferences, so one individual may prefer *A* over *B* over *C* and so on. But others will have different rankings. The difficulty is that if these preferences are randomly spread then it is impossible to find a fair and accurate mechanism that will enable a choice to be made. You could just take first preferences, but that might result in a system where the choice was backed by 34 out of 100 voters but opposed as the worst possible choice by 66 out of 100 voters. In any case if you are trying to identify the popular will then, from a moral and democratic standpoint, you should try to capture the subtlety of it. You could start taking into account lower-ranking preferences, but here the outcome will not be determined by people's preferences in the purest sense but by the way that the preference counting rules work: again, this is a violation of democratic rights. Different rules will yield different versions of the popular will and therefore populist democracy can never be anything other than a process leading to arbitrary outcomes.

Riker's second argument against populism is that even if a voting system was chosen to form the basis for making collective decisions, the results can be manipulated by agenda-setting and strategic voting. Say, for example, there are three voters and they face a choice over what type of meal to have in the evening. *A* is beef, *B* is chicken and *C* is vegetarian. Bethany and Robert favour *A* over *B*. Bethany and Ben favours *B* over *C*. Finally Robert and Ben favour *C* over *A*. There is no collective choice that therefore emerges. But if Bethany can determine the order in which votes are taken, then she can determine the result. So she shouts out 'let's vote over whether to choose *B* or *C* first', and that is what happens. The result is she wins, with Ben's support, in getting *C* kicked off the agenda. It is then a straight fight between *A* and *B* that inevitably leads to *A* winning as Bethany votes for it along with Robert. In more complex situations, agenda-setting is joined by strategic voting to control results. People gang up against the preference that most threatens their top choice. According to Riker, this capacity for manipulation renders the claim that the popular will is being discovered by voting meaningless.

For Riker, populist democracy is an inferior way of deciding anything. In general, he favours the market as the mechanism for making decisions in society. The best you can do is to argue for limited government and as much protection of people's interests against government as possible through a liberal constitution that defends the citizens' freedoms. Beyond that when collective choices have to be made democracy, in the form of voting for leaders, is justified so that at least politicians and governments are given incentives to do what people want for fear of being kicked out of office.

There are two main counter-arguments to Riker's position taken.[16] The first is empirical. Voters' preferences are not often completely randomly distributed and therefore different voting systems, much of the time, produce similar results. People may well have similar preferences, so theoretical impossibility is in practice resolved. Second, to say that powerful interests can manipulate democracy or that people may vote strategically in the light of the circumstances they find themselves in is not a claim against democracy as such, but rather a reflection of the reality of democratic politics.

Dowding's Argument

Keith Dowding takes the argument against Riker a stage further, by pointing out that the market also involves similar constraints to democracy:

> It only reveals our preferences given the constraints under which we buy and sell. If I buy a pint of beer rather than a bottle of champagne, does this reveal that I prefer beer to champagne? No. It shows I prefer beer to champagne given my budget constraints. It reveals my preferences given the products on offer, and given my resources (which are relative to others' resources). Similarly, voting reveals my preferences for the alternatives on offer given the constraints under which I vote. These include what candidates are standing for what policies, and the way I think others are going to vote. We operate strategically in markets, just as we do in elections.[17]

In the case of markets, as argued in Chapter 4, the rationing process is internalized rather than imposed, but it still is a constraining influence on individual choice: in markets you are expected to make your choices according to the circumstances you are in. Moreover, as Dowding goes on to argue, you might well face misinformation as a consumer from sellers who are aware, for example, of cheaper prices elsewhere for the goods or service they are trying to sell you. But the rule in the market that is widely accepted is 'buyer beware': it is up to you to check on alternative prices and the possibility of manipulation. If that rule applies in market settings, suggests Dowding, then it could equally be held to apply as part of the realist practice of democratic politics.

So there are grounds for arguing that ambitions of populists for democracy cannot be ruled out as impossible or unachievable. The problem with populists in general is rather that they do not understand how democracy requires contrasting styles of politics and that democratic politics cannot survive on the diet that populists serve up.

Pragmatic and Redemptive Politics

Democracy requires two styles of politics, according to Margaret Canovan.[18] One is *pragmatic* and the other is *redemptive*. Both are value-laden. The pragmatic tendency is to that extent slightly misleadingly labelled, in that it is driven by values of toleration, peace, respect and stability. The pragmatic way of looking at democracy promotes it as a form of governing that enables conflicts to be managed between antagonistic interests without resort to violent exchanges. Democracy in this vision is a form of conflict management or a 'nonaggression pact among different political groups'[19] that avoids more destructive ways of resolving disputes. It works through the contingent processes and institutions that bind people into the political process. The history of democracy is the history of making institutions that enable that 'binding' to work and be sustained through institutions such as elections, assemblies, lobby group organizations and access to constitutional protection of freedoms and rights. The great virtue and claim of pragmatic democracy is that it provides the conditions for people to live their lives and do the best for themselves and their families. This pragmatic understanding of democracy has a modest level of expectation about what governments can do, and is suspicious about the concentration of power even if democratically controlled.

The redemptive vision of democracy takes a rather more ambitious line on what democracy can achieve. Democracy can lead to a better world by giving the people the power to take control of their lives: it is a politics of faith, built on the belief that the world can be a better place and that if people work together they can achieve a superior life. Redemptive democracy glorifies the sovereignty of the people and wants to see people engage in politics with passion and commitment.

These two sides of politics need to live together. Political mechanisms for resolving conflicts become empty and devoid of the capacity to stimulate participation if there is no hope built into the system. Some hope of transformation or commitment to a wider ideal of the possibility of meaningful change is essential. In the face of the challenges and difficulties of achieving change, politics needs the passion and commitment of the redemptive understanding of politics. People need to believe that the promise of power through democracy is not illusory, and that if they engage they can make a difference. The result is a paradox: 'unrealistic visions may be a condition of real achievement as well as a recipe for disappointment'.[20] On the other hand, the political will needed to achieve the ambition of conflict management in the pragmatic vision needs a certain faith that the game is worth all the effort. Equally the ambitions of redemptive politics have to be made real through the institutions and practices of the pragmatic vision of politics. Romantic commitment to 'people power' will not wash in the long run if; change is going to be effective and lasting, then the organization and input of the pragmatic side of politics is central.

So pragmatism and redemption must exist side by side in the politics of democracies. Populism mistakenly rejects that perspective and puts all its faith in redemptive politics. Democracy should deliver what the people want: failure to deliver means, according to the logic of populist thought, that democracy has been usurped by corrupt politicians, do-gooders, 'big business' – take your pick. There is in populism a frustration with the institutions of pragmatic politics and a sense that a strong leader will resolve all known implementation problems, a faith in the power of personality over institutional arrangements.

Populism feeds off the tensions between these two understandings of democracy. It is ironic in many ways that the silent majority or the common people – so central to populist rhetoric – would in everyday exchanges align themselves with the values of pragmatic politics yet end up backing a redemptive form. They are, after all, by their own definition, the pragmatic, no-nonsense, down to-the-earth people. Yet their politics is built on a one-sided faith that politics can produce miracles and with very little effort on their part.

Concluding Note

In Chapter 7, I rejected the stance of the cynic on the sidelines with an attitude of aloof moral superiority towards the political process. Modern-day populists engage when goaded or encouraged to do so by their leaders or in response to a particular crisis or issue. The result can be great waves of passion and commitment that are often short-lived. Populism tends to be a *reactive* form of politics. As a type of engagement it has its attractions, as it speaks to one of the great claims of democracy, to give power to the people. Yet as a form of politics its often aggressive, antagonistic and intolerant tone makes it an uneasy element in democratic politics, as does its common commitment to the idea that simple solutions to complex problems can be found if only the commonsense of the people is given a chance.

The attraction of populist politics in today's democracies tells us something very important. Citizens need a democratic politics that can deliver, but what is required is more than the pragmatic case for politics that claims that it enables us to get by and rub along. Democracy cannot be sold solely on the grounds that it is a recipe for a quiet life. The case for a liberal, tolerant political system is attractive and positive but it's not enough if the excitement embedded in democracy is going to be sustained. Democratic politics also needs to deliver the prospect for a redemptive capacity, a sense that popular control is achievable, on some occasions, at some point and over some issues. The great claim of democracy is that those affected by a decision should have the right to a say in it; that is its power. Populism produces too often a distorted and illiberal response to that ambitious hope; it creates a politics of blame and scapegoating. Underneath it all, nonetheless, there is a message: giving scope for the realization that the popular will matters. People in democracies do not take kindly to being told that politics – engaging in collective decision making – is not for the likes of them.

Part III

Searching for Solutions

9

Politics for Amateurs

E. J. Dionne, Jr., *Washington Post* syndicated political colum-
nist, [once] gave the commencement address at George
Washington University's Graduate School of Political
Management. After his speech, Dionne was presented with a gift
from the student body, a T-shirt with the words 'Graduate School
of Political Management' on the front and 'Because politics is
not for amateurs' on the back. Dionne graciously accepted the
gift, but then said he hoped the T-shirt's slogan was mistaken.[1]

Dennis Johnson, *No Place for Amateurs*

E. J. Dionne is right that politics is not just for experts. Democracy should
give ordinary people a say in the affairs that govern their lives. You don't
have to be an expert. You don't have to be a professional. You don't have to
be wealthy. You don't have to be socially gifted. Admittedly having any one
of these characteristics might well give you an advantage when you do
engage, but they are not a precondition for entry. The era of mass democracy
has established a commitment to realize the great democratic norm: 'every
individual potentially affected by a decision should have an equal opportunity to affect that decision'.[2]

The magic in that formula appears to have been lost in the practice of
democratic politics if the analysis presented by Parts I and II of this book is
anything to go by. Part III of the book, therefore, focuses on the search for
solutions, and is premised on a conviction that we need to construct a politics fit for amateurs. Politics in democratic societies needs more than effective leaders and activists and a silent and patient citizenry. It also requires
citizen engagement, without which the spirit of democracy that created
support for the idea of democratic governance in the first place will be lost.
It needs to feed a commitment to a politics of toleration and willingness to
compromise and at the same time reaffirm a sense that we can use our collective decision making capacities to make the world a better place. Politics
needs to become less a vocation for the few, and more an opportunity for the

many. However, most citizens want only to engage in politics occasionally and not as specialists: they want to be political amateurs, not professionals.

'Amateur' is a word that carries a complex of meanings. On the positive side, 'amateur' can mean someone who does things because they are interested and care and not because of any financial reward. For the amateur, engaging in their chosen activity is just one part of their wider life; they are part-time, occasional activists and come with a fresh pair of eyes, a range of experiences and a wider sense of what is important in life. On the other hand, 'amateur' can mean an unskilled person. There is nothing wrong with being an amateur and we should celebrate the value and perspective that amateurs bring to all walks of life, including politics. But there is a difference between a vaguely competent amateur and a completely inadequate layperson (remember the Introduction). Politics is a place for amateurs, but we need to design institutions, structure processes and develop support systems so that amateurs can engage and improve their skills.

Up until now, the book has striven to describe and understand what is, but we now need to consider what should be, and how positive change can be delivered. My prescription starts from where people are – amateurs – and then seeks to ask how we can mould political institutions and a wider civic infrastructure to enable people to engage in politics more effectively.

This chapter makes the general case for constructing a politics for amateurs. It begins by arguing against the idea that democracies have something to fear from citizen engagement. Citizens may well lack skills and competencies; many may hold limited and narrow understandings of their situation. But citizen engagement brings too many positive benefits to the decision making process to be feared. For democratic governors at local, regional, national and international levels it provides that crucial 'feedback loop' without which our governance systems will fail. In today's world, the complexity of what governments are trying to do, the connectedness of different parts of society, the nature of the social and economic issues we face and the cultural fabric of society make engagement not an optional extra but an essential. 'Engineers use a technical term to describe systems without feedback mechanisms: "stupid".'[3] Citizen engagement, if designed appropriately, may cement the relationship between citizens and their commitment to the democratic political process.

The second part of the chapter argues that there is only so much engagement that citizens should be expected to provide and that we should not be overly prescriptive as to the form that that engagement should take. Since the 1950s, the dominant trend in thinking about democratic politics among academics and theorists has been to argue for more participation, extensive deliberation, deepening democracy and a new public domain. My objections to these reform ideas, if pushed too far, are covered in the next two sections of the chapter. Arguments for more participation too often reek of a sort of moral conviction about how citizens should conduct themselves and engage in the world. Demanding that people conform to your image of what is 'appropriate behaviour' can be encouraging and supportive, but it also can be oppressive and undermining. There may be many different ideas about a legitimate way of coming to a judgement.

Insisting that people are something they are not can also lead to desperately unrealistic expectations. There are practical arguments against participation, given the cognitive limitations and difficulties faced by citizens, and complexity and dilemmas of the modern political process. More participation is not always the right or even the viable option.

Engagement needs to be targeted and built on realistic premises. Think back to the evidence presented in Chapter 5. Most people don't want to spend all their time on politics, they cannot and would not wish to claim the depth of knowledge and understanding available to experts, they are comfortable with a division of labour. They want to engage directly over the issues that are most salient to them but would prefer to rely on the judgements of representatives and activists over most issues, most of the time. The challenge of the twenty-first century is to design a political system that can more readily meet those aspirations.

Political Engagement is Good (Up to a Point)

Should we want People to Engage?

In Chapter 1, I celebrated democracy because as a system of governance it provides citizens with a 'voice' in the processes and institutions that determine how power is exercised and how decisions are made in their societies. Activism and engagement, as we saw, are central to the very rationale of democratic politics. However some people take the position that politics is something best left to the professionals. It is up to our leaders and representatives to decide, once we have chosen them. This very narrow view of democracy is often justified because the scale of modern democracies means that it is not practical for everyone to be involved in decisions. But it sometimes rests also on a fear and distrust of the public:

> The main reason for . . . downgrading the role of ordinary people in democratic politics is straightforward enough: it is because most people are ignorant about issues, irrational in their opinions and preferences, and easily swayed by manipulative appeals from unscrupulous politicians.[4]

The implication of this position is that people should vote, choose their government and then get out of the way.

There are some who also argue that where things went wrong was in imagining that people wanted to get more engaged in politics. As Morris Fiorina puts it:

> It is time to abandon the notion of political participation as part of human nature. It is not, it is an unnatural act...Contrary to the suggestions of pundits and philosophers, there is nothing wrong with those who do not want to participate; rather there is something unusual about those that do.[5]

Fiorina goes on to argue that many academics and practical politicians think that democracy would work better if all people were asked to do was vote. But in the end he concludes that there can be no turning back, in part because although citizens may not always engage they do value that opportunity in the abstract, and would oppose any restriction on it.

Citizens see the power that democracy gives them as individuals to raise issues that concern them: democracy is justified not just as an opportunity to choose their governors but as a chance to have a say themselves. The academic/theoretical narrative of democracy, as Michael Saward shows, has now moved towards a more participative, expansive understanding of democracy.[6] The importance of freedom of association and free speech to making democracy work is now accepted and, for many pressure or lobby groups composed of representatives of different citizen interests provide a vital link between citizens and government. Robert Dahl,[7] in particular, has expanded the narrow focus on elections of earlier theorists such as Joseph Schumpeter.[8] For Dahl, a democratic world requires not only free elections and competition for political office but also an active citizen group environment to gather information and express views *between* elections. Everyday politics is not just a matter for elected leaders; it is also a matter for organized groups that can help give voice to the citizens' concerns.[9]

Too narrow a view of what citizens can or should be expected to do does not sit well with the ideals of democracy; nor it is necessarily right when it comes to judging the citizens' capacity. Citizens can certainly be uninformed about issues and have half-baked ideas about solutions, but then so can governments – that is what the decline in deference in the later part of the twentieth century enabled everyone to see more clearly. Citizens can be critical, challenging and knowledgeable about their own interests and concerns: we need our democracy not to save governments from the public, as some would like, but rather to create the context for mutual challenge and respect between governors and governed.

Writers that take an elitist approach to democracy by underplaying the role of participation rest their views on a profound distrust of people, and produce a very limited vision of democracy. From the 1950s, the Cold War and the threat of communism were used by such thinkers to support such a negative view, and there is a danger that the threat of international terrorism after 9/11 2001 may be used to argue that we should risk only a limited democracy, for fear that our security is undermined or we show weakness by displaying divisions of opinion to our 'enemies'.

The Positive Case for Activism

At its best, democracy enables people to see beyond their immediate self-interest and engage in collective decision making that is transformative and positive. Democracy should also be about more than simply voting for leaders: it should be about providing the opportunities to get involved and engaged in a whole range of institutions and decisions, from neighbourhood to global. The positive case for activism rests on several of grounds. First, and most fundamentally: 'democratic decision-making requires knowledge of the interests of the people'.[10] Those interests cannot be assumed, and they often reflect a particular local knowledge and understanding that only the citizen has. Asking citizens their opinion enables their knowledge and preferences to be registered in the governance process.

This practical case for gathering public opinion has become more relevant given the complexity of our governance systems and the fact that more participation might lead to more effective learning and better decisions. A properly organized democracy should increase our capacity to address fundamental social problems. It might have been appropriate to limit democracy to a 'protective' role when the government itself was restricted to such a role but with the rise of welfare and other public spending to between a third and a half of national gross domestic product (GDP) government is no longer an institution that can be separated off – it is *de facto* a part of every aspect of our lives. We therefore need a more extended capacity to debate and exchange with it other than that afforded by the simple act of voting.

Second, the state is no longer a local or even a national institution, it also takes a supranational form – the development of the EU being the strongest expression to date. We need a way of influencing those institutions that take decisions for us on that terrain as well as at national, regional, local and neighbourhood levels.

What is the appropriate form and role of democracy in this our changing world? The focus on engagement in modern democratic theory rests on a conception of democracy as a process of *continuous exchange* between governors and governed: democracy helps to provide solutions by enabling us to exchange and learn from one another. As Paul Hirst argued: 'Democracy in this sense is about government by information exchange and consent, where organized publics have the means to conduct a dialogue with government and thus hold it to account'.[11] What is required to confirm the democratic credentials of governance is a way of extending the rights to consultation to the widest possible range of issues and the construction of a dialogue that allows space for the involvement of the disorganized many as well as the organized few.

A democratic system does not require the participation of all the people or all of the time; rather, its defining characteristic is its openness to all. If representative politics is working then on many occasions further public participation may be unnecessary. The value of openness does not require or assume large-scale and continuous direct participation; it rests its case on the availability of options for extending participation. These options should operate without making overwhelming time demands and in a way that enhances the broad representativeness of those involved. Activism enables people to achieve a fuller expression of their interests by debating and sharing ideas with others; but it also enables people to come to terms with the complexities and challenges of the modern government. Engagement is not something to be afraid of: rather, it is something to be welcomed.

Over-Prescription of Citizen Engagement

We need a politics for amateurs because, for most people, politics is not their first choice of activity. There are trade-offs between 'time spent at a political meeting and the joys of private life, including time spent with family and friends'.[12] My concern is not just about over-doing engagement, however; it goes deeper than that. There are practical but also normative issues to consider. Advocates of engagement over-prescribe particular forms of engagement and they misjudge the extent and nature of the engagement, that people want. These arguments are pursued in the next two sections.

Too Much Emphasis on the 'Good' Citizen

According to Matthew Crenson and Benjamin Ginsberg, the problem in mature democracies such as the USA is that democracy has been 'downsized' and 'privatized': citizens make their interventions to get a better service or win something for themselves but they are no longer engaged in collective battles. Governments have also made their institutions more responsive to customers, and as a result citizens can often get their concern heard as individuals rather than through collective protest:

> We are approaching the end of a political epoch, one in which citizens jointly inhabited a public sphere. They gathered there because they mattered . . . The public sphere was an artefact of modernity. It provided a place in which mere political subjects evolved into political actors and full citizens.[13]

This view sounds a bit like 'today's citizens are just not what they used to be', a classic complaint of one generation about the next. But it also is a form of argument that places a special value on the need to enter the political arena as other-regarding citizens engaged in collective action rather than as private individuals.

This tradition of thinking about politics as a special and separate arena is very strong. Many of those writing in recent years have argued that we have lost this special sense of the 'public realm'.[14] The public domain in this discourse has its own culture and codes. It provides a framework of norms which guide behaviour where citizenship trumps market power or the bonds of clan and kinship. A sense of service and civic duty are the driving forces of this world – a gift of history – and they are in danger of being fatally undermined by individualism and disengagement. People need to be brought back into politics, so this line of argument goes, but only in a way that expresses the noble and collectivist traditions of citizen politics.

Given what I argued in Chapter 4, I can readily concede that politics is conducted according to a different set of rules to those which operate in the market. The case for politics having a distinctive flavour is strong, but the argument about the nobility of politics and the sacredness of the citizen a bit hard to swallow. Politics has rather more prosaic and pragmatic ends than heroic deeds at its heart. I also find it difficult to trust anyone who says they are behaving altruistically or in an other-regarding manner. I can accept mixed motivations, but I don't like the idea of those who engage in politics being able to claim that they are working for higher, benign purposes alone. Thirdly, I am rather pleased that in some areas of their life people can now raise personal complaints and issues as individuals rather than always having to go through collective channels. Engagement can be empowering when it is done as an individual just as much as when it is done collectively.

People engage in politics with a range of motivations but they can learn to do it better. This way of understanding of what it means to be a citizen rests on a view that people seek to frame their responses to problems by reference to a 'mental map', an understanding of the way that life works that makes sense to them. They need cues from other citizens, the media and wider societal and political institutions in order to frame their response. They need to recognize that politics is a different space, but they do not need to be constrained to engage through collectivist forms alone or in a way that demands that they and others are nobly pursuing the public interest.

Should Citizens Deliberate?

The second strand in the engagement debate that deserves to be questioned is the emphasis on *deliberation*: 'The deliberative model of democracy has been the dominant new strand in democratic theory over the last ten to fifteen years'.[15] Proponents of deliberation argue that democratic politics must involve discussion and an exchange of views. The problem comes when deliberation is put on a pedestal as the most vital democratic act: public deliberation between citizens on an equal and inclusive footing is seen as the central and legitimate expression of politics. The assumption appears to be that people through deliberation can develop a deepened awareness and confidence to engage in public affairs and come to a new shared position: 'Deliberative democracy looks to *transform* people's (possibly ill-informed) preferences through open and inclusive discussion, not merely to design electoral procedures to *reflect* them'.[16] Some deliberation theorists emphasize the importance of rationality in exchange and others are willing to allow for a wider range of discursive forms, from careful reasoning to rambling anecdotes.[17] But they all share a faith in the value of transforming debate that moves people towards a new consensus, or at least a working agreement.

There is undoubtedly value in this emphasis on deliberation. Opportunities for deliberation should be part of the toolkit of any democratic governance. But it may be more suited for some situations than others. On many occasions, the goal in politics is not so much consensus but more a willingness to fudge and make a messy compromise that enables all sides to move on and live to come back and fight another day. The conflicts of Northern Ireland, for example, are unlikely to be resolved through the emergence of a consensus given the differences between the sides but politics works in this setting by finding weasel words and obscure and temporary settlements rather than full blown deliberation.

Deliberation theory also suffers from the same problem faced by those who see politics as requiring 'noble citizens': its (often academic) advocates often talk about transforming people rather than accepting them as they are. The image of the good citizen emphasizes reason, reflection, open and challenging debate and careful weighing of the evidence. (In practice, of course, much academic exchange is based on misunderstanding other's positions, breaking into separate and adversarial schools of thought and generally talking past one another.) As one young academic advocate of deliberation in public administration pondered:

> If we (and in this instance, by we I mean those of us within the academic communities who are interested in various deliberative, discourse-based democracies) cannot engage in a conversation without resorting to . . . making exaggerated representations of each other's positions, how can we expect citizens to do any differently?[18]

Deliberation in this light is something to be aspired to but, difficult to achieve, and is thus a rather weak base on which to build our ambitions for the revival of democracy. Deliberation brings out in me an unease I have generally about transformational forms of politics: surely we need to start from where people are and not attempt to construct a politics around 'new model citizens'? People can certainly learn new skills and capacities but there are also limits within which we can realistically expect human behaviour to change.

Many writers who promote the cause of deliberation are keen to avoid the charge that they are mere dreamers and focus their efforts on the practical institutional innovations of deliberation.[19] Archon Fung and Erik Olin Wright have promoted the case for 'empowered participatory governance'.[20] They see empowered and deliberative forms of engagement for citizens as a way to draw teeth from neo-liberal calls for the state to withdraw and cut back on its public spending by showing how the state and government decisions can be handed over to citizens who are in turn empowered to make decisions and services more responsive to their needs. I suspect because these writers are concerned that deliberation may be a slightly unnatural act for citizens, they explicitly articulate and address fears that the deliberation processes will be taken over by strong community interests or manipulative state officials. As a result there is a considerable emphasis in their models of engagement on constraining and controlling the process through prescriptive rules.

Strict rules promote the primacy of deliberation: people are supposed to choose between options not on the basis of self-interest but rather on the basis of a judgement about which of the options are most reasonably going to advance the group's agenda. Whether they do or not depends on 'participants following the procedures and norms of deliberation'.[21] There is a keenness to have local decision makers place their decisions under the oversight of a higher government body, in part so that best practice can be spread and bigger issues can be raised and dealt with, but also for the much less benign-sounding reasons of coordinating the distribution of resources and 'rectifying pathological or incompetent decision-making in failing groups'.[22] There is also a lot of emphasis on education and practice on the part of the citizens because 'individuals' capacities to deliberate, and make public decisions, atrophy when left unused'.[23]

There is much to admire in the schemas and practice that Fung and Wright describe, but as the rules pile up one on top of another, their institutional frameworks for 'empowered participatory governance' do give you a sort of feeling of being back at school. The advocates of deliberation are clearly aware that it is not easy to deliver, is open to abuse and may not be appropriate for all contexts. In trying to design out these difficulties, there is a danger that they will foster forms of governance that in practice become rigid and deeply constrained and not all that participatory, since only 'acceptable' behaviour and 'reasonable' demands will be allowed.

The normative case for citizen engagement in politics is powerful and convincing. What is less convincing is some of the more detailed argument and prescription that surrounds the case for engagement. Insisting on public, deliberative and rule-bound forms of citizen engagement smacks of a very particular understanding of human nature and human society that is not automatically attractive or desirable. It also suggests, probably mistakenly, that people like politics.

Intensive Engagement is not Always Effective or an Option Open to All Citizens

Do People Want to Engage?

The advocates of engagement are prone to over-estimate the extent and intensity of political engagement that most people desire, or are even comfortable with. The assumptions built into the argument for engagement are not necessarily borne out in studies of the way that people do actually engage. John Hibbing and Elizabeth Theiss-Morse summarize a range of findings, and conclude that 'people's dislike of politics runs deep and is unlikely to be eliminated if only they would get involved with other people in political procedures'.[24] They identify a number of potential *cognitive stumbling blocks* in the path of greater engagement. In the introduction, we used their work to support the contention that people often have a very naïve understanding of the way that politics works, struggle to see the world through the eyes of others and are fearful that somehow they are going to be duped by the political process. We now need to consider whether offering people greater chances of engagement will automatically be grabbed with open arms by them, or even improve political decision making.

The positions taken by Hibbing and Theiss-Morse are quite controversial; they go against much of the accepted wisdom of both political theorists and other political scientists. Analysts commonly see a positive connection between people participating in groups that are non-political as training for wider political involvement: it is through workplace, church and voluntary organizations that people learn the skills of talking, debating and negotiating – skills that can be transferred to the political sphere. One of the most well-known exponents of this position is Robert Putnam who, as we saw in Chapter 3, argues that it is people's declining associational activity that has robbed them of the opportunity of developing social capital that in turn gives them the motivation and skills necessary to engage in politics.[25]

Hibbing and Theiss-Morse are not so convinced that associational activity is a good training ground for politics. When people do meet in associations and groups they often, for fear of stimulating too much controversy or open discussion of troubling issues, put a lot of pressure on members to stick to a limited range of topics and matters where regular, unassuming citizens can feel at home and unchallenged. This observation plainly applies to associations dealing with leisure, sports or hobbies matters, but also applies to many more overtly political organizations where issues of ideology or policy are debated less frequently than more practical issues of administration and fund-raising. People in associations and groups often confine their interactions to a limited set of topics and more practical issues partly as a means of coping with the unknown views of group members and the uncertainty created by conflict and division. They prefer to stick to nearer-at-hand issues and to the uncontroversial, and gravitate towards groups that are populated by like-minded people. They are learning to get along with one another, and in that sense they may be gaining in social capital, but that is not necessarily being transferred into *political capital*, which is an ability to deal with the challenges and conflicts of political choices.

If many people are not inclined to discuss politics in their everyday memberships of groups and associations, will they do so in the more ordered and ruled environments favoured by deliberative theorists? The answer is 'yes', and many studies of deliberation experiments show that political efficacy measurably grows among the participants in the deliberative exercise.[26] Political engagement at the community level, in particular, makes people feel better about their political effectiveness, more knowledgeable about their local community and clearer about how local officialdom could, or should, respond to them.[27]

Hibbing and Theiss-Morse, however, again offer a number of important counter-arguments. Deliberative groups can become dominated by one particular voice and not encourage group reflection but rather encourage a sort of 'group-think' where people abandon their ordinary standards of judgement and go along with a line of argument or a conclusion that may be ill-judged. Just think of the mixed record of citizen juries in deciding criminal cases: deliberation can produce bad as well as good decisions.

Deliberation is also much more difficult over controversial and challenging issues, as many advocates are happy to admit.[28] Participation can leave people feeling humiliated and brow-beaten. People may be required to 'open up' in a way that they do not feel comfortable with. Many people do not react well when faced by opposing views: they find it very challenging, preferring to believe that most people agree with them. When faced by opposing views they can retreat into silence. Hibbing and Theiss-Morse conclude that deliberation 'in real-world settings tends to disempower the timid, quiet, and uneducated relative to the loquacious, extroverted and well schooled'.[29]

These potential limits to engagement should lead those who advocate engagement to pause. Those who are over-ambitious or overly optimistic about the prospects for engaging the vast bulk of people in politics need to think again. A politics for amateurs needs to offer opportunities to participate, but should not assume that they will be taken up. Politics tends to raise troubling, difficult and complex issues. Citizen engagement, and in particular deliberation, may not be the most appropriate or effective way of dealing with them.

Towards a Strategy of Engagement: Public and Civic Politics

Dimensions of Engagement

The point of this book is not to argue that people are apathetic so let's not expect them to engage in politics. Nor do I argue that people are far too irrational or ignorant to be trusted to engage. Many people remain interested in politics and most want to engage when they perceive that an issue directly affects them. The heart of democracy's appeal is the right to engage. However, I do not think that we can conclude that people are happily becoming critical and challenging citizens and that the loss of trust in the political system is a mere reflection of this more critical and challenging perspective. We should not be sanguine about the disenchantment in our democracies, we are not moving to an appropriately more robust phase in our political exchanges, escaping from an earlier era of deference. We need an active strategy for re-engaging people in politics, but one built on realistic premises and normative concerns about the range, quality and equality of the engagement.

The dimensions of citizen engagement that we should care about are identified in a work prepared by the American Political Science Association that examines the critical issues that are putting US democracy at risk.[30] The overall quantity of engagement is an issue. The legitimacy of the political system rests on participation, at least in some elements of the political process, being widely practised. Given the complexity of modern governance, citizen input is often not only required in the development phase of policies but also in the implementation phase. Environmental change, more healthy lifestyles and better education are all areas that require an input from both government and from the citizen if positive change is to be achieved. Political engagement does not always have to be intensive or deliberative, but it should not be uninformed and divisive, either. The quality of participation matters. How can we design into our systems an element of competition and challenge and at the same time allow scope for participation that binds people together and supports its overall legitimacy and health? Issues of equality are also important. We should be concerned if the evidence points to obstacles blocking particular groups from engagement – the poor; the less well educated; racial and ethnic minorities; or perhaps, in some societies, young people or women.

I have argued that we need to develop a realistic response and construct a politics for amateurs, and would-be reformers need to keep several principles in mind.[31] First reformers need to understand that effectively designed changes recognize the diversity of people's motivations. Institutional mechanisms can appeal to people's self-interest but also their sense of identity, what is right and what is socially appropriate. Second, as Bob Goodin argues, 'revisability is an important principle of institutional design':[32] institutions can learn by doing and adapt over time. Effective learning will not always occur, but we should build in a process of evaluation and reflection when changes are introduced. We need to observe the consequences of reform carefully to guard against undesirable outcomes, but we need also to recognize that good things occasionally happen by accident and unexpected positive lessons may emerge.

Third, in designing institutions the cognitive strengths and limitations of people need to be recognized. There is no point designing institutions that require super-human capacities for information-processing and analytical reasoning. We need to start from where citizens are, rather than premise our plans on the hope that a more noble and able citizen will automatically emerge. People use mental short-cuts to help them make decisions, and we need to design institutions that work with the grain of human behaviour rather than against it. We also need an ergonomic approach; we need ways of engaging in politics that are comfortable and easy to use, yet efficient and appropriate to meeting the challenges.[33]

Finally, we need to recognize that we can outline appropriate changes in terms of broad principles but their application requires another level of detailed analysis and understanding. History matters, and the context of past institutional forms needs to be taken into account.[34] So although Chapters 10 and 11 provide the outlines of a reform agenda, they are premised on this point. Although I provide some ideas and directions for reform, the practice and particular form of change will need to be appropriate to the circumstances of different countries.

Chapters 10 and 11 explore the institutional reforms, devices and contextual framing that may help to deliver a politics for amateurs. Chapter 10 is premised on the idea that we can do a great deal by revamping representative processes. Many collective decisions do not require direct democratic input and there is a need for a division of labour between a representative political process and more participative forms of engagement. Representative politics can do a lot better in making citizens believe that politics is being conducted in their name and with their interests in focus. Chapter 11 explores how the civic arena can be made supportive of a politics for amateurs. It notes the range of options that exist for engaging people in politics without expecting them to give up their lives to the endeavour, and it examines how the media and practices of civic education can be reformed to make a politics for amateurs both better informed and more sustainable.

10

Reviving Political Institutions

[T]he opposite of representation is not participation. The opposite of representation is exclusion. And the opposite of participation is abstention. Rather than opposing participation to representation, we should try to improve representative practices and forms to make them more open, effective, and fair. Representation is not an unfortunate compromise between an ideal of direct democracy and messy modern realities. Representation is crucial in constituting democratic practices.[1]

David Plotke

The bulk of this chapter is taken up with measures that will enable people to re-engage with representative politics. The divide between professional politicians and amateur voters is too great, and we need reforms that will give amateurs greater confidence in systems of representation and in their capacity to exercise influence through them. Representation involves an active exchange between citizen and representative.[2] Too often our thinking has been clouded by the minimalist understanding of representation outlined in Chapter 9, whereby all that matters for the citizen is the act of choosing their representative: once chosen, the representative acts and citizens are passive. But it should not be assumed that citizens are mere passive players. As David Plotke suggests, the divide between representative and participative democracy is not as great as some believe. If representation is going to be meaningful and powerful – to do its democratic job – it requires a sustained connection between the representative and those who are represented. Citizens should have the capacity for an active exchange with their representative, not just as supplicants looking for a helping hand to cope with a maze of government polices and services but as constituents whose interests the representative is there to represent.

Making representation work better is attractive because it meets a key challenge of a politics for amateurs: it enables citizens to wield influence through getting others to act on their behalf. A division of labour is a smart and obvious option with the representative doing the bulk of the work and the citizen made part of the process. The substantial benefit is decision making undertaken by those representatives that is informed and coherent and yet focused on the concerns of their constituents. That is what effective representation offers: the challenge is to make it so.

I assume here that representatives are more than delegates, there to follow the direct instructions of citizens, and that most citizens would favour representatives who exercised judgement. Survey and other evidence supports this contention but what is equally clear is that most people expect their representative to follow their constituents' preferences and interests.[3] People are clear that representative democracy should not be replaced by direct democracy and they appear to recognize that representation is a complex process. What they do want is to be communicated with and to be dealt with greater openness than occurs in established systems of democratic governance.

The great value of representation is that it enables politics to work for all without an intense input from all. As Mark Warren explains:

> Because individuals cannot attend to all the collective decisions that affect our lives, it follows that they must rely on the representations and judgements of others and do so with most issues, most of the time. The ideal circumstance for individuals would be a society that empowers and equips them to spend their participatory resources (their time, attention, interest and knowledge) on the issues most salient to them. But on most issues at any given time, individuals must trust others to participate on their behalf.[4]

If representation is made effective then people can focus on passively and sporadically monitoring rather than engaging with intensity at all times: in short, it is the ideal mechanism for delivering what the amateur political citizen wants. The challenge of doing it, however, is greater than ever in a globalized world with the complex layers of government.

The challenge is to get some system loyalty back into the political process and institutions. According to David Plotke, the key to effective representation is a system where representatives seek primarily to pursue their constituents' interests as defined by their expressed preferences. To deliver such a system requires 'expanding participation in representative forms; enhancing communication between representatives and constituents;

increasing effective participation by previously excluded or underrepresented groups; and increasing sites and modes of representation'.[5]

In the first section of the chapter I consider critically certain reforms that might be on other people's wish lists. I do not think that so-called 'sunshine' laws to give information about the decision making process should be pushed too far, nor do I think that new assembly or parliamentary procedures are necessarily the key to reform. The idea of making voting compulsory has some attractions, but many downsides. Nor do I think that attempts through gimmicks and campaigns to make registration and voting easier will necessarily work.

I next present a set of reform ideas that rest on getting representative politics right. There are three mainstream reform issues to consider: how to make elected politicians more socially representative; how to ensure that the highest ethical standards are observed by our elected representatives; and how to make elections more competitive. Attention then turns to three slightly more unconventional ideas for reform. First, I suggest some measures to enable a more effective style of communicating with citizens between elections. Second, I argue that we need to ensure that more of the representatives' time is spent more effectively. Third, we need to challenge citizen and lobby groups to demonstrate their claims to represent interests more effectively.

The chapter then moves on to consider reforms to the architecture of representation, to cope with the twin challenges of localism and globalization. I argue that democratic practice needs to move beyond a narrow focus on national institutions and become more effective locally and globally, and strategies for achieving these goals are outlined.

My agenda is radical in some respects, but I do not propose to create a new type of direct, deliberative or associational democracy, as promoted by others, although I do draw on elements of these alternative visions.[6] It is more important to get the processes of representation right than assume that people have the stamina or interest to engage in even more politics and political activity. I assume a territorially based representative political system – built around nation states – achieved through open and fair elections that provide the basis for decision making and a liberal constitutional framework that guarantees citizens' freedoms and rights. Again, this is fairly conventional: the aim is to make the existing institutions of democracy – those that triumphed at the end of the twentieth century – work better, rather than propose that we start all over again and abandon the core ideas of democratic governance. We need a representative politics that works, and is capable of working through a more complex architecture of governance.

The penultimate section of this chapter grapples with the issue of whether reform can be achieved. It deals with those who point out that institutional reform often goes wrong and does not deliver the promised benefits. It also recognizes that reforms often meet resistance because of the mobilization of interests who perceive them to be a threat. It explores the prospects of finding strong enough *change agents* – the people and forces to carry through contested reforms.

Making Representation Better

Reforms that Fail Fully to Convince

More 'sunshine laws' and other procedural reforms

Constitutional reformers quite commonly call for so-called 'sunshine laws' that ensure that citizens get the fullest information possible about not only policy and administrative issues but also about the processes of decision making undertaken by their representatives. I do not want to argue against the idea of basic freedom of information provisions in the laws of any country, as these are often important in enabling people to protect and assert their rights. However, I do not think that 'sunshine laws' aimed at exposing always and everywhere the processes of decision making are either realistic or desirable. Nor do I think that broadcasting – on TV or the web – of the work of assemblies or council chambers does, or will, make much difference. It is not undesirable, but it is likely to have no real effect. Another possibility is to consider reforms to parliamentary procedures to make them more open – by, for example, strengthening the hand of the assembly against the executive or more generally modernizing the way that parliaments work. There is much to commend these reforms, but I do not think they are likely to impact on the pivotal relationship between the citizen and the representative.

As John Hibbing and Elizabeth Theiss-Morse argue, 'we should not look to new ways of exposing people to every nook and cranny of the decision-making process as a solution to people's negative views of government. People do not need and do not want to be satiated in politics'.[7] Overloading citizens with information or access to decision making processes ignores the attraction of the division of labour that is provided by representative politics. From the citizen's viewpoint, somebody else – their elected representative – is taking the time and trouble to investigate the issues. Asymmetry of knowledge and information between representative and citizen is an inevitable result of this process and accountability becomes more difficult, but the citizen remains able to make a judgement about the representative. Having access to all information themselves, or having the opportunity to witness the process of decision making live on TV, rather defeats the purpose of this division of labour. Calls for open and public access to decision making are of limited value given the analysis of political disengagement offered in this book, virtues that command two rather than three cheers.

Making voting compulsory and lowering the voting age

Another reform option that is advocated – in the light of non-voting, in particular – is the suggestion that voting be made compulsory.[8] Compulsory voting would certainly increase turnout, although it is difficult to judge by how much. Compulsory voting is part of the established practice of democracies in Australia and Belgium, but introducing a system of compulsion for the first time in countries such as the UK, might be perceived as an imposition out of tune with the existing culture of politics. A determined non-voter could still avoid their 'civic duty' by failing to register themselves as a voter.

There have been some high-profile advocates of compulsory voting in political science. Arend Lipjhart used his position as president of the American Political Science Association in 1997 to push the idea.[9] The main argument appears to be that if everyone voted then representatives would have to be interested in the full cross-section of society, not just those who regularly vote. Compulsion would thus overcome inequalities in voter turnout. Young people might be drawn into politics more if the voting age were to be lowered to, say, 16 years and then required to vote as well. Shortage of space dictates that the difficult issues about when people become 'adults' and whether you need to be an adult to exercise your full democratic rights cannot be discussed here. Lowering the voting age would, however, not be on my list of top reforms.

Compulsion could be deemed an assault on individual freedom, although perhaps that criticism might be tempered if the voter were required to vote but allowed to spoil their ballot. My main objection is simply that it will do nothing to close the gap between representatives and citizens, and indeed runs the danger of encouraging representatives to believe that the problem has been solved. In a similar way, lowering the voting age would formally allow more to participate but a better relationship between representative and citizen would not automatically follow; what might emerge is an even wider and larger pool of alienated voters. Finally, it seems strange to insist that an alienated population participate; making somebody like something by forcing them to be involved in it has a certain authoritarian tone that sits uneasily with democratic ideals and strikes the wrong note compared to measures aimed at coaxing or encouraging participation.

Gimmicks and incentives to stimulate voting

What about giving people encouragement and incentives to vote? We could offer electronic voting, postal voting or voting in supermarkets. We could give people a holiday on voting days or arrange for it to take place on existing leisure days.[10] There is no harm in trying these methods if any issues of vote fraud can be managed effectively but it seems unlikely that such measures will ever make a truly reluctant elector vote. Some go further and suggest that voters could be given small financial incentives as a reward for voting.[11]

In any case, making voting more convenient is likely to solve only part of the problem. Lack of time to vote is a factor for many but there are deeper factors at work, as earlier chapters in this book indicated. This is not to argue against the development of easier and more 'modern' ways for people to vote but such measures for increasing turnout appear not to tackle the entire problem. The idea of providing financial incentives for people to vote smacks of desperation and does not address the fundamental problems of disaffection and alienation.

Three Mainstream Reforms

Social Representativeness

One school of thought sees representation as a relationship between citizen and representative in which the latter promises to deliver effective representation in return for the citizen's support. It does not really matter who the representative is, as long as they do their job effectively and can be removed by citizens if they fail to deliver. There has, however, always been another line of thought: that a representative assembly should be a microcosm of the wider society. The social characteristics of that society should at least find some reflection in the construction of an elected assembly.[12]

We know that we need to build up trust between elected representatives and citizens, and a strong case can be made for the argument that having more socially representative politicians could aid that process. In diverse communities – with a mix of ethnic groups – it would be better for the legitimacy of politics if a range of minorities found direct representation in the elected assembly. The case for social representativeness rests on recognizing that identity matters in developing trust: citizens have to feel that politicians represent *them*. Ensuring a full opportunity for women to take up positions as elected representatives and, more generally, for all to have equal access to positions of representation, positively expresses a commitment to political equality. The key issue is finding ways of enabling our political representatives to reflect the diversity of our societies without claiming in any sense that it would be possible or even desirable to move to a group of elected representatives that were a statistical representative sample of society. The measures that have to be undertaken include positive encouragement to women or other underrepresented candidates and measures to ensure that working conditions and the institutional environment of representative assemblies reflect the concerns of diverse groups in society. A concern with social representativeness is a way of making politics more engaging for all sections of society. People need to be able, to some extent, to identify with their representatives, and that is more likely if those representatives reflect the diversity of existing society.

Maintaining Ethical Standards[13]

Outright corruption, and the more general fear of being 'played for a sucker' by politicians that only look after their own interests, are barriers to an effective and trusting relationship between elected representatives and their voters. A key challenge for any democracy is to maintain an ethical environment around decision making. Ethics can be institutionalized and are not just an individual matter. The commonly espoused principles of public life – honesty, integrity, disclosure of interest, openness, fair dealing and accountability – cannot all be 'lived-out' by individuals acting alone. An individual cannot unilaterally decide to be accountable, for example, because they need others to hold them to account. Principles of good governance have to become everyday practice.

There are several organizational ingredients to building an ethical environment. First, leadership matters. An ethical environment may make particular demands of leaders by virtue of their having a higher profile and specific powers. Leaders can set the tone for ethical behaviour in their organizations by encouraging compliance with ethical rules.

Transparency in government is also vital to sustaining an ethical framework. Mechanisms designed to allow greater transparency include the registration of interests and gifts and the recording of external interests and sponsorship received by representatives, intended to allow the identification of undeclared conflicts of interest. Some support for 'whistle blowers' who reveal wrong-doing and a commitment to 'freedom of information' can act to provide generic support for organizational openness. Transparency also facilitates after-the-event examination of decisions and decision making processes, making it easier to both attribute (positive or negative) responsibility and to learn from past problems and successes. Second, greater transparency, by allowing this backward-looking scrutiny, can act as an incentive for individuals to behave in an ethical manner. Third, people may be more likely to behave in a principled manner when they are subject to public oversight, not just because they have a self-interest in not wanting to get caught behaving badly but also because they are reminded that they are there to serve the public.

The focus on transparency needs to be balanced against other considerations. There may be tensions between the institutional mechanisms for openness and the perceived reality of political life. The leadership of an organization may have genuine concerns about the distortion and partial use of information by people or groups, or may worry that the wider public will misunderstand policy issues. Formal openness may also prevent people at the top of an organization from properly and comprehensively considering all the options for a controversial policy decision.

Leadership and transparency mechanisms often need to be joined by a commitment to independent oversight. Independent monitoring and support for ethical behaviour is essential for underwriting ethical standards. Those that do audits benefit from being seen as independent and impartial and such qualities make the process of audit more plausible to the general public.

Competitive Elections

The value of representative politics is lost if citizens do not feel that their vote counts in some way: the political amateur needs to believe that voting makes a difference. We need electoral systems that help to create a healthy relationship between elector and political representative.

Electoral systems vary considerably throughout the democratic world, and are generally composed of three elements.[14] The first is the size and construction of *electoral units*, since most elections in a territory (local, regional, national, or international) rest on administrative divisions within it. The second reflects the *choice* given to voters. It is categorical – that is, do they choose between either one candidate or party or another? Or is the system ordinal, in which voters rank their preferences for candidates? The third and final building block of an election system reflects the way of translating votes cast into *seats*. We therefore have three broad families: the *single-member plurality* system, where the candidate with the largest number of votes in an electoral unit wins; the *majoritarian* system, where the candidate must get an overall majority of voter support to win the seat; and finally various forms of *proportional* system, where the emphasis is on getting the overall numbers of seats for parities and candidates to reflect their share of the votes cast.

Difficulties with any one of these elements of an electoral system can undermine the competitiveness of an electoral system. As Stephen Macedo and his colleagues[15] point out, the US practice of regularly redrawing the boundaries of electoral districts has created too many seats where the elections are not competitive and the incumbent has a strong advantage. This deters people from bothering to vote. Lack of choice over candidates or parties may similarly deter people from engaging as they may feel that that the subtlety of their preferences is not being respected. Party list systems of proportional representation are often criticized on the same grounds. Finally, the choice of electoral system can make a difference. Single-member plurality systems, such as that used in Britain's general election, can mean that for many seats the result is virtually a foregone conclusion as, given the make-up of the voters and the history of their voting habits, one party or candidate is overwhelmingly likely to have more votes cast than the others. Campaigning becomes narrowly focused on those seats where the result is more uncertain. For many in Britain, election campaigns no longer involve the experience of local campaigning and mobilization. Systems that rest on proportionality competitiveness can be rendered point-less if the coalition-building that takes place after the election means that the issues over which a party won support may be set aside in order to reach or sustain a deal with coalition partners. Systemwide competitiveness can be lost if one small party keeps itself in government for a long time by join-ing coalitions formed by larger parties.

In the end, there are normative choices to be made about what outcomes to value from an electoral system. Some emphasize that a voting system should make all votes count by ensuring the strongest possible correlation between votes cast for a party and seats allocated to that party; others argue that voters value stable government more than anything else and that voting systems that are slightly less proportional in allocating votes and seats might be attractive if they delivered strong government. Counter-claims about the virtues of different systems abound; for the present, let us look at mecha-nisms that might deliver more competiveness because it is difficult other-wise to see how citizens can feel that voting makes a difference.

Adaptations to existing electoral systems might help. Macedo and his colleagues suggest that a combination of more independent control over the construction of electoral units, a shorter timetable for presidential primaries and elections and a shift in the pattern of allocating college votes to give presidential candidates more incentives to campaign everywhere, combined with better polling-day organization, might increase competition and US voter participation.

The case for a change to make the system more competitive in Britain's general elections is substantial. A more proportional system, if properly designed, could deliver the crucial shift to a system where parties were encouraged to campaign vigorously everywhere and in which all electors could see that their votes counted.[16] A changed voting system is no panacea, and it is implausible to suggest that any one system could 'cure' the problem of political disengagement. But if getting citizens to take representative politics seriously matters then some reform of the electoral system to deliver competition should be part of a UK package of reform.

Above all, we need electoral systems that encourage candidates and parties to engage citizens more directly. Donald Green and Alan Gerber[17] have launched a number of experiments directed towards persuading people to get out and vote. In a number of studies using random assignment of an intervention (including for example leaflet delivery, phone calls and personal contact), they have shown that personal contact has the greatest impact in encouraging people to be active. In particular, contacting people by canvassing or by telephone can have an effect, although the former may have more impact than the latter. The core of the experimental method is to assign the voters randomly to 'treatment' and 'non-treatment' groups, which allows the researchers to observe whether an intervention raises turnout in a group that is identical in all other observed respects to the one where there is no intervention. A repeat of this type of experiment in the UK by Peter John also found that telephone canvassing or a personal call to the home by an independent, non-partisan organization can raise turnout by about 7 per cent.[18] At the heart of all these experiments is the view that people can be mobilized to engage. We need an electoral system that is sufficiently competitive, in as many electoral seats as possible, to encourage political parties and candidates to build contact with the voters.

Three Unconventional Reforms

Conversational Democracy through ICT

Reinvigorating representative democracy requires the construction of a stronger relationship between representatives and citizens once they are elected. As Stephen Coleman[19] argues, the public need to have the opportunity for a 'sustained conversation' with their representatives, not just an occasional burst of canvassing or consultation. This conversation would reveal issues of concern to the public and give representatives a chance to render an account of their actions (or inactions). Although some representatives attempt to establish such a dialogue – through surgeries, question times and newsletters – in general this has not happened.

Developing a more conversational style in representation is partly also a matter of commitment and learning new skills on the part of representatives, but it also could be facilitated by the digital technology and information communication technology (ICT). Using technology for making representation more effective is more attractive because it allows citizens still to remain as citizens rather than ultra-activists and the argument here is not about the simple right to email your representative or watch webcasts of them in action. It is to recognize that the *interactivity* built into ICT opens up unprecedented opportunities for elected representatives to construct a conversation with the public:

> As relatively inexpensive and increasingly convergent media technologies have become accessible, and the rigid division between producer and audience evaporates, opportunities for self-representation, such as blogging or making videos and distributing them via mobile phone, become more realistic . . . Citizens tend to be more innovative and sophisticated in their use of ICT than the politicians who represent them. The danger for the political class is the emergence of a subterranean sphere of discourse from which they are excluded.[20]

Politicians need to recognize that the terms of political communication can be rethought and restructured in a digital age. By developing a more extensive conversation, representatives could begin to deliver that sense of 'connection' that is so often absent from current political practice.

However, getting the practice right is going to be a hard challenge. A study of some initial blogging sites established by British politicians suggests that while they may excite the occasional interest of a journalist they are not attracting a great deal of engagement from ordinary citizens. Ross Ferguson and Barry Griffiths found after testing blogs against the opinions of cross-sections of the public that most 'did not find the content or the bloggers engaging, and while they could envisage the technology's potential to stimulate greater political engagement, their experience of the sample blogs was disappointing'.[21]

Re-engineering Representative Politics

Representatives could also take a long and hard look at the way they spend their time. In the public and private sector, people talk about business process re-engineering (BPR). What is involved is a breakdown of a production or service process into its component parts to see if the connections are right and if their efficiency could be improved by changing ways of working. Applied to political representatives, the questions would be: how do they spend their time performing their role, and are there tasks that they could do more effectively? It is difficult to imagine that such a process would not reveal more opportunities for representatives to spend more time focused on building connections with their constituent representatives than they do at the moment.

A Representativeness Challenge to Campaign and Civic Groups

Some of the campaign and civic organizations that claim to represent us need to be a little more aware of how good or effective their own processes on internal democracy actually are. The onus should be on some of the major civic organizations to demonstrate that they actually do consult and reach out to their own members.

A New Architecture of Multi-Level Governance

The future of democratic governance institutions rests on building a more complex, multi-level architecture for decision making in which citizens can be engaged. Several of the conventional features of democratic governance remain essential: the protection of fundamental citizen rights and freedom of organization and assembly for groups and individuals. But we need different answers to two fundamental questions: what are the institutional building blocks in which to practice democracy, and what is the nature of accountability? The conventional answer to these two questions sees the nation state, national assemblies and national government as the ultimate building blocks of democracy and accountability, as led by elected representatives being held to account by their electorates. This one-dimensional 'top-down' view of democracy is not sufficient when we think about making democracy work in our modern complex societies.

Complexity is inevitable because of the range of activities in which governments and public services are now engaged.[22] Many organizations are involved in delivery, not all of them are formally part of the public sector. Decisions are made by an array of institutions that might be held formally accountable through the nation state in some way but in many respects are autonomous and powerful decision makers in their own right.

Complexity also reflects the sheer technical difficulty of what we now attempt to do in the public sphere. We have moved in advanced industrial democracies from 'hard-wiring' challenges to a concern with 'soft-wiring' society. It is hard enough to build schools, roads and hospitals and ensure the supply of clean water, gas, electricity and all the other requirements of modern life ('hard-wiring'). It is harder still when what we are trying to do is about 'soft wiring': getting healthier communities, ensuring that children from their early years get the right stimulation and the right environment in which to grow and develop, finding ways in which our economy can grow in a way that meets the challenges of globalization and the need for sustainability. The challenge of governance requires a different form of organization and accountability in the light of these 'soft-wiring' challenges.

There are also major complexities around jurisdiction and who should be involved in a decision.[23] What happens to rainforests in Brazil matters to people in that region and nation, but also to many beyond the borders of the individual nation state. When US-based companies such as Microsoft change the way they work this can have profound economic implications for others. Can these decisions be solely the responsibility of an individual nation state? Issues such as global climate warming require action beyond the nation state. Globalization and the forces of global economic change, discussed in Chapter 3, have changed the landscape of decision making. Many seemingly 'domestic' issues are now global, and the need for international and global cooperation concerning major issues confronting humanity is now paramount.

Accountability cannot any longer easily be captured within the boundaries of a nation state: it needs a multi-dimensional character and also a more flexible exchange between governors and governed. Accountability can be about kicking out leaders that fail, but it also needs to get governors to give reasons for their actions. The lines of accountability are multiple and overlapping, and do not all lead back to a single small collective group of political leaders to be held accountable for their failures and limitations. In our modern complex world, more subtle and varied forms of accountability are required.

We do not need to change our fundamental understanding of democracy in the light of these complexities, but we do need to shift the pattern of our engagement with political institutions. The essence of the democratic creed – that those affected by a decision should have a right to have a say in that decision either directly or indirectly through elected representatives – remains in place. What becomes a lot more challenging is deciding who is affected by a decision, and how and at what level they can exercise influence over it. David Held offers a general solution:

> The principle of inclusiveness and subsidiarity points to the necessity of both the decentralization *and* the centralization of political power. If decision-making is decentralized as much as possible, it maximizes the opportunity of each person to influence social conditions that shape his or her life. But if the decisions at issue are translocal, transnational or transregional, then political institutions need not only to be locally based but also have a wider scope of operation.[24]

The future is one of *multi-level governance*. Nations states and their associated democratic institutions will remain important, but there needs to be a greater capacity for democratic input into decisions both at the local and at the global level.

The Case for a New Localism

Democracy must have a strong local dimension; the sole institution of democracy is no longer the nation state. This commitment to 'new localism' can be characterized as a strategy aimed at devolving power and resources towards front-line managers, local democratic structures and local consumers and communities,[25] and the case for it rests on three grounds. First, it is a realistic response to the complexity of modern governance: only through more local decision making capacity can local knowledge and action be connected to a wider network of support and learning. We can then get solutions designed for diverse and complex circumstances.

Second, it provides an open base for engagement in politics. 'Local' in this case means a territorial-based unit in a neighbourhood or community, but it also refers to a more functional base around an issue such as crime prevention or park management that finds expression in local organization. The advocacy of the local is not premised on giving a strong role to formal elected local government institutions, although in many cases that may be appropriate. It is also about viewing the local as providing a wide range of sites where people can engage. The role of formally elected local government becomes an enabler and supporter of a wide range of local institutions of governance.

Finally, the new localism enables the dimensions of trust, empathy and social capital to be fostered. The essential insight of the social capital theory, which was discussed in Chapter 3, is that the quality of social relations makes a difference to the achievement of effective outcomes when a complex exchange of ideas and the coordination of a variety of actors is involved. To come to a judgement about the use of open space in a community, or to take on a project to clean up the local environment requires effective networks of information flow, trust and some shared norms. Local or community governance can deliver that capacity and help to meet challenges that 'top-down' government simply lacks the strength of social relations to deliver.

There are two common grounds for objecting to local decision making. One argument is that the perspective of communities is inherently limited and limiting. Too much local decision making can open up too much decision making to the parochial concerns of narrow-minded individuals and threatens the ideas and practice of a wider welfare politics. Behind the romantic notion of community lurks a real world of insular, 'not in my own back yard' (NIMBY) politics. Most forms of progressive politics may need a wider canvass than local politics can provide.

The 'new' localism advocated in this chapter is crucially set in the context of a wider system of multi-level governance. There is nothing in the 'new' localism that automatically makes local politics devoid of the tensions that characterize politics at other levels: conflict between interests and their resolution remains at the heart of politics, wherever it is conducted. 'New' localism does not imply a sort of romantic faith in communities to come up with solutions for the common good, and nor is it incompatible with a redistribution of resources provided through higher levels of government.

The argument for 'new' localism is one for a shift in the balance of governance, one that allows more scope for local decision making and local communities. It is premised on the idea that involving people in the hard, rationing choices of politics in a shared sense of citizenship can deliver a more mature and sustainable democracy. Meeting the challenge of equity does not mean treating all communities or individuals the same, but rather it involves tailoring solutions to meet particular needs. 'New' localism can play a part in ensuring that the tailoring process succeeds and is responsive to local needs and circumstances.

A second objection to the kind of localism advocated here is that there is a need for interventions to address the inequalities faced by particular communities. To tackle inequality requires national or even international intervention, and creating more scope for local decision making simply helps to foster (or even reinforce) existing inequalities: rich areas will stay rich and poor areas will be allowed the freedom to spend non-existent resources on addressing the problems they confront. The vision of 'new' localism needs to be carefully specified in a way that recognizes both diversity in communities and a concern with equity issues. The argument is about a central and growing role for local involvement in decision making about the public services and the public realm as part of a wider system of multi-level governance.

It is difficult to develop detailed proposals here for what such local governance should look like. Local devolved institutions need to build around an often complex and layered sense of identity: we need a local government system that enables us to act in our neighbourhoods and that has the strategic capacity to frame our local response to globalization.[26]

A Better Global Governance?

It is not possible to talk in any meaningful sense of the creation of a 'global civil society', notwithstanding growing evidence of protest and NGO activism at the global level, as discussed in Chapter 6. The starting point is to think about the possibility of a better set of global political institutions and then how democratic governance can be made more effective through the practice of those institutions.

As David Held[27] points out, problem solving at the global level is beset with difficulties. First, the existing institutions of global governance are fragmented, have mandates that frequently compete. The goals of the World Bank in terms of health and social policies are not the same as those of the World Health Organization (WHO) or the UN's UNESCO organization or the International Labour Organization (ILO), for example. The G7 group of advanced industrial economies might be clear about its economic and social aims, but they are often very different from those of the G77, the coalition of southern developing states. Global institutions, secondly, often have an 'inability to mount collective problem-solving solutions faced with disagreement over means, objectives, costs and so on.'[28] A third major difficulty is the accountability deficit surrounding the institutions and the scale of power imbalances between both nation states and states and non-state organizations.

Given the scale of these difficulties, it is not possible to imagine short term simple solutions. But, as Held suggests, the reform agenda has to grapple with each of these challenges. We need to encourage more effective and coordinated international organizations, to develop the capacity to act more effectively and globally and we need rules that give all stakeholders a locked-in function in the decision making process.

This large-scale reform agenda could be joined by a range of more pragmatic reforms aimed at making the prospects for democratic governance on the global scale more than just a daydream. As Jan Aart Scholte argues, a number of initiatives could make democracy more viable.[29] The first is to engage in public education, because if citizens are uncertain about the institutions of democracy at local and national levels they are largely ignorant of what the institutional framework and pressure points at the global level are. Second, and connected to this, there could be more transparency in the way that these organizations work through the provision of clear and accessible information. National parliaments and assemblies could debate and scrutinize the actions of global institutions more thoroughly and effectively than they do. More support could be provided to civil society organizations so that they could speak more effectively concerning a full range of global interests. Scholte concludes that 'a number of eminently feasible measures are available to bring greater public participation and accountability to the regulation of transplanetary affairs'.[30]

The Prospects for Reform

This chapter has opened up a discussion about a range of reforms. Some argue that designing better political institutions is a 'mission impossible' because it is not feasible to establish any clear understanding of cause and effect between intervention and outcome in order to guide our judgements. Moreover even if the design challenge is met, forces of resistance to change are likely to be encountered.

Albert Hirschman[31] reminds us that opponents of change tend to frame their arguments along set lines. Sometimes they claim that any change will jeopardise key valued elements of existing arrangements. At other times they argue that the reforms will be futile; they will not achieve their stated purposes. Finally they argue that the reforms will have perverse, unintended consequences.

The first argument is a useful reminder that any process of institutional design for governance is unlikely to start with a blank sheet and has to meet the challenge of being better than the existing system. We can perhaps be confident that reform, if done well, will preserve what is good in the current system and move us on to a better level of democratic practice. More troubling are last two arguments, because they suggest that whatever we do, it won't work and could even make things worse. But is that fair?

There are certainly good grounds for doubting whether intentional institutional change can be easily achieved. The connection between designers' intentions and outcomes is rarely straightforward.[32] First, the designers of change may not be clear in their thinking or objectives. Research and evidence shows that reorganizations can often be muddled and not well thought through, and may be undermined by short-term thinking.

A second issue is that there is often likely to be a substantial temporal gap between the design of an institution and any reward its designers may receive for its effective operation. Institutional change takes time to work its way through, yet designers remain keen to bind their successors. Long-term potential benefits are often argued for on the basis of short-term planning and time horizons.

It is also often argued that institutional effects cannot be anticipated, and are generally unpredictable. There are in fact some who define political studies as driven by the 'sour law of unintended consequences'.[33] The world changes, but never quite as we intended, and change is inherently unpredictable. Moreover, short-term and long-term effects may take very different paths.

You may, at this stage, be thinking that reform is a type of complicated accident. Bob Goodin[34] suggests change can appear to happen almost by accident: events, and therefore institutional developments, are a matter of *contingency*. Something happens simply because the circumstances and situation were right to make it happen. Generally speaking, we would be well advised not simply to settle for creating the conditions for a sustainable democracy by accident.

Can we rely on evolution? Using a biological analogy, change occurs, institutions adapt and the most effective or efficient mechanisms are selected because they have a better fit with the environment. As Goodin[35] comments, many changes have occurred along these lines. It is undoubtedly true that there is a perception in both established and newer democracies that better ways of doing things have evolved over time. The traditional way of 'doing democracy' can be enabling; it can also be a blockage to effective modern democratic practice. Institutions such as political parties may have served a purpose, but be now past their 'sell by date', as Chapter 6 suggested. From an evolutionary perspective, it appears that some of our selection mechanisms have not been sufficiently sharp to cull practices that may have made sense in the past but make little sense now – many would say that the UK House of Lords was a prime example. We would clearly be wise to not entirely rely on evolution to deliver us the institutions we need for the twenty-first century.

The irresponsibility of leaving reform to accident or evolution brings us back to intentionally designing better institutions. Change can be put in place by individuals or organized groups in a planned and rational way. Reformers identify a problem and then define a solution and give it institutional expression. The idea that we can design our way to better democratic institutions is not universally accepted, but institutions can be modified and enhanced and designers can find better processes and procedures. Drawing lessons from earlier mistakes is always possible.

Yet even if the design challenge is met, reforms often meet resistance. The perceived loss of power that some reforms imply means that those that hold power will refuse to accept change. A key lesson for reformers is thus to organize alliances and coalitions of support for change.

The seeds of resistance, however, may reflect forces deeper than simple calculations of self-interest. A deeply ingrained sense of legitimacy can surround current political arrangements.[36] Resisters often ask: how can you think about changing the way our established political institutions work given their long democratic history?

Institutions, however, are not permanent and are always in a potential state of flux. They achieve stability through the processes of influencing the way their members think and act. But these are human processes: surprise and shocks can drive change. Politicians may think they are doing a good job but eventually it dawns on them – when no one else agrees – that they are not. The constant drip, drip of such challenges can turn people in an organization from one way of understanding to other, stimulating radical change.

Conclusions

Probably the most important lesson in achieving change is to be clear about your aims. The most crucial challenge is the promotion of political institutions and mechanisms that will enable citizens to experience a greater engagement with the political process, the conditions for a 'politics for amateurs'.

My solution to the problem of disenchantment with politics is thus deceptively simple. We need to change our political institutions to 'give people more opportunities to have a say about the issues they care about'. The phrase to 'have a say' carries with it a message: for most people, having a veto or being the final judge is not what they want. As amateurs, citizens are cautious about claiming decision taking responsibility. 'Having a say' means wanting to influence, but not having to decide, which is why getting representative politics to work better, at a range of levels in challenging circumstances from the local through to the global, is so important.

In most democracies, the challenge of making representative politics work better will have to be met by political parties and citizen groups. Both are potential sources of resistance to the reforms outlined in this chapter, but equally they could be supporters and catalysts for the changes envisaged. It is difficult to see politics existing without such intermediary institutions – a loose coalition of protest organizations cannot fill the vacuum. Given their pre-eminence in making democratic politics work, it would be a great challenge to construct a reform momentum without the cooperation and engagement of high-intensity activists. Reframing parties and the citizen lobby seems the most desirable way forward, but key players in those organizations need to be responsive to change. We need to 'open out' politics and we need sufficient activists in parties and citizen lobby organizations to commit to reforming our institutions and the wider elements of representative politics in order to deliver an attractive and viable future.

11
Creating a New Civic Arena

> What is meant by civil society . . . is not always clear . . . It is an arena of associations, of individual and community agency . . . there is agreement, in a broad sense, that it comprises socio-political institutions, voluntary associations and a public sphere within which people can debate, act and engage with each other . . . Civil society is crucial for democracy because it is the space between the public and private spheres where civic action takes place.[1]
>
> Jean Grugel, *Democratization*

Jean Grugel's rather tentative definition of the civic arena nevertheless provides a valuable launching point for this chapter, because it reminds us that making democracy work is not just a matter of tinkering with political institutions; it also involves strengthening the *civic base* for politics. Creating the conditions for a politics for amateurs is not just about reviving formal political institutions; it is also about taking seriously the idea that it is not just politics that needs to change but also the *environment* in which citizens operate. This chapter is not about to provide moral exhortations about the need for us all to improve our behaviour and get active, or offer romantic visions of how communities can learn to live with one another in harmony.[2] My understanding of how to create a new civic arena is more pragmatic and practical in its focus and premised on the idea that it is faulty design rather than faulty citizens that has created the political problems that we face.[3] The three sections of the chapter suggest some particular ways in which we can 'open up' processes of citizen engagement, encourage civicness and voluntary activity and enhance the institutional context for information exchange and debate.

The first set of reforms is premised on the idea of an ergonomic approach to politics. We need ways of getting people more directly involved in policy making and implementation without at the same time expecting them to give up their lives and become professional politicians. Five new types of citizen engagement are outlined, from better forms of consultation to advances in e-democracy. The second set of reforms rests on the idea that getting people to be civically active, even if that activity is not directed at political engagement, is a good thing in itself in that it delivers immediate benefits but may also have a wider value in building a sense of a *capacity to act* among a wide groups of citizens. The third set of reforms is premised on the idea that a free flow of information and understanding are essential to the operation of democratic politics; it examines the role of the media and prospects for civic education.

New Forms of Citizen Engagement

How can we directly engage citizens in the construction and implementation of public policy? In work with colleagues from De Montfort University, I have shown how the variety of officially sponsored forms of citizen engagement has expanded considerably in recent years.[4] An excellent pamphlet by Graham Smith takes the argument a stage further. He shows how there has been innovation in forms of public engagement worldwide and offers the following categorization for these schemes: consultative, deliberative, co-governance, direct and e-democracy schemes.[5] It is worth looking at each method in a little more detail, and it is also valuable to focus on some examples of effective practice from several countries. After the discussion of the five techniques of engagement I will briefly discuss the strengths and limitations of these new forms of civic engagement.

Consultative Innovations

These approaches aim to inform decision makers of citizens' views and at their best use a combination of methods to explore public opinion. The range of methods stretches from public meetings to web-based consultation. Innovation comes in finding new ways of putting these consultation methods together to ensure that the widest range of public opinion is heard. The trick is to recognize that some mechanisms – like a public forum – are attractive to some citizens but not to others who find the idea of public speaking, for example, daunting. Mechanisms such as on-line consultation or surveys of public opinion can, however, ensure that a wider range of voices are heard.

An interesting case study is provided from the UK.[6] Following public hostility to the introduction of genetically modified (GM) foods and crops in Britain, a government advisory body, the Agriculture and Environment

Biotechnology Commission, was influential in persuading the government of the need for a widespread public debate on the future of GM technology. An independent steering committee was established to oversee the programme and developed an innovative approach to consultation that included:

(1)   Nine foundation regionally based discussion workshops, eight of which recruited members of the public representing different stages of life and two broad socio-economic groups. The ninth workshop involved participants 'actively involved' in the GM debate.

(2)   Some 675 regional and local community open meetings, many of which were stimulated by a specially made film and other materials. Participants completed a questionnaire, the results of which were collated nationally.

(3)   A series of ten closed-focus groups involving a total of seventy-seven citizens (chosen to represent different stages of life and socio-economic groups) to provide more structured analysis of issues and to act as a control to compare with the results of the local meetings.

(4)   Background material and a questionnaire, available by post or on the internet for citizens who were unable to attend local meetings. The website received over 2.9 million hits and 24,609 unique visitors, 60 per cent of whom submitted feedback forms. In total 36,557 feedback forms were returned and analysed. The results of the debate conclusively showed the general unease about GM crops and food among the public, with little support for early commercialization of GM crops in the UK.

Another example of using a combination of consultative methods is provided by a study of large-scale initiatives in three US cities, Eugene (Oregon), Sacramento (California) and Fort Collins (Colorado). Research showed how public consultation could have an input into local government policy towards community issues.[7] Eugene and Fort Collins are of similar size and are relatively wealthy college cities. Sacramento, with a population of 400,000, over three times larger than the other two cities, is racially and ethnically diverse, with nearly 25 per cent of the adult population educated below high-school standard. Eugene's and Sacramento's debates concentrated on the relationship between public services and the willingness to pay for them. Eugene alongside Fort Collin focused on how the communities would like their cities to develop over the next decade. Throughout the initiatives a mixture of telephone and questionnaire survey techniques were used, along with participatory workshops and deliberative processes, and the results were fed into local government processes. Although community responses were lower in Sacramento, all the initiatives had significant and positive effects on local government decisions in each city.

What these varied forms of engagement show is that, with a little imagination and commitment, political leaders and officials can get beyond viewing consultation as a routine exercise of sending out a leaflet that will often remain unread or calling a public meeting that will be sparsely attended. The range of consultation techniques and the capacity to reach out to access groups are such that no government can hide behind the claim that they consulted and nobody was interested. What is required is the commitment and intelligence to design consultation techniques suited to the decision at hand.

Deliberative Innovations

The aim with these mechanisms is not just to consult, but to get citizens to deliberate and reflect on issues in the hope that the outcomes will influence policy makers. The emphasis is on enabling a cross-section of citizens to have the time and opportunity to reflect on an issue by gathering opinion and information in order to come to a judgment about an issue. Deliberative techniques can be used in some instances to go further, and offer a statistically valid, representative sample of the population. However one constraint on this form of engagement is that it can directly involve only a limited number of people in its most intensive forms. One option is to use the internet to expand the range and scope of those engaged in deliberation; another option is to run alongside a deliberative mechanism something to test the ideas that emerge on a wider body of public opinion. Deliberation can also be targeted on groups and interests that might not generally engage in political discussion; a well-designed deliberative forum suited to the circumstances, style and culture of different groups can bring out opinions that would otherwise be hidden in more formal or mainstream settings. A further strength of this mechanism is that it allows citizens to explore and extend their engagement skills. One of the most common findings about this deliberative form of engagement is that participants often gain a lot in terms of a sense of their own political capacities.

The case study that illustrates this form of mechanism comes from British Columbia (Canada), where The Citizens' Assembly was established in 2004.[8] Over eleven months, 160 citizens (two citizens from each electoral district in British Columbia, plus two Aboriginal citizens) were given the task of reviewing the province's electoral system. The Citizens' Assembly was charged with producing a report and from the start of the exercise the government of British Columbia had committed itself to a popular referendum based on the Assembly's recommendations. The final report made a strong case for a proportional system of election, using a single-transferable-vote system. When the vote was put to the electorate of British Columbia in May 2005 a majority (57.69 per cent) favoured the reform but that was not sufficient to get over the threshold of 60 per cent in favour needed for the proposed reform to pass.[9] The deliberation efforts thus achieved no change to the voting system yet, as Graham Smith concludes:

> The main lesson that can be drawn from this experiment is that it provides evidence that citizens are willing and able to deliberate on controversial policy issues and to provide a reasoned decision. The Assembly was carefully designed to ensure that citizens were able to learn about the issue, receive evidence from the wider population and interest groups and deliberate effectively amongst themselves.[10]

Nothing guarantees success when it comes to political change, but the initiative did show that citizens could engage in an intensive and complex form of deliberation.

Deliberative forums can operate in slightly more relaxed and informal ways than the procedures followed in the Canadian case. Some, rather than seeking to get a clear view of a whole society's perspective on an issue, try to 'open out' the opportunities for particular sections of a society to find a voice. One interesting example is the Hip Hop Summit Action Network (HSAN) founded in 2001, that uses Hip Hop music as a vehicle to address both problems in society and the needs of vulnerable young people at risk, while initiating deliberation and youth action. The network is a non-profit, non-partisan grouping of artists, youth workers, the music industry and those involved with education and civil rights. HSAN receives external funding from a number of organizations and has held large summits in nine US cities including New York, Los Angeles and Miami which have been well attended by the young and numerous high-profile figures in the industry. One held in Detroit, where the population is predominantly black, received extensive backing from the city's Mayor, the 32-year-old Kwame Kilpatrick. Although criticized by some for his enthusiasm for such a project he has received a lot of support for his efforts, from both observers and the young community he is trying to reach. In the most recent mayoral race, voting turnout of 18- to 40-year-olds increased by 40 per cent.[11]

Deliberative techniques in their more developed and formal forms offer an opportunity for intense engagement by a few. They address issues about the quality of citizen engagement by giving an opportunity for more informed and reflective activity. They can involve testing ideas out in a survey of a representative sample of the population[12] or going further still and putting the judgement of the smaller deliberative group to the whole electorate, as occurred in British Columbia. In providing an informal gathering point for often excluded or unheard voices deliberative techniques are also valuable, because they address issues of inequality of access to engagement. They are not a panacea leading to a new form of decision making, in that they are largely reliant on other arenas for the final decision to be made, but they provide a useful and varied tool for engagement.

Co-Governance Innovations

Co-governance arrangements aim to give citizens significant influence during the process of decision making, particularly when it comes to issues of distribution of public spending and service implementation. Whereas deliberation initiatives tend to be focused on the *design* of programmes and policies and allow citizens to propose changes, co-governance schemes encourage citizens to share power with elected decision makers and take responsibility for making *choices* about what to do in their communities. Co-governance arrangements tend not to simply provide one-off opportunities to engage citizens but on-going opportunities to take part in decision making.

Participatory Budgeting (PB) provides a good illustration of the type of engagement that is involved in co-governance. PB started its existence in Porto Alegre (Brazil) in the late 1980s but by 2004 it was estimated that over 250 cities or municipalities practised some version of it.[13] The essence of PB rests on an annual opportunity for citizens to engage in the process of public spending decision making in their neighbourhoods, and more broadly their locality.

The mechanisms of the PB in Porto Alegre are clear, though complex and original.[14] There is a cycle of three types of PB meetings annually – regional and thematic citizen meeting, forums of regional delegates and the budget council (the COP). The first round of citizen plenary meetings, held in each of the sixteen regions of the city, takes place in March. These meetings focus on the previous year's spending. Government officials, flanked by citizens' delegates, explain the timing and quality of the delivery of the actions agreed by the neighbourhood the year before. Has it gone according to plan? This first plenary in the year also elects regional delegates for the next stage in the process: the delegates' forums, at which each region will establish its priorities. In addition, this first meeting elects two city delegates to be members of the COP.

Before the regional delegates take decisions about regional priorities, they meet with their groups to seek out their views on areas such as road-building, schools, health provision, sewerage, economic development including cooperatives and leisure and sports facilities. The regional delegates meet together monthly, or more often, to work out the proposed priorities for the region. The delegates then gather together at the delegates' forum, where they work out budget priorities by combining two objective criteria (population size and statistically measured need) with one subjective criterion (the priority given to different issues by the community). They apply a weighting system so that quantitative weights can be given to different areas of investment. The same criteria are applied across the city. This weighting system, sometimes known as the 'budget matrix', plays a crucial role in creating awareness of the needs of both the different regions and of the city as a whole.

The municipal government also holds citizen meetings, bringing together people from across the city with a common interest: common themes are education, health, culture and economics. These important thematic meetings also elect delegates to the COP, which starts work in July or August. The COP is a powerful body that negotiates the final investment priorities for the city on the basis of input from the regions and the thematic groups. In addition, it considers some projects proposed by the government itself. Through an open process of negotiation and reporting back, the COP draws up the overall budget and puts it to the mayor and municipal council for final agreement.

PB thus provides a powerful example of co-governance, because citizens are drawn into a process of agenda- and priority-setting. As Graham Smith comments:

> Perhaps the most interesting lesson that can be drawn from PB is the way in which it gives citizens an incentive to participate. First, levels of participation have an effect on the probability of investment – not only do citizens choose their own neighbourhood priorities, but they also elect representatives who decide on budget allocation – the number of representatives is related to levels of participation in local forums. Second, PB started small, with investments where return was quick and visible. Thus neighbourhoods who did not initially participate were able to see that participation could lead to investment. PB offers a clear response to the question 'why participate?'[15].

Participatory budgeting is no longer just a trendy idea but a sustained practice in a number of localities. There is a need for commitment from both citizens and public authorities for the process to work; allocating monies and budgets is plainly an area where it is possible to build engagement even among relatively disadvantaged or disengaged citizens. Being involved in decisions that make a difference is an offer that many citizens can be attracted by.

One more illustration brings home how co-governance can capture people's imagination and commitment.[16] Kerala is one the poorest states in India. The left-wing government of the state introduced a programme in 1996 whereby 40 per cent of the Kerala state public budget was taken from traditionally powerful line departments in the bureaucracy and devolved to nearly 900 village-level *gram panchayats*. In order to spend these monies, each village had to produce detailed development plans, which were then approved or rejected by direct vote in popular village assemblies. In 1996, the Planning Board estimated that more than 2.5 million participated in the process. More than 100,000 trained volunteers have played active roles in development committees, task forces and technical review committees since then, and nearly 14,000 elected *panchayat* officials have seen their powers, resources and responsibilities vastly expanded. New procedures and mechanisms of accountability have increased overall representation in both the *panchayats* and in the critically important beneficiary committees (that help in the formulation of the village development plan), although it is somewhat less clear how far these new institutions of participatory governance have created new spaces and opportunities for civic associations.

Co-governance techniques are attractive because they give citizens a direct say over issues that are important to them, and over which they can see some immediate return. Budgets can be applied to the management of nearby open spaces, parks, crime prevention, housing schemes and many other public services and programmes. Plainly they make demands on citizens' time, but the tying of engagement with other desired benefits means that a valuable additional tool in the range of forms of engagement has been created.

Direct Democracy Innovations

We are all familiar with the idea of referendums called by governments to approve a constitution or agree a treaty. But referendums can also be called by citizens, and provide examples of direct democracy. They come in two broad forms. The first, usually called *popular initiatives*, are about citizens mobilizing to recall or block some decision made by their elected representatives. The second, generally called *citizens' initiatives*, allow citizens to set the agenda and put an issue up for public decision even if their elected representatives have been overlooking or sidelining the issue. In both cases citizens have final decision making power.

Citizen-sponsored referendums are used widely in Switzerland and a number of US states, and allow a whole population of voters to make a final decision on a proposal. Citizen initiatives usually require a campaign to get an issue placed on a ballot, and then a campaign in the build-up to the ballot vote itself. In order to call a referendum, citizens normally need to be able to demonstrate the support of a significant number of people (say 5 or 10 per cent). Some barriers are necessary to limit the number of issues that can be decided in this way; a referendum should be used by citizens when the political decision making process is going very wrong. The resources available to groups both to set the agenda and influence the vote may be unequally distributed, and this factor leads some to doubt the value of this way of making decisions. However, citizen initiatives certainly give a powerful incentive for people to get involved in decision making, because if they can win the argument for their position with their fellow citizens they may win the day in terms of the final vote.

The big attraction of direct democracy is that it gives the amateur citizen the ultimate comfort that if the political process appears to heading in the wrong direction there is a mechanism available that they and their fellow citizens can use to challenge their elected representatives. It is a tool that if used all the time would undermine the spirit of politics for amateurs, but as a fallback tool it is of considerable value.

E-Democracy Innovations

These innovations are characterized by their use of ICT to give citizens new opportunities to engage in policy debates and practices. The prospect of using ICT to meet the ergonomic challenge outlined at the start of this chapter seems to be very positive. By allowing the free exchange of information and ideas at relatively little time or cost to individuals, ICT appears to offer opportunities for engaging citizens in democratic governance that were not available in earlier decades. Using computers and the internet, it is possible to see how citizens could debate and discuss issues as well as inform themselves about what decisions are at stake without having physically to meet.

Graham Smith identifies Minnesota E-Democracy as a good example of the potential offered by this style of virtual engagement.[17] MN-POLITICS in Minnesota is run by a non-partisan, independent organization established in 1994 that aims to enable internet-based dialogue and debate between citizens and groups. As Graham Smith explains, it has three separate e-mail lists dealing with announcements, state political discussions and national and world affairs discussions.

MN-POLITICS discussion forums are moderated by a list manager who ensures that basic rules and guidelines of engagement are followed by users. Like many e-democracy initiatives, Minnesota E-Democracy attracts those already interested in political activities. But it does seem to have had a more general impact:

> Although difficult to assess, there appears to be evidence that Minnesota E-Democracy has, at times, played an agenda-setting role – for example, the press has covered online debates. There is also anecdotal evidence that debates have had an effect on local political decisions. In a recent survey (the representativeness of which is unclear), users state that Minnesota E-Democracy 'is a good forum to spot political undercurrents not appearing in other media' and that it provides 'quicker responses and interactions among political actors'. There is recognition that the discussion forums provide 'much more equal access for all viewpoints and opinions than traditional media' . . . Although there is a tendency to overstate effects in surveys, there appears to be evidence that Minnesota E-Democracy plays an important role in civic life and engagement in the state.[18]

There are many other examples of how the internet has helped to encourage democratic exchange and debate. One thing that should be stressed is that the internet can be used to reach out to groups that are often excluded from the political process. The potential is enormous, especially in those societies where access to the internet through broadband has become relatively widespread.

In 2003, the Hansard Society in the UK produced a pilot scheme called 'HeadsUp' to investigate the use of online deliberation platforms by young people and how ICT might be used as a platform for dialogue between citizens and elected representatives on topical political events, issues and policies.[19] 'HeadsUp' revolves around regular three-week debates. Topics are put forward by the young people themselves and these are then filtered so that the direction and timing ties in with government and parliamentary business. One example is provided by the 'children's commissioner' debate in September 2004; parliamentarians consulted directly with young people on the proposals within the Children Bill for a children's commissioner. Findings were shared on the floor of the Commons during the Bill's readings, and the Department for Education and Skills included the forum contributions in the application material sent to candidates for the Commissioner position that was eventually created. Hansard Society's Ross Ferguson concludes that:

> The input directly derived from HeadsUp on policy making and scrutiny may be modest but it is measurable and uptake amongst young people and elected representatives is increasing. With genuine commitment and backing over the lifetime of this Parliament, we can be confident of the positive impact 'democratic innovations' like HeadsUp can make to democratic renewal.[20]

This illustration clearly suggests that e-democracy can facilitate the engagement of those often unlikely to take up more established and formal forms of politics.

The big attraction of the internet as a tool of participation is that it requires only a modest amount of effort to become engaged. A great deal of debate and information exchange can be facilitated, and over geographical areas beyond those normally covered by politics. We are only beginning to really understand the potential of political exchange through these forms of technology and they offer the hope of further advances in the future.

Judging the Success of Citizen Engagement Techniques

From better methods of consultation to new forms of e-democracy the range of ways of engaging citizens is considerable. The civic arena does not have to be dominated by boring public meetings in draughty community halls. There are imaginative and effective techniques available that open out new opportunities for citizens to engage in a way that does not demand from them a change of lifestyle and goes with the grain of how they live their lives.

Increasing the quantity of engagement is a laudable goal, but it is not the only objective that could be met if these techniques of engagement were more widely used in our systems of democratic governance. As Stephen Macedo and his colleagues put it:

> At least as important as the overall amount of political and civic engagement are the quality and distribution of these activities. Those who would reform democracy must think not only about how much popular political activity there is but also about who is participating and how they participate.[21]

Several of the schemes outlined above could make some claims to improve the quality of engagement. More complex forms of consultation, deliberative methods and various forms of e-democracy can open up opportunities for exchange and debate that give engagement a richer quality. The participatory budget schemes, especially if done on the scale and with the commitment of the original in Porto Alegre; offer an intensity of engagement that also encourages citizens to make budget choices and not simply agree that more should be spent on their neighbourhood. The big attraction of citizen initiatives is that they grant formal equality to all citizens, in that they rely on the principle of 'one person, one vote' in order to decide the matter at hand.

New techniques of citizen engagement do not, of course, remove the inequalities in society, and these inequalities can be reflected in the practice of engagement, as often is the case with the more standard forms of citizen engagement analysed in Chapter 5. There are dangers that unequal access to the internet is likely to reflect wider inequalities in society, so using the internet needs to be managed with care. But equally, as the schemes from the Hansard Society show, e-democracy can be used to reach previously inaccessible groups. E-democracy schemes can have special features built into them to ensure that access is not simply being granted to those with the resources to engage in the electronic world. Deliberative techniques can also address the issue of inequality by either being targeted at often silent groups or through moving the more intense deliberation to a higher level of judgement, drawing in a representative sample of citizens to reflect on the outcomes of the more detailed deliberation by a smaller group. The Porto Alegre case of participatory budgeting or the forms of mixed consultation practised in many places shows that it is possible to draw citizens from all walks of life into well-constructed schemes. It is not a good argument against these schemes that they somehow promote more inequality in political practice; the issue is how they are designed, and well designed schemes can offer access to a wide range of citizens.

The variety and range of techniques will ultimately be judged by citizens by two overwhelming criteria: Did they allow them to make a difference to decisions that they cared about? Did they do so without demanding of citizens that they become what they do not want in most cases to be, high-intensity activists? It is important to avoid making a fetish out of a particular technique or form of engagement. Different techniques will be appropriate in different circumstances, but all mechanisms have to meet the demand that was also identified as part of the CLEAR model in Chapter 5: is there evidence that citizens' efforts to engage have been responded to by the public authorities to whom they were addressed? The biggest challenge in engaging the public is making sure that public authorities are geared up to respond, because without that no technique is going to be sustainable.

Encouraging 'Civicness' and Voluntary Activity

Sustaining capacity in the civic arena can be about giving citizens the opportunity to engage with each other rather than directly with a public authority. Encouraging civicness and participation makes sense for its own sake, because it helps to build capacity for engagement and delivers immediate benefits when citizens come together to deliver shared goals and projects. The idea of capacity-building has been an integral part of development theory and practice for a number of decades. Capacity-building 'is an essential element if development is to be sustainable and centred in people'.[22] The capacity of local citizens to engage and take control of the aid projects that are directed at their communities is a key ingredient in their success.

Given Robert Putnam's argument (Chapter 3) about how social ties in industrial societies are becoming increasingly fragmented and narrowly focused, there is a wider argument for capacity-building that enables bridging connections to be built between different communities. Robert Putnam and Lewis Feldstein describe several projects to mobilize communities throughout the USA, and stress the importance of bridging social capital: the building of networks between different groups and communities is 'especially important for reconciling democracy and diversity'.[23] The schemes described include the 'Do Something' programme that encourages young people to be organized and active in many parts of the USA, and the mobilization of Mexican Americans in the Rio Grande valley.

For many years, European governments have sponsored community organizations and voluntary associations and more generally encouraged volunteering. In the UK, a further wave of community initiatives were unleashed as a response to the civil disturbances in several towns and cities in the summer of 2001.[24] Local investigations were set up in some areas, and the findings proved disconcerting. The disturbances occurred in areas known to have become fragmented in terms of race, generation, religion and culture; there was little dialogue between these groups, and racial attacks were common. Far-right activity had also been identified in some instances. The conclusion was that the isolation of inner-city housing estates and the segregated nature of community, voluntary, educational, cultural and religious networks had resulted in culturally defined micro-communities living alongside each other without integration. A number of community initiatives were set up to try to combat these problems but the divisiveness increased and the micro communities chose to segregate themselves further.

Community cohesion was identified as being the crucial factor for bringing about inter-culture contact, insight and respect and, accordingly, civic responsibility and a sense of citizenship. The government implemented a number of immediate community-based measures and then encouraged local institutions and communities to develop a community cohesion framework for medium- and long-term action.

Another case of community capacity building, called the 'The Wired High Rise Project', comes from Australia. This scheme was an initiative of the 'Reach for the Clouds' Project and was born out of a partnership between a not-for-profit agency, community groups, local government, state government and commercial agencies. It was designed to develop an empowered and cohesive 'networked community' in an ethnically diverse, low-income population, mostly dependent upon social security who resided in high-rise public housing blocks in Melbourne. Over 40 per cent of households were headed by single women and almost as many had children residing within them. The area was regarded as unsafe and a target for crime, drug-dealing, vandalism and 'stereotyped' negative attention from the media. Most welfare facilities were under-used yet residents voiced a need to know more about tenancy issues, health opportunities and legal services. Furthermore, they had suggested that they would benefit from literacy and information technology (IT) classes. By connecting apartments and tenants it was felt that an alternative to pamphlets and inadequately attended meetings might be found, along with a support structure counteracting loneliness and a perceived lack of safety.

Another idea that has attracted a lot of interest in several countries is the Japanese/US 'Time Swap Bank' , a modern bartering system that is tackling the problems of social exclusion in people who can, for example, swap errands for housework, letter-writing for woodwork. As journalist Roger Cowe explains:

This innovative idea is simple. Like many others it originated in the US, and has been copied in Japan. After 10 years, there are now said to be about 1,000 schemes running in those two countries. In Brooklyn, New York, bereavement counselling is available for time dollars, and a Baltimore housing estate allows tenants to pay rent in time. The Japanese government has backed a time currency which translates as [a] 'ticket for caring relationship'. It works rather like a baby-sitting circle. You do three hours for one member, then you can claim three hours back, either from that member or any other.[25]

The basic idea behind the scheme is that the possibility of getting practical help is combined with a mechanism that encourages community connection and capacity.

What has all this got to do with tackling the problem of political disenchantment? Essentially these kinds of schemes – capacity-building initiatives in all their various forms – are about persuading people that engaging is worthwhile. The assumption is that if people – even those that are segregated by cultural and other divisions or are weighed down by various disadvantages – can see that their engagement can make a difference, then a basis is there for the kind of political engagement that appears to be beyond the experience and practice of many citizens in our current systems of democratic governance. Some of these schemes work better than others, and many may be difficult to sustain once an initial level of funding and support has gone or as the challenges and problems that are tackled become harder. But it is difficult to deny that encouraging civicness and voluntary activity would seem to be a worthwhile part of any package aimed at creating and sustaining an active civic arena.

Information Flow and Understanding: Citizen Education and the Media

A third set of reforms that needs to be considered is premised on the idea that a free flow of information and understanding are essential to the operation of democratic politics. By getting more involved, the argument goes, we can get citizens not only to engage but to understand the demands of politics in a collective setting to a greater degree. But we should also examine the wider context in which political engagement is framed. This section examines the potential of two framing institutions: citizenship education and the media.

Citizenship Education: Operating at the Margins

Citizenship education has come back in vogue in recent years. There appears to be increased attention to it in the USA;[26] in England, increased interest in citizenship education has it origins in the report of the government appointed Advisory Group on Education for Citizenship and the Teaching of Democracy in Schools, which was set up in 1997 and chaired by Professor (now Sir) Bernard Crick, author of the book *In Defence of Politics* mentioned in the Introduction. From September 2002, schools in England were legally required to deliver citizenship education for all 11–16-year-olds. A series of pilot development projects was started in 2001 to explore what an entitlement to citizenship education might look like for all young people involved in 16–19 education and training.[27]

The impact of these schemes does not appear to be earth-shattering. The early evidence from England shows that 'provision is uneven, patchy and evolving' and that

> despite the frantic policy activity concerning citizenship in the curriculum and in other education and training sectors, there is a common acceptance that citizenship education in England is still in its infancy in terms of the development of effective practices in schools and colleges.

Moreover it appears that 'students in all year groups associate citizenship more with rights and responsibilities and issues of identity and equality than with formal political processes'. Researchers concluded that 'it is perhaps no coincidence that the topics least taught – voting, elections, government and the EU – are those that students least associate with the concept of citizenship and the groups and institutions that students trust the least'.[28]

In many ways, the key to school citizen education might be to focus on the experience of democratic engagement rather than democratic theory. Many schools appear to be taking this approach by encouraging engagement about school matters, but also by picking up and working on issues relevant to the wider environment beyond the school gates. As argued earlier in the chapter, real opportunities to engage will deliver far more than general constitutional lessons. The same truth applies to young people as to older citizens: doing it is more important than talking about it.

It is difficult not to see these efforts as likely to remain marginal, even if implementation picks up and schools become better at delivering citizenship education. Schools operate in the context of many competing influences. Commenting on the US situation, but a point with general applicability, Stephen Macedo and his colleagues argue that schools' citizenship efforts need to be put in a broader framework: 'Schools did not create our current civic engagement crisis single-handedly, and they cannot solve it on their own.'[29]

Perhaps what we need is citizen education for all and not just for the young in schools? Universities could do a lot more to turn the learning, knowledge and understanding created by research into material that is useable and accessible to citizens in their engagement and debates; too often the emphasis in universities is on research rather than contributing to the debates that are taking place in society. Voluntary organizations or not-for-profits or think tanks could be encouraged to get universities to make more of a public impact: the challenge should be not only to encourage good-quality academic teaching and research but to enrich the public realm with informative and insightful public intellectuals.

The Media: A Journalism That is Civic?

In Chapter 7, I argued that a free and varied media was essential to the operation of democratic governance. As Pippa Norris[30] argues, the news media can potentially bring three benefits to democracy. They 'provide a civic forum in which to hear serious and extended political viewpoints from all voices in society'. They should also offer 'a watchdog to check abuses of civil and political liberties'. Finally, they should stimulate interest in public and political affairs. It is difficult to argue that all of these functions are delivered effectively in our current news media. In the UK, the 'watchdog' function is perhaps the most effectively delivered; the other two functions are met only to a degree, and with significant limitations.

Norris is right to suggest that 'blaming the news media is too easy',[31] if you are looking to explain the problems of the modern democratic systems. For Norris, a killer finding appears to be that those that pay more attention to news media – who watch more TV news and read about politics in newspapers – are more interested in politics. Contact with the media cannot be putting people off politics; on the contrary, she concludes it is a 'virtuous circle' – the more contact you have, the more you are inclined to engage in politics. I am not convinced by this reasoning, for two reasons. First, the issue of *causality* is unclear: does contact with the news media lead to interest in politics, or is it the other way round? Second, the 'virtuous circle' may be enjoyed by political activists more than ordinary citizens. The range and variety of the media in many democratic countries, and the additional resources available on the internet, mean that if you want to be informed about most issues, then you can. But from the perspective of a politics for amateurs the diet offered up on a mass basis by the news media is thin gruel. As I argued in Chapter 7, mainstream media offerings encourage a rather simplistic understanding of politics and ultimately a cynicism that politics can never deliver. The mixing of reporting and comment probably also encourages a skewed debate, in which there is no evidence or facts, just opinions.

We do not want to create incentives for the media to be in the pocket of government, but drawing on the ideas of *Financial Times* journalist John Lloyd[32] it is possible to make several suggestions.

First, the questioning of public figures needs to be aimed more at drawing out their ideas and identifying difficult issues rather than a gladiatorial struggle between interviewer and politician in which the former sees their job as slaying the latter. That is not to say that political interviews should not be challenging; indeed it would be excellent if the questioning of experts, pressure group lobbyists and even academics, was designed to be as balanced and challenging as it should be for elected politicians. Too often, these voices are left to say what they have to say without any serious challenge.

Second, there should be less emphasis on stirring up controversy and more on trying to explain the subtleties of politics. Shifting your position does not always have to be 'a climb down' or a 'U-turn'; it can reflect a spirit of compromise, the great resource of politics, or that even rarer but even more laudable political quality: changing your mind in the light of evidence and argument.

Third, the mixing of news reporting and commentary should be done with great care; they have different goals. The former should be about a stab at objective truth, the latter is about opinion and debate. Understanding the difference is vital for journalists and there also needs to be a clear set of signals given to the audience when journalists are moving from one form to the other.

Finally, journalists need to see themselves less as the heroic protagonists shedding light on the dark issues that no one else wants to address and view themselves more as servants of society (not, I emphasize, politicians) and so enable people to better understood the issues of the day and make up their own mind about them.

John Lloyd asks: 'can we imagine a journalism that is civic'? A journalism is required that offers a first draft of history in all its complexity and subtlety and acts as a stimulus to engagement and informed debate. Without it, a democratic governance suitable for political amateurs will be much harder to achieve.

Concluding Note

To become more effective, politics requires an attempt to support the civic arena alongside new political institutions. This chapter has shown that a range of techniques for citizen engagement are available that offer new opportunities for building that civic arena. There are also wider policies that can be adopted to encourage 'civicness' and volunteer activity. And although not a matter for government intervention there are debates to be pursued about the way that the media informs the public about politics. Above all, this chapter argues against the idea that formal school-based civic education will make much of a difference and for the idea that providing a wider range of opportunities for engagement – political and non-political – will do much more to sustain a civic arena that in turn might encourage a more civic journalism aimed at explaining and supporting democratic politics, rather than rubbishing it. It also suggests that universities might take a more major role in informing debates in the civic arena.

Conclusions

The first thing to say is that there are many possible reasons to disagree with what I have been arguing in this book. There are other routes to understanding the issue of disenchantment in democratic societies, and associated paths for reform, and it is important to recognize the choices that are being made here. Some would argue that there is not much that can be done given that citizens have become more critical and challenging, stimulating disenchantment and dissatisfaction as a result: politicians just need to accept it and learn to live with it. Others might argue that the structural inequalities inherent in capitalist free-market societies demand a more radical approach to reform that will enable citizens to challenge the power of corporate business and business-funded and business-friendly politicians. Still others will argue for a deeper, more deliberative expression of public politics than my limited vision of a politics for amateurs. Finally some will say that I am crazy even to think that the formal apparatus of politics can again be made attractive to citizens. In a post-modern, post-material world, citizens are developing their own looser and more diverse forms of politics, whether through using consumer power by boycotting goods and services to make a political point in the market or through new single-issue groups and new forms of protest and or through internet and mobile media-supported exchanges. These are only some of the lines of attack that might be brought against the arguments of this book.

The second thing to say, of course, is that I remain convinced that my diagnosis of the problem, and the set of solutions I provide, are better than those offered by others. I think that the critical citizen thesis is wrong, and that the attitudes of most citizens to politics are not driven by a new confidence and assertiveness. There is something in the thesis for some parts of some societies, but overall I do not think that the thinking offered by the critical citizen perspective is helpful. The argument that structural inequalities are blocking progress has again something to commend it, but I think it overplays the power of business and the corruption of politics. In the end, in a democracy the people count, and the issue is how to ensure that people power has the maximum chance to make a difference. Inequalities hinder an accessible politics, but they do not make it impossible. The argument for citizens to become more intensely engaged in a deeper politics of the public realm comes up against one telling point: citizens (and the evidence is overwhelming) do not want it. Finally for those that say that 'old' politics is dead, long live the new, I reply that I, too, see changes in the forms of politics. But

201

I see those changes as a complement to, rather than a substitution for, more traditional representative political processes. The old rules of politics have not changed; politics remains about people expressing conflicting ideas and interests and then finding a way to reconcile those ideas and interests in order to rub along with one another.

What however I am happy to concede is that this book only scratches the surface in the analysis and understanding that it offers. In expressing an extensive mix of arguments and evidence I have undoubtedly sometimes over-simplified and certainly not dealt at sufficient length with important lines of debate and valuable bodies of evidence. Moreover, I am conscious of generalizing from my British standpoint, Although I have taken the trouble to try and understand the political challenges of other countries, I look forward to people telling me how I need to develop a more nuanced and detailed understanding of what is going on elsewhere: especially, of course, if it is accompanied with an opportunity to visit!

I am also clear that the reform measures outlined in Part III of the book are not on their own adequate to the task of getting people re-engaged with a democratic politics. Given the scale of the problem that we face, a bit of institutional tinkering, a few new opportunities to engage, a bit of a push on better information and media are not on their own going to do the trick. They are necessary parts of a programme of reform, but they are not sufficient. Moreover, the ideas floated in Chapters 10 and 11 should be regarded as on trial; they are reform ideas that may be worth putting into place rather than proven techniques that, if introduced, will transform our politics.

The argument of this book is that the malaise in our democratic politics has deep roots in the culture, assumptions and mindsets of our societies. Much of the book has been about how to understand the way that we currently engage with politics. Politics appears to be, for most of us, a rather unedifying process that we would rather not have much to do with. Our attempts to engage in politics – that is, most of our forays into collective decision making – are ad hoc and sporadic. Most substantial politics is done by a mixed, but small, cadre of elected politicians, unaccountable officials, specialist lobbyists, narrowly focused experts and professionalized protesters. That world, in turn, is reported to us by a media that focuses on personality conflicts, controversy and a mix of reporting and commentary that can enlighten, but more often confuses. The average citizen is alienated from politics and far from convinced of its value.

This understanding that there is something substantially wrong with the way we do politics is joined by a deeper sense that somehow or other we have forgotten what politics is capable of doing – and, perhaps more importantly, we are unclear about what it can't do. At its most extreme you could argue that the malaise afflicting democratic governance today is that many citizens rather wish that they could do without politics.

As a long-time student of politics I find the 'anti-politics' perspective of many of my fellow citizens possible to understand, but deeply worrying. Politics is prone to crises because it faces one of the toughest challenges available to human societies. It is about how, given our inherent interdependence, we can learn to manage conflicts and construct pillars of cooperation. There is no end-game in politics, but rather a cycling of issues and solutions that produces one temporary fix after the other, with an occasional and powerful expression of some more permanent institutionally reinforced boundary markers. Politics has a natural rhythm that tends to create a certain level of dissatisfaction and disenchantment. It imposes collective decisions on us all, its processes of communication and exchange are time-consuming and irksome and implementation and decision outcomes involve resource distributions and practical actions and interventions that cannot always be either comprehended or valued by those on the receiving end of them. Politics, as I argued in Chapter 4, is almost designed to disappoint. Yet it does an important job for us by enabling our voice to be heard among many and then compromises to be made and deals struck so that in vital areas conflicts can be contained and cooperation achieved.

Part of the core purpose of this book is about getting people to accept a more realistic and positive understanding of politics. I appreciate that I am swimming against a tide of counterforces in presenting this argument. They include difficulties with the practice of politics, covered in depth in Part II of the book, that hardly present the process in the best light, and a widespread cynicism that is promoted by many elements of the modern media and more broadly by the culture of our societies. Underlying both these elements, and even more damaging, there is impact of the growing individualization of society.

The biggest challenge facing democratic governance is the spread of global capitalism that lionizes self-advancement and appears to move key decisions out of the control of the collective. The individualized world is experienced through the eyes of the sovereign consumer, able to choose the ingredients that make up a unique lifestyle. The post-modern goal is to construct our expressive self and take responsibility for own values, lifestyle choices and circumstance. Politics is reduced to the personal: it is about what we think and how we act. If in this individualized world, in addition, we lose faith in the capacity of our collective agency because of the forces of globalization and other developments, then politics becomes a hopeless and inevitably frustrating charade. If there is no collective capacity, there is no point to politics. Politics is about collective decisions, balancing conflict and cooperation, in order to promote human purposes. If all there is, is individual choice, and the rest is fate – a product of forces that we cannot hope to understand and should not desire to control – then no wonder citizens are becoming disenchanted with, and alienated from, politics in democracies.

As I argued in Chapter 3, the forces of economic globalization and the increasing reliance on unsustainable technologies to bolster our societies are a massive challenge, but they are not inherently uncontrollable and unmanageable. There is no need to collapse into a fatalistic view that nothing can be done. What matters more is that we throw off the shackles of ideas that so privilege the individual that it makes the collective unsustainable. In that sense, a further obstacle to restoring faith in politics is the persistence (and, indeed, dominance) of neo-liberal thinking, perhaps the most successful ideology of the last twenty-five years. It has proved to be extremely influential in the domestic policy thinking of many democratic governments – reflected in the commitment to privatization and cutting back the state – and has been since the 1980s the unofficial ideology of globalization, reflected in the commitment to *laissez-faire* economic policies.

Neo-liberal thinking offers a powerful critique of the idea of the civic and the public realm. As Raymond Plant[1] explains, the starting point for neo-liberal thought is that liberty is the key goal, and that the only form of liberty that can and should be promoted is freedom from coercion. The collective is about imposing your values on others, and as such is undesirable since all values are subjective, a matter of individual choice. Individuals, when entering collective bargaining, do not become more heroic or other-regarding; they remain selfish and self-interested. So when the collective is constructed it needs to be done so in a way that keeps what can be done by government to a minimum. A framework of non-coercion and civil rights to protect citizens from interference is all that is needed. The goal of neo-liberals is a minimal state to frame and support free markets and to allow individuals to pursue their own good. In short 'there should not be collective aims but only a set of rules of law to define in detail what mutual non- coercion entails in practice'.[2] The power of this ideology is considerably reinforced since it rides on the back of a rampant capitalism and marketization in our societies. It undermines the case for politics, and any faith that politics might deliver something of collective value.

The neo-liberal vision needs to be challenged – and, indeed, it increasingly has been at both a domestic and global level. Markets are not quite the perfect instrument that the ideology proposes and in practice are constructed around corporate power and structural advantage as much as the free choice of individuals. Moreover, government – and, more generally, the state – can achieve far more and more effectively than neo-liberals give the public realm credit for. Many of us are lucky enough to benefit from effective government action to deliver health, education and numerous other benefits. Above all, we need to recognize that community, solidarity and common humanity are just as much an expression of the condition of humanity as self-interest and self-actualization. Values may be subjective, but they can be shared or combined; we can agree about things that are important to us all and we can recognize that some things are important to others and need to be protected or promoted.

Politics cannot afford a fatalism about the prospect of effective collective action, yet equally it cannot rely on faint-hearted appeals to create a new type of citizen to get us out of the hole that, as disappointed citizens of democracies, we appear to be in. Many reformers advocate forms of political engagement that are intensive, time-consuming and demand 'new model citizens'. I think we are better off assuming that citizens will not transform themselves, but are more or less competent for the task of engaging in democratic politics, and very clear that the one thing they do not want is a more intense engagement. In short we need a politics designed for amateurs so that citizens can engage in politics and retain a life.

The sharp divide that has grown up between professional politicos and ordinary citizens in the practice of politics should become fuzzier, and needs to be bridged by a wider range of channels of communication between the two sides through better representative politics and new forms and opportunities for citizen engagement. We also need to construct an architecture of politics to cope with the twin demands of localized and globalized decision making, alongside the more traditional focus on decision making through the nation state. Finally, we need to find support through the media and a viable practice of citizen education that enables people to understand, rather than be alienated by, democratic politics. I do not see politics as somehow noble; it is a pragmatic and practical response to the human condition. It exists because we need to find ways to resolve conflicts and coordinate our actions for our mutual benefit. As John Dunn argues:

> Political understanding requires us . . . to seek to know the price of everything and the value of everything . . . It should sober, move, perhaps sadden and certainly embolden us: make us warier, but not less kind, more self-reliant, but also more grateful for what we do prove able to rely on in our fellows. It is a discipline of the heart as much as a discipline of the mind.[3]

Politics ultimately requires us to think beyond simple and immediate self-advancement, but it does not assume a noble, self-sacrificing countenance. It merely requires us to value others and believe that desirable collective action can be willed. Politics is not about truth-seeking or about deciding what is right. It is about constructing ways in which in an inter-dependent world we can live more effectively with one another. In the busy world of markets and individual self-expression, and in the public culture which capitalism has fashioned in our societies, there is a danger that we are losing not only the will but also the skills and subtleties of mind and heart to do politics. But doable it is, and this book argues that we can construct a politics and a democracy that works even for the majority of us who will remain amateurs in its practice.

This book has identified a challenge facing all democracies. The ideals of democracy are valued and supported by most citizens, however, the practice of democratic politics is currently a massive turn-off. We want democracy, but we are not sure that we have the political capacity to deliver it. Getting politics right matters to the future working of democracy and it would appear that to make democracy sustainable in the twenty-first century we need to find a new accommodation with politics.

A person needs many things to live in a good life in a good society. Among the core requirements are sustainable technological and scientific advancements to aid understanding and make things easier. People also need love, friendship and emotional support. They also need a moral philosophy of some sort to guide their choices and enable them to understand their place in the world. The argument of this book is that they also need an effective democratic politics. We need the collective capacity offered by politics to protect our liberties, express our interests and views and enable ourselves to cope with the demands of living in a shared world. Politics matters because it, too, is an ingredient in what is needed for a good life. It is about recognizing that those affected by a decision have a right to a say about it and that in a complex world where our lives overlap and intersect with so many others we need to find ways to communicate, to agree to disagree and to cooperate. Achieving mass democracy was the great triumph of the twentieth century. Learning to live with it will be the great achievement of the twenty-first.

Notes and References

Introduction

1. Brian Whitaker, 'Politicians are voted the world's least trusted people', *Guardian*, Thursday 15 September 2005 (available at http://politics.guardian.co.uk/polls/story/0,11030,1570316,00.html).
2. John R. Hibbing and Elizabeth Theiss-Morse, *Stealth Democracy: Americans' Beliefs about How Government Should Work* (Cambridge: Cambridge University Press, 2002).
3. These reflections draw on Hibbing and Theiss-Morse, *Stealth Democracy*, p. 131.
4. The section draws on John Dunn, *The Cunning of Unreason: Making Sense of Politics* (London: HarperCollins, 2000).
5. Dunn, *The Cunning of Unreason*, p. 133.
6. See Ulrich Beck, *The Reinvention of Politics* (Cambridge: Polity, 1996).
7. These reflections draw on Hibbing and Theiss-Morse, *Stealth Democracy*, pp. 222–3.
8. Dunn, *The Cunning of Unreason*, p. 65.
9. Bernard Crick, *In Defence of Politics*, 5th edn (London: Continuum, 2000), pp. 30–1.
10. Max Weber, 'Politics as a vocation', in H. H. Gerth and C. Wright Mills (trans. and ed.), *From Max Weber: Essays in Sociology* (New York: Oxford University Press, 1946), p. 128.

1 The Triumph of Democracy?

1. Amartya Sen 'Democracy as a universal value', *Journal of Democracy*, 10(3) (1999), pp. 3–4.
2. Larry Diamond, 'Universal democracy?', *Policy Review* (June–July 2003), p. 119.
3. See Kenneth Newton and Jan W. van Deth, *Foundations of Comparative Politics* (Cambridge: Cambridge University Press, 2005).
4. Diamond, 'Universal democracy?'.
5. Jean Grugel, *Democratization: A Critical Introduction* (Basingstoke and New York: Palgrave Macmillan, 2002), p. 241.
6. For a discussion of various concepts of democracy, see Michael Saward, *Democracy* (Cambridge: Polity, 2003).
7. Grugel, *Democratization*.
8. Sen, 'Democracy as a universal value', p. 5.

9.   Sen, 'Democracy as a universal value', p. 12.
10. Samuel P. Huntington, 'A clash of civilizations?', *Foreign Affairs*, 72(3), (1993), pp. 22–49.
11. Huntington, 'A clash of civilizations?', p. 41.
12. Sen, 'Democracy as a universal value', p. 15.
13. Saward, *Democracy*, p. 30.
14. See Timothy Besley and Masayuki Kudamatsu, 'Health and democracy', 10 January 2006 (unpublished paper, available at http://econ.lse.ac.uk/staff/tbesley/index_own.html#pubs).
15. Sen, 'Democracy as a universal value', p. 8.
16. Diamond, 'Universal democracy?'.
17. See Diamond, 'Universal democracy?'.
18. See David Beetham (ed.), *Defining and Measuring Democracy* (London: Sage, 1994).
19. One of the anonymous reviewers of an earlier draft of the book kindly pointed out that Winston Churchill's exact words were: 'No one pretends that democracy is perfect or all-wise. Indeed, it has been said that democracy is the worst form of Government except all those other forms that have been tried from time to time.' As the reviewer went on to explain, the survey question offers a rather gentler judgement on democratic governance than that offered by Churchill. There are reasons to think that Churchill was not necessarily the greatest advocate of rule by the people, since another of his well-known quotations is: 'The best argument against democracy is a five minute conversation with the average voter.'
20. Ronald Inglehart, 'The worldviews of Islamic publics in global perspective' (2005) (available at www.worldvaluessurvey.org).
21. Grugel, *Democratization*, pp. 238–47.
22. Michael Mann, *The Dark Side of Democracy: Explaining Ethnic Cleansing* (Cambridge: Cambridge University Press, 2004).
23. Mann, *The Dark Side of Democracy*, p. 3.

2   Global Dissatisfaction with Politics

1.   Russell J. Dalton, *Democratic Challenges, Democratic Choices: The Erosion of Political Support in Advanced Industrial Democracies* (Oxford: Oxford University Press, 2004), p. 17.
2.   Dalton, *Democratic Challenges, Democratic Choices*, p. 18.
3.   Michael Mann, *The Dark Side of Democracy: Explaining Ethnic Cleansing* (Cambridge: Cambridge University Press, 2004).
4.   See Susan Pharr and Robert Putnam (eds), *Disaffected Democracies: What's Troubling the Trilateral Democracies?* (Princeton: Princeton University Press, 2000).
5.   IDEA, 'Voter turnout – a survey' (available at www.idea.int).
6.   The Electoral Commission, *Election 2005: Turnout* (London: The Electoral Commssion, 2005).

7. Brian Wheeler, 'UK politics: dead or dormant?', BBC News online 25 February 2005 (available at www.bbc.co.uk).

8. Hans-Dieter Klingemann and Dieter Fuchs, *Citizens and the State* (Oxford: Oxford University Press, 1995).

9. Polly Toynbee, 'It is New Labour, as much as the public, that lacks trust', *Guardian*, 22 November 2005 (available at http://politics.guardian.co.uk/polls/comment/0,,1647719,00.html).

10. The Electoral Commission and Hansard Society, *The Audit of Political Engagement: Research Report 2* (London: The Electoral Commission, March 2005), Table 2, p. 20.

11. Susan Scarrow, 'Parties without members? Party organisation in a changing electoral environment' in R. Dalton and M.Wattenberg (eds), *Parties without Partisans* (Oxford: Oxford University Press, 2000), pp. 79–101.

12. Declan Hall and Steve Leach, 'The changing nature of local Labour politics', in Gerry Stoker (ed.) *The New Politics of British Local Governance* (Basingstoke: Macmillan, 2000).

13. Wheeler, 'UK politics: dead or dormant?'.

14. The Electoral Commission and Hansard Society, *The Audit of Political Engagement*.

15. Charles Pattie, Patrick Seyd and Paul Whiteley, *Citizenship in Britain: Values, Participation and Democracy* (Cambridge: Cambridge University Press, 2004), Table 3.1, p. 78. When asked if they had donated money to a political organization or group rather than any organization the European Social Survey found that under 1 in 10 in the UK answered that they had (see Table 5.1, pp. 90–1).

16. Dalton, *Democratic Challenges, Democratic Choices*, p. 1.

17. Pharr and Putnam, *Disaffected Democracies*.

18. Joseph Nye, 'Introduction', in Joseph Nye, Philip Zelikow and David King, *Why Americans Mistrust Government* (Cambridge, MA: Harvard University Press, 1997), p. 1.

19. Robert Lane, 'The politics of consensus in an age of affluence', *American Political Science Review*, 59, (1965), pp. 874–95.

20. Lane, 'The politics of consensus', p. 894.

21. Lane, 'The politics of consensus', p. 877.

22. Robert Putnam, *Bowling Alone: The Collapse and Renewal of American Community* (New York: Simon & Schuster, 2000).

23. Putnam, *Bowling Alone*, p. 36.

24. Putnam, *Bowling Alone*, p. 45.

25. Putnam, *Bowling Alone*, p. 46.

26. Putnam, *Bowling Alone*, p. 47.

27. See Michael Moore, *Stupid White Men* (London: Penguin, 2002).

28. Stephen Macedo et al., *Democracy at Risk: How Political Choices Undermine Citizen Participation and What We Can Do About It* (Washington, DC: Brookings Institution Press, 2005).

29. Centre for Research and Information on Canada, *Voting Participation in*

Canada: Is Canadian Democracy in Crisis? (Montreal: CRIC, 2001) (available at www.cric.ca).

30. The figures are taken from Philippe C. Schmitter and Alexander H. Treschel, *The Future of Democracy: Trends, Analyses and Reforms* (Strasbourg: Council of Europe, 2004).

31. The European Social Survey (ESS) (available at http://naticent02.uuhost. uk.uu.net/index.htm).

32. See ESS.

33. Schmitter and Treschel, *The Future of Democracy*.

34. Susan Pharr, 'Public trust and democracy in Japan', in Nye, Zelikow and King, *Why Americans Mistrust Government*.

35. Scott Brenton, 'Public confidence in Australian Democracy', Democratic Audit of Australia, Australian National University, 2005 (available at http://democratic.audit.anu.edu.au/), p. 1.

36. Brenton, 'Public confidence', p. 7.

37. See a large range of material from the New Zealand political change project (available at http://www.vuw.ac.nz/pols/Research/staff-research/nz-political-change-project.aspx).

38. See www.globalbarometer.org/governance indicators.

39. United Nation Development Programme (UNDP), *Democracy in Latin America: Towards a Citizen's Democracy*, 1st edn (New York: UNDP, 2005).

40. UNDP, *Democracy in Latin America*, p. 25.

41. See www.globalbarometer.org/governanceindicators.

42. UNDP, *Democracy in Latin America*, p. 27.

43. UNDP, *Democracy in Latin America*, p. 131.

44. UNDP, *Democracy in Latin America*, pp. 131–2 and Table 46.

45. UNDP, *Democracy in Latin America*, p. 141.

46. See www.globalbarometer.org/governanceindicators.

47. Afrobarometer, 'Democracy and electoral alteration: evolving African attitudes', *Briefing Paper*, 9 (April 2004), (see www.afrobarometer.org).

48. See www.globalbarometer.org/governanceindicators.

49. Javeed Alam, 'What is happening inside Indian democracy?', *Economic and Political Weekly*, 11 September 1999.

50. A. Gupta, 'Blurred boundaries: the discourse of corruption, the culture of politics, and the imagined state', *American Ethnologist*, 22(2) (1995), pp. 375–402.

51. Pippa Norris (ed.), *Critical Citizens: Global Support for Democratic Governance* (Oxford: Oxford University Press, 1999).

52. A point made by Russell Dalton in a written exchange with my colleague, Peter John.

53. Norris, *Critical Citizens*, p. 268.

54. Dalton, *Democratic Challenges, Democratic Choices*, p. 10.

3 Explanations for Political Disenchantment

1. Russell Dalton, *Democratic Challenges, Democratic Choices: The Erosion of Political Support in Advanced Industrial Democracies* (Oxford: Oxford University Press, 2004), p. 78.
2. Definition taken from TI (see www.transparency.org).
3. Committee on Standards in Public Life, *Survey of Public Attitudes towards Conduct in Public Life: Summary of Findings* (London: Committee on Standards in Public Life, 2004), Box 5, p. 7.
4. See 'Transparency International poll shows widespread public alarm about corruption' (available at www.transparency.org).
5. Harold Pinter, 'Art, truth & politics', Nobel Prize Lecture (7 December 2005) (available at http://nobelprize.org/literature/laureates/2005/pinter-lecture.html).
6. Pippa Norris, *Critical Citizens: Global Support for Democratic Government* (Oxford: Oxford University Press, 1999), p. 26.
7. Anthony Giddens, BBC Reith Lectures, 'Runaway World, Lecture 5, London, Democracy' (1999) (available at http://news.bbc.co.uk/hi/english/static/events/reith_99/week5/week5.htm).
8. Ronald Inglehart, 'Postmaterialist values and the erosion of institutional authority', in Joseph Nye, Philip Zelikow and David King, *Why Americans Mistrust Government* (Cambridge, MA: Harvard University Press, 1997), p. 218.
9. Inglehart, 'Postmaterialist values', p. 236.
10. Jean Grugel, *Democratization: A Critical Introduction* (Basingstoke and New York: Palgrave Macmillan, 2002), Chapter 5.
11. Michael Edwards, *Civil Society* (Cambridge: Polity, 2004), pp. 14–15.
12. Grugel, *Democratizatio*, p. 115, emphasis in the original.
13. Robert Putnam, *Bowling Alone: The Collapse and Renewal of American Community* (New York: Simon & Schuster, 2000).
14. See Bob Edwards, Michael Foley and Mario Diani (eds), *Beyond Tocqueville: Civil Society and the Social Capital Debate in Comparative Perspective* (Hannover: Tufts University Press, 2001).
15. See Yaojun Li, Mike Savage, Gindo Tampubolon, Alan Warde and Mark Tomlinson, 'Dynamics of social capital: trends and turnover in associational membership in England and Wales, 1972–1999', *Sociological Research Online*, 7 (3) (2002) (available at http://www.socresonline.org.uk/7/3/li.html) and Alan Warde, Gindo Tampubolon, Brian Longhurst, Kathryn Ray, Mike Savage and Mark Tomlinson, 'Trends in social capital: memberships of associations in Great Britain, 1991–98', *British Journal of Political Science*, 33 (2003), pp. 515–34.
16. Charles Pattie, Patrick Seyd and Paul Whiteley, *Citizenship in Britain: Values, Participation and Democracy* (Cambridge: Cambridge University Press, 2004), p. 265.

17. Warde *et al.*, 'Trends in social capital', p. 525.
18. Warde *et al.*, 'Trends in social capital', p. 525.
19. Robert Putnam (ed.) *Democracies in Flux* (Oxford: Oxford University Press, 2004), p. 412.
20. Putnam, *Democracies in Flux*, p. 412.
21. Andrew Gamble, *Politics and Fate* (Cambridge: Polity, 2000), p. 1.
22. Jan Aart Scholte, *Globalization: A Critical Introduction*, 2nd edn (Basingstoke and New York: Palgrave Macmillan, 2005), p. 3.
23. For a discussion of this position, see Peter Dicken, *Global Shift: Reshaping the Global Political Map in the 21st Century* (London: Sage Freidman, 2003), pp. 11–14.
24. See Dicken, *Global Shift*.
25. Dicken, *Global Shift*, p. 12.
26. Dicken, *Global Shift*, p. 122, emphasis in the original.
27. For a brief overview of the vast literature in this field, see Andrew Gamble 'Economic governance', in Jon Pierre (ed.), *Debating Governance* (Oxford: Oxford University Press, 2000), pp. 110–37.
28. Dicken, *Global Shift*, p. 130.
29. For a clear introduction to the concerns and issues of anti-globalization campaigners, see http://en.wikipedia.org/wiki/Anti-globalization_movement.
30. Gamble, *Politics and Fate*, p. 46.
31. Joseph Stiglitz, *Globalization and its Discontents* (London: Allen Lane, 2002).
32. Gamble, *Politics and Fate*, p. 115.
33. Andrew Dobson, *Citizenship and the Environment* (Oxford: Oxford University Press, 2003).
34. Quotations and argument taken from 'Science communication – to or with the public?', 14 November 2005 (available at http://www.euractiv.com/Article?tcmuri=tcm:29-147978-16&type=News&_print).
35. Gamble, *Politics and Fate*, p. 119.
36. The discussion below draws on Andrew Dessler and Edward Parson, *The Science and Politics of Global Climate Change* (Cambridge: Cambridge University Press, 2006), pp. 34–8.
37. Gamble, *Politics and Fate*, p. 119.
38. Anthony Giddens, *The Third Way and its Critics* (Cambridge: Polity, 2003).
39. Gamble, *Politics and Fate*, p. 37.
40. For a start on the governance literature, see Gerry Stoker, 'Governance as theory: five propositions', *International Social Science Journal*, 155, 1998, pp. 17–28.

4   The Politics of Mass Democracies: Designed-In Disappointment?

1. John Dunn, *The Cunning of Unreason: Making Sense of Politics* (London: HarperCollins, 2000), p. xii.

2. See, for example, Michael Moore, *Stupid White Men* (London: Penguin, 2001) and Michael Moore, *Dude, Where's my Country?* (London: Penguin, 2003).
3. David Beetham, *Democracy: A Beginner's Guide* (Oxford: Oneworld, 2005).
4. Adam Przeworski, *States and Markets* (Cambridge: Cambridge University Press, 2003), p. 80.
5. Przeworski, *States and Markets*, p. 80.
6. Albert Hirschman, *Exit, Voice and Loyalty* (Cambridge, MA: Harvard University Press, 1970).
7. Bernard Crick, *In Defence of Politics* (5th edn) (London: Continuum, 2000), p. 18.
8. David Marquand, *Decline of Public* (Cambridge: Polity, 2004).
9. Michael Saward, *Democracy* (Cambridge: Polity, 2003), p. 121.
10. Michael Laver, *Private Desires, Political Action* (London: Sage, 1997), p. 1.
11. For accessible reviews of that literature, see Laver, *Private Desires* and Przeworski, *States and Markets*.
12. Peter Hall and Rosemary Taylor, 'Political science and the three new institutionalisms', *Political Studies* (1996), 44(5), pp. 936–57.
13. Niccolò Machiavelli, *The Prince*, trans. William Connell (New York: St Martin's Press, 2005).
14. Hall and Taylor, 'Political science'.
15. Hall and Taylor, 'Political science'.
16. C. Mantzavinos, *Individuals, Institutions and Interests* (Cambridge: Cambridge University Press, 2001).
17. Charles Lindblom, *The Intelligence of Democracy: Decision Making through Mutual Adjustment* (New York: Free Press, 1965).
18. Lindblom, *The Intelligence of Democracy*, p. 99.
19. Perri 6, Diane Leat, Kim Setzler and Gerry Stoker, *Holistic Governance* (Basingstoke and New York: Palgrave Macmillan, 2002).
20. Lindblom, *The Intelligence of Democracy*, pp. 33–4.
21. J. Pressman and A. Wildavsky, *Implementation* (Berkeley: University of California Press, 1973).
22. Peter John, *Analysing Public Policy* (London: Pinter, 1998), pp. 28–9.
23. Przeworski, *States and Markets*, pp. 84–5.
24. David Beetham, *The Legitimation of Power* (London: Macmillan, 1991).
25. Hirschman, *Exit, Voice and Loyalty*, p. 80.
26. Paul Pierson, *Politics in Time* (Princeton: Princeton University Press, 2004), pp. 154–7.

5 The Decline of Citizen Engagement?

1. John Hibbing and Elizabeth Theiss-Morse, *Stealth Democracy: Americans' Beliefs about How Government Should Work* (Cambridge: Cambridge University Press, 2002), p. 2.

2. The average figure also includes data for an additional nine countries. For full details of the European Social Survey, see http://naticent02.uuhost.uk.uu.net/publicity/index.htm.
3. Charles Pattie, Patrick Seyd and Paul Whiteley, *Citizenship in Britain: Values, Participation and Democracy* (Cambridge: Cambridge University Press, 2004), p. 265.
4. Pattie *et al.*, *Citizenship in Britain*, Table 3.2, p. 81.
5. Pattie *et al.*, *Citizenship in Britain*, p. 266.
6. Sidney Verba, Kay Schlozman and Henry Brady, *Voice and Equality: Civic Volunteerism in American Politics* (Cambridge, MA: Harvard University Press, 1995), p. 281.
7. Pattie *et al.*, *Citizenship in Britain*, p. 109.
8. Vivien Lowndes, Lawrence Pratchett and Gerry Stoker, 'Diagnosing and remedying the failings of official participation schemes: the CLEAR framework', *Social Policy & Society*, 5(2) (2006), pp. 1–11.
9. Vivien Lowndes, Lawrence Pratchett and Gerry Stoker, 'Local political participation: the impact of rules-in-use', *Public Administration*, 84(3) (2006).
10. Pattie *et al.*, *Citizenship in Britain*, pp. 275–80.
11. Matthew Crenson and Benjamin Ginsberg, *Downsizing Democracy: How America sidelined its Citizens and Privatized its Public* (Baltimore: Johns Hopkins University Press, 2002), Chapter 1.
12. NIMBY stands for 'Not In My Back Yard', a reference to the desire of people to protect their own situation regardless of wider community concerns.
13. Pattie *et al.*, *Citizenship in Britain*, p. 276.
14. Crenson and Ginsberg, *Downsizing Democracy*, pp. 2–3.
15. Crenson and Ginsberg, *Downsizing Democracy*, p. 19.

6   The Professionalization of Activism?

1. Paul Whiteley and Patrick Seyd, *High-Intensity Participation: The Dynamics of Party Activism in Britain* (Ann Arbor: University of Michigan Press, 2003), pp. 1–2.
2. Michael Moran, *Politics and Governance in the UK* (Basingstoke and New York, Palgrave Macmillan, 2005), p. 7.
3. Paul Webb, David Farrell and Ian Holiday, *Political Parties in Advanced Industrial Democracies* (Oxford: Oxford University Press, 2002).
4. Paul Webb, 'Conclusion: political parties and democratic control in advanced industrial societies', in Webb *et al.*, *Political Parties in Advanced Industrial Democracies*, p. 442.
5. Wainer Lusoli and Stephen Ward, 'Digital rank-and-file: party activists' perceptions and use of the internet', *British Journal of Politics and International Relations*, 6 (2004), p. 454.
6. Lusoli and Ward, 'Digital rank-and-file', p. 454.

7. Webb, 'Conclusion', pp. 442–4.
8. Lusoli and Ward, 'Digital rank-and-file'.
9. Dennis Johnson, *No Place for Amateurs* (New York: Routledge, 2001).
10. Richard Katz and Peter Mair, 'Changing models of party organization and party democracy: the emergence of the cartel party', *Party Politics*, 1, pp. 5–18.
11. Peter Mair, 'Political parties, popular legitimacy and public privilege', *Western European Politics*, 18 (1995), p. 54.
12. Webb, 'Conclusion', p. 441.
13. Russell Dalton and Martin Wattenberg (eds), *Parties without Partisans* (Oxford: Oxford University Press, 2000).
14. Theda Skocpol, 'Advocates without members: the recent transformation of American civic life', in Theda Skocpol and Morris Fiorina (eds), *Civic Engagement in American Democracy* (Washington, DC/New York: Brookings Institution Press/Russell Sage Foundation, 1999).
15. Peter John, *Analysing Public Policy* (London: Pinter, 1998), Chapter 4.
16. John, *Analysing Public Policy*, p. 66, and the Amnesty International example is taken from p. 77 of this work.
17. Jeffrey Berry, *The New Liberalism: The Rising Power of Citizen Groups* (Washington, DC: Brookings Institution Press, 1999), p. 17.
18. Berry, *The New Liberalism*, Table 6.8, p. 145.
19. Berry, *The New Liberalism*, Table 2.1, p. 20.
20. Berry, *The New Liberalism*, Table 2.2, p. 24.
21. Berry, *The New Liberalism*, p. 32.
22. These figures are taken from Grant Jordan and William Maloney, *The Protest Business? Mobilizing Campaign Groups* (Manchester: Manchester University Press, 1997), Table 1.1, p. 13 and Table 1.5, p. 20.
23. See Jordan and Maloney, *The Protest Business?*, pp. 17–25.
24. Berry, *The New Liberalism*, p. 155.
25. Berry, *The New Liberalism*; see Chapter 4 in the book for detailed evidence on the power of citizen groups.
26. Jordan and Maloney, *The Protest Business?*, p. 193.
27. Skocpol, 'Advocates without members', pp. 491–2.
28. Skocpol, 'Advocates without members', p. 496.
29. See Jordan and Maloney, *The Protest Business?*
30. Skocpol, 'Advocates without members', pp. 499–504.
31. Skocpol, 'Advocates without members', p. 503.
32. Jordan and Maloney, *The Protest Business?*
33. Theda Skocpol and Morris Fiorina, 'Making sense of the civic engagement debate', in Skocpol and Morris Fiorina (eds), *Civic Engagement in American Democracy*, p. 14.
34. Marilyn Taylor 'The art of dissent', Lecture, mimeo.
35. See Neil Stammers and Catherine Eschle, 'Social movements and global activism', in Wilma de Jong, Martin Shaw and Neil Stammers (eds), *Global Activism: Global Media* (London: Pluto, 2005), pp. 50–67.

216   *Notes and References*

36. Pollyanna Ruiz, 'Bridging the gap: from the margins to the mainstream', in de Jong, Shaw and Stammers (eds), *Global Activism*, pp. 194–207.
37. Jan Aart Scholte, *Globalization: A Critical Introduction*, 2nd edn (Basingstoke and New York: Palgrave Macmillan, 2005), p. 219 and, more generally, pp. 218–21.
38. Scholte, *Globalization*, p. 369.
39. Scholte, *Globalization*, p. 370.
40. Martin Shaw, 'Peace and western wars: social movements in mass-mediated global politics', in de Jong, Shaw and Stammers (eds), *Global Activism*, pp. 143–4.
41. Michael Shellenberger and Ted Nordhaus, *The Death of Environmentalism: Global Warming Politics in a Post-Environmental World* (2004) (available at www.breakthrough.org).

7   The Dangers of Cynicism

1. Taken from http://www.wisdomquotes.com/cat_politics.html.
2. All the data in this section come from the European Social Survey, 2002 (see p. 38, where I make some cautionary comments about the data). The work on the figures and tables comes from my statistician and daughter, Bethany. Using the same data, she combined three responses: those that thought most or all politicians were only interested in your vote; those that thought most or all politicians did not care what you think; and those who in addition did think that politicians could be trusted (they additionally ranked their trust in politicians as 'No trust at all' to at most a low 3 out of 10). 'Cynics and with a fondness for conspiracy theories', she called them, and they came out at about a third of European respondents to the survey (33.9 per cent to be exact).
3. Niccolò Machiavelli, *The Prince*, trans. William Connell (New York: St Martin's Press, 2005), p. 87.
4. James Buchanan, 'Market failure and political failure', *Cato journal*, 8 (1998), pp. 1–13. The arguments below draw heavily on Andrew Hindmoor, 'Public choice', in Colin Hay, Michael Lister and David Marsh (eds), *The State: Theories and Issues* (Basingstoke and New York: Palgrave Macmillan, 2006), pp. 79–97.
5. Michael Taylor, 'When rationality fails', in Jeffery Friedman (ed.), *The Rational Choice Controversy* (New Haven: Yale University Press, 1996), pp. 229–30.
6. Donald Green and Ian Shapiro, *Pathologies of Rational Choice Theory* (New Haven: Yale University Press, 1994).
7. Colin Hay, 'Theory, stylized heuristic or self-fulfilling prophecy? The status of rational choice theory in public administration', *Public Administration*, 82(1) (2004), p. 43.
8. Peter Oborne, *The Rise of Political Lying* (London: Free Press, 2005).

9. Oborne, *The Rise of Political Lying*, p. 137.
10. Libby Purves, 'Be honest: you're not, are you?', *The Times*, Tuesday 17 May, 2005, p. 19.
11. Richard Rose, *Do Parties Make a Difference?*, expanded 2nd edn (London: Macmillan 1984), p. 65.
12. John Lloyd, *What the Media Are Doing to Our Politics* (London: Constable, 2004), p. 161.
13. Oborne, *The Rise of Political Lying*.
14. Meg Russell, *Must Politics Disappoint?* (London: Fabian Society, 2005), p. 30.

8 The Perils of Populism

1. Richard Allan 'Kilroy-Silk launches his own party', Times online, 2 February 2005.
2. This analysis draws on material on populism taken from www.en.wikipedia.com.
3. Quotation taken from www.heraldsun.news.com.au.
4. Information in this section is taken from www.en.wikipedia.com.
5. Information on Chávez is taken from www.en.wikipedia.com.
6. Marta Harnecker, 'After the referendum: Venezuela faces new challenges', *Monthly Review*, 56(6) (2004).
7. Harnecker, 'After the referendum'.
8. Margaret Canovan, 'Trust the people! Populism and the two faces of democracy', *Political Studies*, 47 (1999), p. 6.
9. Cas Mudde, 'The populist zeitgeist', *Government and Opposition* (2004), pp. 541–63, emphasis in the original.
10. Canovan, 'Trust the people!', p. 5.
11. Mudde, 'The populist zeitgeist', p. 558.
12. Mudde, 'The populist zeitgeist', p. 556.
13. Canovan, 'Trust the people!', p. 8.
14. William Riker, *Liberalism Against Populism: A Confrontation Between the Theory of Democracy and the Theory of Social Choice* (San Francisco: W. H. Freeman, 1982).
15. Kenneth Arrow, *Social Choice and Individual Values* (New Haven: Yale University Press, 1951).
16. Gerry Mackie, *Democracy Defended* (Cambridge: Cambridge University Press, 2003).
17. Keith Dowding, 'Can populism be defended? William Riker, Gerry Mackie and the interpretation of democracy', *Government and Opposition* (forthcoming, 2007).
18. This section draws on Canovan, 'Trust the people!', pp. 9–16.
19. Norberto Bobbio, quoted in Canovan, 'Trust the people!', p. 10.
20. Canovan, 'Trust the people!', p. 13.

9   Politics for Amateurs

1. Dennis Johnson, *No Place for Amateurs: How Political Consultants Are Reshaping American Democracy* (New York: Routledge, 2001), p. ix.
2. Mark Warren, 'What can democratic participation mean today?', *Political Theory*, 30(5) (2002), p. 678.
3. Michael Shellenberger and Ted Nordhaus, *The Death of Environmentalism: Global Warming Politics in a Post-Environmental World* (2004) (available at www.breakthrough.org), p. 12.
4. Michael Saward, *Democracy* (Cambridge: Polity, 2003), p. 41.
5. Morris Fiorina, 'Extreme voices: a dark side of civic engagement', in Theda Skocpol and Morris Fiorina (eds), *Civic Engagement in American Democracy* (Washington, DC/New York: Brookings/Russell Sage, 1999), pp. 415–16.
6. Saward, *Democracy*, Chapters 2 and 3.
7. Robert Dahl, *A Preface to Democratic Theory* (Chicago: Chicago University Press, 1956).
8. Joseph Schumpeter, *Capitalism, Socialism and Democracy*, 5th edn (London: Allen & Unwin, 1976).
9. Saward, *Democracy*, pp. 48–50.
10. Stephen Macedo *et al.*, *Democracy at Risk* (Washington, DC: Brookings Institution Press, 2005), p. 4.
11. Paul Hirst, 'Democracy and governance', in Jon Pierre (ed.), *Debating Governance* (Oxford: Oxford University Press, 2000).
12. Macedo *et al.*, *Democracy at Risk*, p. 5.
13. Matthew Crenson and Benjamin Ginsberg, *Downsizing Democracy* (Baltimore: Johns Hopkins University Press, 2002), p. 241.
14. David Marquand, *Decline of Public* (Cambridge: Polity, 2004).
15. Saward, *Democracy*, p. 121.
16. Saward, *Democracy*, p. 121; emphases in the original.
17. See John Hibbing and Elizabeth Theiss-Morse, *Stealth Democracy* (Cambridge: Cambridge University Press, 2002), Chaper 7.
18. Campbell, K. (2005) 'Nobody said it was easy: examining the Matryoshka dolls of citizen engagement', *Administration & Society*, 3795, p. 647.
19. See Archon Fung and Erik Olin Wright, *Deepening Democracy: Institutional Innovations in Empowered Participatory Governance* (London: Verso, 2003); Hilary Wainwright, *Reclaim the State: Experiments in Popular Democracy* (London: Verso, 2003); Frances Moore Lappe, *Democracy's Edge: Choosing to Save Our Country by Bringing Democracy to Life* (San Francisco: Jossey-Bass, 2006).
20. Fung and Wright, *Deepening Democracy*.
21. Fung and Wright, *Deepening Democracy*, p. 18.
22. Fung and Wright, *Deepening Democracy*, p. 21.
23. Fung and Wright, *Deepening Democracy*, p. 28.
24. Hibbing and Theiss-Morse, *Stealth Democracy*.

25. Robert Putnam, *Bowling Alone* (New York: Simon & Schuster, 2000). To demon-
     strate group support among political scientists for this position see, for a recent and
     strong statement of this position, Macedo *et al.*, *Democracy at Risk*, p. 120.
26. See Graham Smith, *Democratic Innovations* (London: Power Inquiry, 2005).
27. See Macedo *et al.*, *Democracy at Risk*, p. 120.
28. Fung and Wright, *Deepening Democracy*.
29. Hibbing and Theiss-Morse, *Stealth Democracy*, p. 203.
30. Macedo *et al.*, *Democracy at Risk*, pp. 8–10.
31. This section draws on Gerry Stoker 'Designing institutions for governance in
     complex environments: normative, rational choice and cultural institutional
     theories explored and contrasted', *ESRC Fellowship Paper*, *1*, June 2004
     (available at www.ipeg.org.uk).
32. Robert Goodin, 'Institutions and their design', in Robert Goodin (ed.), *The Theory
     of Institutional Design* (Cambridge: Cambridge University Press, 1996), p. 40.
33. Discussions with Matthew Taylor and David Halpern, both senior policy advi-
     sors to the UK Labour government, have emphasized the importance of these
     points. See, in particular, David Halpern *et al.*, *Personal Responsibility and
     Changing Behaviour: The State of Knowledge and its Implications for Public
     Policy* (London: Cabinet Office, 2004) (available at www.strategy.gov.uk).
34. See Paul Pierson, *Politics in Time* (Princeton: Princeton University Press,
     2004).

10   Reviving Political Institutions

1. David Plotke, 'Representation is democracy', *Constellations*, 4(1) (1997),
    pp. 19–34.
2. Hannah Fenichel Pitkin, *The Concept of Representation* (Berkeley: University
    of California Press, 1972) is a classic study. For a very interesting review of
    where the debate has reached at the start of the twenty-first century, see Dario
    Castiglione and Mark Warren, 'Rethinking representation: seven theoretical
    issues', a paper prepared for delivery at the Midwest Political Science
    Association Annual Conference, Chicago, 6–10 April 2005 (available at
    www.huss.ex.ac.uk/politics/research/reading).
3. See, for example, Stephen Coleman, *Direct Representation: Towards a
    Conversational Democracy* (London: IPPR, 2005).
4. Mark Warren, 'What can democratic participation mean today?', *Political
    Theory*, 30(5) (2002), p. 693.
5. Plotke, 'Representation is democracy'.
6. For a review of the main options, see Michael Saward, *Democracy*
    (Cambridge: Polity, 2000), Chapter 5.
7. John Hibbing and Elizabeth Theiss-Morse, *Stealth Democracy: Americans'
    Beliefs about How Government Should Work* (Cambridge: Cambridge
    University Press, 2002), p. 213.

8. For a wider discussipon of these issues and a review of the evidence, see Lewis Baston and Ken Ritchie, *Turning Out or Turning Off: An Analysis of Political Disengagement and What Can be Done About It* (London: Electoral Reform Society, 2004); Martin Wattenberg, *Where Have all the Voters Gone?* (Cambridge, MA: Harvard University Press, 2002).

9. Arend Lijphart, 'Unequal participation: democracy's unresolved Dilemma', *American Political Science Review*, 91 (1997).

10. Wattenberg, *Where Have all the Voters Gone?*

11. Baston and Ritchie, *Turning Out or Turning Off.*

12. For a much fuller discussion of these issues, see Anne Phillips, *The Politics of Presence* (Oxford: Clarendon Press, 1995).

13. This section draws heavily on work by Stephen Greasley that is reported in joint work with Lorraine Johnston, Gerry Stoker and Francesca Gains (available at www.ipeg.org.uk).

14. David Farrell, *Electoral Systems: A Comparative Introduction* (Basingstoke and New York: Palgrave Macmillan, 2001), pp. 6–7.

15. Stephen Macedo *et al.*, *Democracy at Risk* (Washington, DC: Brookings Institution Press, 2005).

16. Baston and Ritchie, *Turning Out or Turning Off*, Chapter 9.

17. Alan Gerber and Don Green, 'The effects of canvassing, telephone calls and direct mail on voter turnout: a field experiment', *American Political Science Review*, 90(3) (2000).

18. See this work by Peter John, reported at www.ipeg.org.uk.

19. Stephen Coleman, *Direct Representation*.

20. Coleman, *Direct Representation*, pp. 14–15.

21. Ross Ferguson and Barry Griffiths, 'Thin democracy? Parliamentarians, citizens and the influence of blogging on political engagement', *Parliamentary Affairs*, 159(2) (2006), p. 1.

22. On the issue of complexity, see Saward, *Democracy*, pp. 98–101.

23. David Held, *Global Covenant* (Cambridge: Polity, 2004), pp. 96–7.

24. Held, *Global Covenant*, pp. 100–1, emphasis in the original.

25. These ideas are developed much further in the work on the think tank New Local Government Network, of which I am a founding member (see www.nlgn.org.uk). For a fuller statement of my own ideas, see Gerry Stoker 'New localism, progressive politics and democracy', in Andrew Gamble and Tony Wright (eds), *Restating the State?* (Oxford: *Political Quarterly*/Blackwell, 2004), pp. 117–30.

26. See Gerry Stoker, *Transforming Local Governance* (Basingstoke and New York: Palgrave Macmillan, 2004), for a more detailed account of recent reforms in England; for a broader comparative analysis, see Bas Denters and Lawrence Rose (eds), *Comparing Local Governance* (Basingstoke and New York: Palgrave Macmillan, 2005).

27. Held, *Global Covenant*, Chapter 6.

28. Held, *Global Covenant*, p. 95.

29. Jan Aart Scholte, *Globalization: A Critical Introduction*, 2nd edn (Basingstoke and New York: Palgrave Macmillan, 2005), pp. 410–17.

30. Scholte, *Globalization*, p. 417.
31. Albert Hirschman, *The Rhetoric of Reaction* (Cambridge, MA: Harvard University Press, 1991).
32. The discussion below draws on Paul Pierson, 'The limits of design: explaining institutional origins and change', *Governance*, 13(4), (2000), pp. 475–99.
33. Peter Hennessy, *Never Again* (London: Jonathan Cape, 1992), p. 453.
34. Robert Goodin, 'Institutions and their design', in Robert Goodin (ed.), *The Theory of Institutional Design* (Cambridge: Cambridge University Press, 1996).
35. Goodin, 'Institutions and their design'.
36. Mary Douglas, *How Institutions Think* (London: Routledge, 1986).

11 Creating a New Civic Arena

1. Jean Grugel, *Democratization: A Critical Introduction* (Basingstoke and New York: Palgrave Macmillan, 2002), p. 93.
2. Courses of action that Michael Edwards wisely suggests we should avoid. See Michael Edwards, *Civil Society* (Cambridge: Polity, 2004), p. 93.
3. On this point, see Steve Macedo *et al.*, *Democracy at Risk* (Washington, DC: Brookings Institution Press, 2005), p. 160.
4. See Vivien Lowndes, Lawrence Pratchett and Gerry Stoker, 'Trends in public participation: part 1 and part 2', *Public Administration*, 79 (1&2) (2001).
5. Graham Smith, *Democratic Innovations* (London: Power Inquiry, 2005) (available at www.powerinquiry.org).
6. For a fuller description, see Smith, *Democratic Innovations*; for more information, go to http://www.gmnation.org.uk/.
7. See E. Weeks, 'The practice of deliberative democracy: results from four large-scale trials', *Public Administration Review* (July–August 2000).
8. See again Smith, *Democratic Innovations*; see also http://www.citizensassembly. bc.ca.
9. Result obtained from http://www.elections.bc.ca/elections/ge2005/ finalrefresults.htm.
10. Smith, *Democratic Innovations*, p. 121.
11. This description is taken from Gerry Stoker and Karin Bottom, 'Community capacity building: notes for a talk', Municipal Association of Victoria Conference, Lorne, Australia, 25-27 July 2003 (available at www.ipeg.org.uk).
12. On these ideas, see James Fishkin, *Democracy and Deliberation* (New Haven: Yale University Press, 1991).
13. Yves Cabannes, 'Participatory budgeting: a significant contribution to participatory democracy', *Environment & Urbanization*, 16 (1) (2004), pp. 27–46.
14. This description is taken from Stoker and Bottom, 'Community capacity building'. See also Hilary Wainwright, *Reclaim the State: Experiments in Popular Democracy* (London: Verso, 2003), pp. 42–69.

15. Smith, *Democratic Innovations*, pp. 120–1.
16. See paper by Vasudha Chhotray on participatory governance (available at www.ipeg.org.uk).
17. See Smith, *Democratic Innovations*; further information is available at www. e-democracy.org.
18. Smith, *Democratic Innovations*, pp. 103–4.
19. The following draws extensively on material from The Hansard Society, provided to me by Ross Ferguson, the director of their e-democracy programme (see also www.HeadsUp.org.uk).
20. See Ross Ferguson, *New Mechanisms for New Citizens?*, mimeo. The Hansard Society.
21. Macedo *et al.*, *Democracy at Risk*, p. 164.
22. See Deborah Eade, *Capacity-Building* (Oxford: Oxfam, 1997), p. 1.
23. Robert Putnam and Lewis Feldstein, *Better Together: Restoring American Community* (New York: Simon & Schuster, 2003), p. 279.
24. This description is taken from Stoker and Bottom, 'Community Capacity Building'.
25. See Stoker and Bottom 'Community Capacity Building'; the report comes from the *Guardian*, Wednesday 30 August 2000.
26. Macedo *et al.*, *Democracy at Risk*, p. 6. This book also recommends various web sites including www.civicyouth.org and www.civiced.org.
27. For more background and an on-going study of these initiatives in England, see The National Foundation for Education Research's website, http://www.nfer.ac.uk/publications/.
28. David Kerr, Elizabeth Cleaver, Gabrielle White and Michelle Judkins, *DCA – Connecting with Citizenship Education – A Mapping Study* (London: Department for Constitutional Affairs/National Foundation for Education Research, 2005), pp. 15–18.
29. Macedo *et al.*, *Democracy at Risk*, p. 6.
30. Pippa Norris, *A Virtuous Circle: Political Communications in Postindustrial Societies* (Cambridge: Cambridge University Press, 2000), p. 311.
31. Norris, *A Virtuous Circle*, p. 319.
32. John Lloyd, *What the Media are Doing to Our Politics* (London: Constable, 2004), Chapter 4.

Conclusions

1. Raymond Plant, 'Neo-liberalism and the theory of the state', in Andrew Gamble and Tony Wright (eds), *Restating the State?* (Oxford: Blackwell/*Political Quarterly*, 2004).
2. Plant, 'Neo-liberalism and the theory of the state', p. 34.
3. John Dunn, *The Cunning of Unreason: Making Sense of Politics* (London: HarperCollins, 2000), p. 360.

Index